# FOUR LEGS
## MOVE MY
# SOUL

# FOUR LEGS
## MOVE MY
# SOUL

The Authorized Biography
of Dressage Olympian
Isabell Werth

Isabell Werth and Evi Simeoni

Translated by Lena Rindermann

**TRAFALGAR SQUARE**
North Pomfret, Vermont

First published in the English language in 2019 by
Trafalgar Square Books
North Pomfret, Vermont 05053

Originally published in the German language as *Vier Beine Tragen Meine Seele* by Piper Verlag, Munich

ISBN: 978 1 57076 956 6

Library of Congress Control Number: 2019937924

Design by Tim Holtz
Cover design by RM Didier
Index by Andrea M. Jones (www.jonesliteraryservices.com)
Typefaces: Veljovic, Cantoria, Blair

Printed in the United States of America

10 9 8 7 6 5 4 3 2 1

In memory of
Dr. Uwe Schulten-Baumer

# CONTENTS

*Do you love the dance? The horse is a dancer in your hand: a dancer into eternity. From the momentum that you communicate follows effortlessness, follows floating. You feel all power unite under your saddle. The land falls behind you. The world flows past you. Your dancer carries you away.*

—From German writer, poet, and horse breeder Rudolf G. Binding's *Equestrian Hymn for My Beloved,* which won a silver medal in the art competition at the 1928 Olympic Games in Amsterdam.

# 1 RHEINBERG

Those who look a good horse in the eye do not need any explanations. A horse is a horse is a horse. The beauty of the horse lies in him being a horse. He looks at us, attentively and calmly, and we see ourselves anew in his dark gaze. We smell his lovely aroma—tangy grass and grain, the cozy warmth of the barn, the sweetness of apples and carrots. And what else? Wanderlust? A longing for closeness? With a satisfied crunch, the horse bites into a carrot while holding our gaze.

The horse allows us to touch his nostrils—so soft, comparable to the skin of a baby. His nose wrinkles when he collects a piece of apple from our hand. He breathes out with a snort.

When the horse slowly moves forward in the field, step by step, eating grass constantly and carefully, he radiates peace. He gives us a sense of quiet presence. When he canters up a hill, he transforms into a cloud of speed and oxygen.

Horses can captivate us, never to let go again.

With hardly any other living being can a human connect as closely over so many years as a rider can with her horse.

The rider takes care of the horse, grooms and brushes him, allows him to rub his nose on her shoulder. She mounts the horse, enfolding him with her legs, sometimes for hours. She follows the fascinating mechanics of the horse's movements with her body—rocked, swayed, tossed, and caught again. The rider does not move her horse, but is moved *by* her horse. The horse is willing to carry her.

But why are horses so interested in us? Why are most of them motivated by the desire to please us humans? To do right by us? Why do so many of them have the need to be led by us? It is a gift they give us, and one for which they have paid a high price over the course of the centuries. Still, they stand by us persistently.

The connection of the rider with the horse is always mutual, physical, sensual. And, ideally, two souls from different worlds correspond in one time and place that only they call their own.

Gold-medal-winning Olympic dressage star Isabell Werth's passion for horses does not start with ambition. She is living a long love story. It is, however, part of this love story that she asks a lot of her horses, that she works them intensely. For her, as an athlete and entrepreneur, discipline and self-criticism are self-evident. The many tears she has cried on all possible winner's podiums during her unparalleled career show exactly this when the performance pressure finally eases off. Euphoric happiness hardly ever waits for her up there on the podium. Up there, she feels pride, gratification, reassurance, satisfaction...and relief. When she does experience perfect moments of happiness, it happens quietly, at home, without an audience, when she is just with her horses in the here and now.

*Imagine winter is over, spring is close, and everything is start-ing to turn green and bloom. You are outside with your horse, you are riding, and you are thinking that it could not possibly be any more beautiful than that very moment. For me, that is utter happiness on a horse—to feel completely independent of competition, to feel only that the horse is with me and I am with the horse. That is bliss.*

Those who visit the horses at Isabell's facility in Rheinberg, Germany, can look forward to ample scratches, pats, and friendly interactions. The herd is all lined up, ears pricked, next to one another in a neat and tidy barn, the superstars of the dressage world: Weihegold, the black beauty. Bella Rose, the Kate Moss of horses. The once unpredictable Satchmo, long since retired and increasingly turning into a "horse-Buddha." Emilio, the shooting star. Belantis, Isabell's great hope for the future, who stands in his stall like a Pegasus in the mist. They all turn a friendly face to their visitor, sniff you, and start to communicate in their individual ways. Obviously, they are just as sociable as the boss herself.

Even Don Johnson, called "Johnny," the cocky hooligan, has a look so gentle and attentive, you would almost believe he was up to no mischief. A closer look in his stall, with its strange safety devices and rubber toys, reveals all: when this horse is overcome by the urge to play, he shreds everything around him to pieces, such as his automatic waterer, regardless of whether he hurts himself in the process. In doing so, Johnny has missed several important competitions—the 2016 Olympic Games among them. There is no piece in his stall that has not had to be replaced. Don Johnson has even managed to kick in a mirror in the indoor arena. Isabell nonchalantly waves this observation aside—yes, he is just a naughty boy. He also likes to buck every once in a while when she is in the saddle, and he has come close to throwing her in the dirt. Of course, she defends herself and puts him in his place: "Johnny, stop this nonsense!" Maybe he knows that, truth be told, Isabell enjoys being his sparring partner from time to time. Later, with a soft smile on her face, she will offer excuses: "He was only offended, as I have not given him enough attention lately."

Isabell has dedicated herself to horses with her head and heart, body and soul. She is a person who radiates a sense of security and peace of mind, a solid groundedness, a steadfast stability. Nothing about her is aimed at trying to make an impression—for her, what counts is what happens. Her nerves seem to be made of steel, she looks out at the world with a confident glance, and she makes absolutely clear that nothing and no one can scare her. And yet, her horses, these large, sensitive animals, throw her into periods of deep doubt, time and again, and sometimes even into despair.

The public hardly knows this side of Isabell. She can be beaming and funny during interviews or at parties and receptions—and sometimes she laughs so heartily that people turn around. This is the cheerful side of her, a characteristic originating in her native Rhineland, rather than the sensitive soul that is hidden from view most of the time. When we see her competing at horse shows or on television, we see her lips pursed in concentration, we see her frowning out of sheer willpower, we see her tongue pushed below her lip, into her chin, and we can tell that every fiber of her body is geared toward maximum performance. This was the way it was when Isabell first picked up the reins at the highest level of dressage sport, and it has not changed three decades and many medals later. It sometimes even seems as if the doses of the "competition drug" she needs to consume regularly have gotten bigger and more frequent. She hungers for that adrenaline, even when it requires a sort of game of cat and mouse: If Isabell has to face the victory of a fellow competitor in a particular class, her opponent better not be so foolish as to think her luck might continue. The Isabell Empire will strike back the next day, shattering her opponent's resistance, all the more painfully. It will seem as if she prepared the carpet and immediately pulled it out from under the other rider. This is how she recharges. This is her very personal warfare.

Isabell Werth, competition monster?

Of course, such results require a horse of superior quality and training to help her control the field, and yet, it is still never guaranteed, not even when the rider is Isabell Werth. She has gone through hard times over and over, periods when success eluded her because of a lack of top-level horses, and where, for a while, only tenacity kept her in the game. Nevertheless, in the later stages of her career, Isabell succeeded bringing several aces to the game. It is not a coincidence that she managed to sit in several top positions in the world rankings at the same time. She became the most successful rider in history following her performance at the Olympic Games in Rio de Janeiro in 2016: She has won six Olympic gold medals in twenty-four years, nine World Championship titles, and twenty European Championship titles. What is most astonishing about this is the plurality: While even the most formative figures of her sport generally ride to top-class international success with only one horse, two at the most, Isabell has qualified a total of eight horses for championships, including Olympic Games, World Equestrian Games, and European Championships. She has brought approximately thirty horses to the highest levels of the sport—a monumental achievement to which no other rider has even come close. This is most likely why, after years of fighting for respect and justifying her success, her role is slowly beginning to change: Isabell is becoming more and more a respected "Grande Dame" of dressage, one who no longer has to prove anything. Sometimes, now having advanced beyond the stages of competition that house envy and resentment, she experiences the third stage of her career—one where, during its best moments, the battle, the competition, and the proven experience are no longer at the forefront. Instead, it seems as though stars rain down on her, as during her win at the World Cup Final in Omaha in 2017. There, all of a sudden, everything seemed to be easy. She beamed on the podium and sprayed celebratory champagne instead of crying painful tears. A new Isabell! She turned the ceremony into a joyful party.

> *It's moments like these where I stop and think sometimes: Have I arrived? Have I come full circle? All those challenges still waiting for me, all the young horses that I still want to bring on, my business and my family—these take up my thoughts in such a way that there is no time for sentimentalities. Most of the time, I collapse into bed exhausted at night, knowing that the next day will be just as precisely timed and organized, whether at a show, in our own arena, or at promotional events. But one thing is clear: Best of all, I like to fall asleep at home, at our farm in Rheinberg, surrounded by my family.*

The podium, on horseback, in the dressage arena—this is where Isabell has belonged since the day she was born on July 21, 1969. It was the same day the first person set foot on the moon. Isabell, however, has remained grounded. She needs the place where she grew up; it mirrors her whole life, her personality, and her dreams. It is where she longs to be when she is racing along a highway somewhere. And it is, where she recharges the energy she needs for a constant and tightly regimented daily routine.

When Isabell was a child, the remoteness of her home sometimes bothered her. She had to be driven everywhere, the riding club included. Today, she is happy about the idyll it provides and feels tremendously privileged to have been raised in such comfort. There might not have been any vacations together with her parents—someone always had to stay home to take care of the animals at the farm—but when she was home, her parents where always there and always available for her, not just when she had problems.

The Werth family is down to earth. They've been farmers for generations and still live on the farm at the Winterswicker Field in Rheinberg on the Lower Rhine like happy islanders, offering each other protection and safety. Family is everything. Four generations lived at the farm at the best of times. Her grandmother, who was one hundred and two, only showed serious signs of weakness and age in her last two years. Her parents, Heinrich and Brigitte, two lively but not very tall people, give the farm every ounce of who they are. Isabell is the "boss" nowadays, with her partner Wolfgang Urban and son Frederik, and her sister Claudia (older by three years) with her family. That Isabell is now the one making the decisions does not bother her father Heinrich—a cheerful man with plenty of natural "Rhineland wit." On the contrary.

"She is the king in our family clan," he says proudly during tea time at Isabell's long dining table.

When Isabell was a child, he tilled over fifty acres of land almost alone. Mother Brigitte ran the household, which was considerable. (Father Heinrich's parents lived in the house for twenty-seven years.) Isabell's father produced barley, oats, corn, and beets in the fields. In addition, there was livestock: dairy cows to manage, pigs to breed and rear, chickens complete with a rooster, geese, ducks, rabbits, dogs, and cats.

"All animals were created by the good Lord," says Heinrich Werth.

For a while, he even bred nutria and pigeons. And, of course, horses, which today are not bred for work, but rather for pleasure only.

Isabell's father operated a classic "mixed" farm, which were once common in their area, remaining unchanged for centuries, but which are almost extinct today. Today, all the farms on the Winterswicker Field are shut down, the buildings have been converted into houses, and the families have leased their land to large agricultural businesses. The "old way of life" is dying. Now, everything is about quantity and large spaces, fertilizers are used intensively, and the land is worked with large machinery—small farms just aren't profitable. Heinrich Werth belongs to the last generation of farmers that operated in the traditional way. He is a farmer, through and through, but his life was even harder than that of his ancestors. Unlike his parents' generation, he could not afford employees. Brigitte Werth also had to go about her tasks differently from her mother and mother-in-law—both had employed a maid for all their lives. The farm no longer yielded that kind of profit. Even using a "swarm" of children as a means of free labour was no longer a solution, as compared to the times where families with twelve or more members were not uncommon, they had few offspring.

As a child, Heinrich Werth witnessed the days when horses were still used to plow the fields. Through all of his work life, he had to carry heavy loads, day in, day out, since the mechanization was not as advanced as it is today. Thus, the arrival of the combine meant a great relief, although Heinrich Werth still worked industriously on his farm, got up at the crack of dawn to feed and to milk, sat on his tractor for days, and was, eventually, exhausted. He reports that he felt way worse at fifty than at eighty. His back refused to function, his discs, his sciatic nerve—he had to use a wheelchair temporarily. But he never complained. Happiness is what is most important to him, he says.

And a family who sticks together.

*My sister and I grew up among all these animals. We loved and cuddled the piglets and the calves, and it was our chore to take care of the bunnies. We could count on a new "fur baby" every day, and we ran over, petted them, and thought they were cute. Of course, we knew that these animals were going to be butchered and, eventually, eaten. But that is how it was; we lived off what the farm produced. We also had no problem providing the obligatory pig eye for our biology teacher's class on dissection in school. (Our classmates were horrified and started to scream!) As soon as a piglet weighed over a hundred pounds, "its time had come." Whenever a pig was slaughtered, we girls looked forward to the vet's attendance, as he examined the meat for trichinae. He let us look through the microscope. Making sausages was a natural next step for us and certainly nothing repulsive—quite exciting, actually, and quite yummy! A piece of the fresh meat was roasted or cooked that night and everyone looked forward to it and enjoyed it.*

Isabell's father knew every single cow and pig and took responsibility for their well-being. It was a life both *with* and *off* the farm animals. Even if they were slaughtered one day, the children learned to never lose respect for them. They were close to the animals physically and not repulsed. If the livestock were sick, they were treated, and nobody rested until they were well again. The family looked after the animals and cared for them three hundred and sixty-five days a year. Nevertheless: They were still livestock and not toys.

*As a child, you are completely impartial; you don't think about it. The horse is there; the dog is there. And you don't develop an inherent kind of fear, but the animal is part of your daily life, almost part of the family. You go into the barn in the morning, the animals are fed; it is a rhythm, it is simply responsibility, and that is how you grow up.*

Isabell knew everything. For example, when the sows had their piglets, they were allowed to romp about in the field. There was also a boar. One aggressive fellow put the fear of God into Isabell one day.

*My dad had bought a new boar. Usually, a boar had his tusks sawn off right away as they can be razor-sharp, but this one hadn't had this done. There was a cow field next door, and this boar apparently had never seen cows in his life. He went completely crazy, and cut open three cows, one so badly she could only go to the butcher. Attempts were made to stitch the others back together. To experience something like that, to see firsthand how fast something can turn on you and become dangerous—I found that deeply impressive.*

Growing up closely with different animals, Isabell developed a natural relationship with them, one that was elemental and instinctual. The animals got involved with her, and she expressed interest in them, opened up to them, formed relationships with them, which cannot be described with words. Rural children approach animals without immediately expecting something from them. They do it simply because the animal exists. It is impossible for a city child to obtain such genuine access. The city child cannot imagine what it is like to grow up so closely together with an animal and to enter into a mutual interdependency.

The affection for all animals that started in her early childhood is the key to Isabell's joy in her life with horses—and also to her success. Over the years, she has further developed this special understanding, has refined it, enriched it with new experiences. And she has made it more professional. *Anthropomorphized*, is what she calls the instrumentalization of a skill she acquired as effortlessly as other children learn Spanish, French, or Portuguese from a nanny. Isabell was able to open up not only one country with the language that came to her, but an entire universe. The animals seem to speak to Isabell, and she seems to be able to hear them.

"A gift," her father says. "We did not teach her it."

"We have been asked where she got it from," says her mother. "It was the Lord who gave her so much feeling."

Isabell's skill to anticipate is legendary. She knows what a horse is about to do, even when an outsider cannot perceive any signs whatsoever. Thus, she is able to take preventive measures, to guide reactions into sensible directions, or to prevent worse outcomes. She can latch onto a horse's sense, understand his individual behavior, and find ways to interpret it.

*I can feel it somewhere in a fiber of my body. In a nerve that was unknown to me before. In my hands, my seat, in my side, somewhere in the body. Somehow, the horse shortly freezes, he*

11

*appears a tiny little bit nervous, reacts a tad differently than usual. I can't explain it, but the feeling is there. Just a small perception sometimes, an instinctive hesitation, a gut feeling, which is confirmed later. Then I say to myself: Look at you, you were right, and I integrate this aspect into my experience. It is a form of communication and instinct. Instinct plays a large role. It has become very refined over time and has developed through the many different horses I have ridden. From my little fat pony to the Grand Prix competitor.*

*Gigolo, my first gold-medal mount, was a generous teacher with regard to communication. He offered himself to me and brought an extremely honest willingness to perform. I listened to him and learned to manage his overboard ambition. He managed to focus on me and the competition situation and always played along. As a Grand Prix debutant, I took this for granted. But the reliable heart of this horse was a great gift for me at that stage of my career.*

Gigolo made it possible for Isabell to withstand Anky van Grunsven's competitive onslaught for years. Anky was her biggest rival from the Netherlands, with whom she "fought" some nail-biting duels in the international ring.

Later, Satchmo would wreak havoc on everything that Gigolo had taught Isabell. Satchmo was also a very forward-oriented horse, but with such a moment of surprise! Isabell listened carefully, sharpened her perception, used her brain, and turned her nervous system on "high"—but he remained unpredictable, even for her.

*Nobody has challenged and sharpened my sense of perception as much as Satchmo has; he was my second great teacher after Gigolo.*

The more sensitive a horse is, the more difficult he is. A horse that has an "ordinary" disposition causes few problems for his rider; however, this type of horse is not ideal for the kinds of requests Isabell is likely to make in the international dressage arena. This horse will be able to learn movements, but he will not be able to "play his part" in the performance in the kind of way that is needed for success on this stage. He will not know when it's all or nothing; he will not fight with all he has left in the decisive moment. He will not unfold magically in a way that touches the audience. He lacks that "something special." And this horse would demand too little in return from Isabell Werth.

Isabell loves and, in fact, *needs* those horses that, amongst riders, are referred to as "hot." She tends to load up on a kind of mental electricity, to work herself into a state of fervor that matches the horse. The hotter her horses, the more impressive their performances together—it is almost to the point where everything falls apart, where Isabell can no longer reach them, and where they lapse into complete hysteria due to pure overeagerness. This is the major challenge for a world-class dressage rider. She must work along this fine line. Every competitive outing is a borderline experience, where the genius of the horse threatens to turn into insanity at any moment. There, on the brink, is where the competitor who is Isabell Werth feels most comfortable. These moments do not leave her paralyzed with fear. She savors them like an acrobat does when waiting to drop from the very top of the circus tent. She draws her own energy from them.

Besides, Isabell does not see her goal as reaching the top as smoothly as possible. Every step needs to have something special. The way she gets there is even more important than getting there: Her pursuit is the art of bringing the most different, and sometimes difficult, of horses beyond their weaknesses to optimal performance.

Isabell's parents are constantly amazed by their daughter.

"She will look at a day-old foal," her father Heinrich says, "and will pretty much tell you where his career path will take him."

As a farmer, he finds this ability especially impressive.

Or consider the story of Amaretto: The poor horse was technically the next "Crown Prince," the one to follow in Gigolo's footsteps, but he was not healthy. Frequent colics tortured the gelding so often that, finally, he had to be taken to live at a veterinary clinic. Whenever she was not on the road competing, Isabell visited him whenever she could, observing her horse in his medical stall for hours, standing next to him and trying to figure out how she could possibly help him. After some time, she took Professor Bernhard Huskamp, the head of the clinic, aside and said: "Whenever Amaretto pulls up his lips and curls them, that is when the next colic episode is about to announce itself." The veterinarian ignored her at first, then began to wonder, and finally took a chair himself and sat down in Amaretto's stall for a few hours. He discovered that Isabell was right. Whenever Amaretto pulled up his lips in a certain kind of way, another colic was about to begin and the horse would lie down soon after.

Her father, the experienced farmer, just said, "You simply cannot learn something like that."

Isabell is deeply concerned whenever horses in her care become ill. After all, one virus can threaten her entire stable. Early in 2018 a mysterious infection spread through Isabell's barn only days after a glorious show performance. The feverish illness manifested itself dramatically—in fact, she lost two horses. The fight against the virus brought Isabell and her entire team to rock bottom—they had no strength left. More than a hundred horses had to be checked several times a day for weeks on end—not only her own, but also precious boarding horses for which she had taken responsibility. It seemed the vet was a permanent guest at the barn—when he was not on site, he was constantly on the phone. At one point, several thermometers actually stopped working due to overwork and had to be replaced.

It was so cold outside the barn that canisters full of disinfectant were frozen. Double-door systems with disinfection mats were put in place to try to eliminate transfer of the virus. Luckily, Isabell's current competition horses had stalls in a separate barn aisle and were given medication to strengthen their immune systems, so they were not affected by the wave of infection. But the entire Team Werth had to fight a downright battle for weeks.

Isabell, the tough one, the woman who accepts any athletic challenge almost with pleasure, was more anxious than she'd ever felt before—she was faced with an uncertain situation and a certain powerlessness. Only days before the outbreak she had told the press that, during her career, she had never been so happy and relaxed than in her current streak of athletic achievements. But only a day later the old wisdom was confirmed: Problems always arise when you least expect them. This can apply to many things but is even more true when you are dealing with vulnerable living beings. It is in those moments that your entire life's experience still will not help you.

The Werth family has always interacted with horses. Heinrich fox hunted. Isabell's mother, Brigitte, the daughter of vegetable and fruit farmers close to the city of Bonn, brought a mare called Palette with her when she married Heinrich. Brigitte rode Palette leisurely on hacks and had some fun with her at the local riding club.

Isabell, somewhat disrespectfully, calls this "housewife riding."

Isabell started riding so early that she can hardly remember her first pony, Illa. She first sat on Illa at five years old. Her first ride was on "a little black horse"—this is all she remembers. Then it was the mare Sabrina. Isabell was not yet eight years old when she had to pass her first crucial horse test: Sabrina got scared right in front of the house for some reason and spooked. Isabell fell off and landed on the stairs, right on her face. She still has a small scar from the little stone that bored into her forehead. Her nose was torn, her lips burst open on the inside—she was taken to the hospital for stitches. In addition to the face wounds, she had a concussion. She had to spend a week in the hospital, eating and drinking with a feeding cup only. She told her dad furiously that she was done with riding, and that he could give Sabrina away. But one day later, remembers Heinrich, she changed her story completely.

"Listen, Dad," she announced from her hospital bed, "I will teach her to listen to me."

Ultimately, however, the gray mare was not allowed to stay. Sabrina was just too spooky for little girls.

Isabell and her sister Claudia grew into the German riding club lifestyle almost automatically, just what you would expect of social butterflies from the Rhineland. A large part of their youth was spent at Graf von Schmettow Eversael, the riding club not far from their farm.

*We smoked our first cigarette behind the indoor arena. And we drank our first apple schnapps behind the embankment.*

*Three times a week, Claudia and I showed up for riding lessons with our ponies: twice for dressage lessons, once for jumping. On the weekend, we went on hacks with ten or fifteen*

*kids, all with backpacks. We played games: skill games, gym-
khana games, jousting, circus tricks. The horses had to wear
hats, hearts, glitter, and glimmer—they were just as fancifully
dressed up as we were. We chased across fields and swam
with our horses in the river. I was always desperate during
pony races because my pony, Funny, was smaller than Claudia's (named Fee), and despite the utmost efforts on my part,
I could not beat my sister. Funny was a 12-hand Welsh pony.
Fee was half an inch taller and more wiry. In best-case scenar-
ios, Funny made it to Fee's tail during our races. But she was
still awesome. Well-behaved, lazy, small, a little chubby. She
did not like jumping at all, and I regularly came off, despite
my persuasive powers (always once, sometimes even twice or
three times in a lesson). It became my personal challenge to
finish a jumping competition, just once, without falling off.*

Despite the challenges of her pony, Isabell remained tough,
and her mother managed to keep calm at the sight of her
daughter being catapulted through the air. She only wondered
where her daughter got the energy to climb back on the horse,
again and again, after she had fallen off! Brigitte did not only
drive her daughters to the riding club but also to their first
horse shows, supporting their passion as best as she could.
With their ponies, the sisters rode against other children on
full-size horses.

Isabell's father's parents, with whom the family shared
the house and who were still rooted in the traditional view of
agricultural, were perhaps less supportive. Keeping horses for
pleasure? Just for the children? Pointlessly driving the kids and
ponies around when the time could be better used for work at
home? Brigitte disregarded their objections, and the girls were
allowed to ride. But, their resolute mother told them, "If you

only want to ride for fun, we do not need to make all this effort. If you want to compete, then it needs to be serious. *Then* we will do it properly and it's not just a game."

From that minute on, the girls and their mother were on the road together every weekend. The question some ask, "Who instilled such ambition in Isabell?" has just become superfluous.

For her early schooling, Isabell studied at night, which is similar to what she would do later in life with her law studies, when she was already reaping international riding success. She always got away with it—although not necessarily with the best possible results. Her sister Claudia specialized in eventing, riding homebred horses, but did not want to devote herself "body and soul" to riding like her little sister did. Isabell rode everything she could get her hands on, no matter the discipline or the horse. Only when Dr. Uwe Schulten-Baumer, the most famous horseman in her neighborhood, took notice of her, did she specialize in dressage. She started riding his horses regularly at seventeen years old. He brought to the table his experience—a long life as a successful riding coach. She had the intuition and the courage. Both wanted to make it to the top. They complemented each other, eventually growing together as a team. They were a terribly successful duo! But Isabell did not only need her exceptional courage to handle the young horses and to take on the seemingly superior opponents in the dressage arena, she also needed it to stand up to Dr. Schulten-Baumer.

Isabell's dad, who supported her vigorously during what were difficult years, said categorically when asked, "You don't need to assess their relationship. It is enough if I do."

Isabell's family supported her when her partnership with Dr. Schulten-Baumer ended in 2001, after sixteen years. And Madeleine Winter-Schulze, who would become Isabell's friend, patroness, and horse owner, came just at the right time. She bought several horses from Dr. Schulten-Baumer and invited Isabell to live and train at her and her husband's facility in Mellendorf, Germany, close to Hanover. It was the perfect way out: it was a way forward into the future.

Dr. Schulten-Baumer paved the way for Isabell in the beginning; he helped her get her foot in the door of major sporting circles. He also taught her everything that she needed to school and train horses herself, and then lead them to success. Madeleine, her friend and sponsor, supported Isabell as she found a newfound freedom, buying horses for her. (Madeleine has Isabell's back to this day.) Other riders often have to compromise and sell horses every now and then to keep their business profitable, but Madeleine ensures that Isabell can fall back on a solid financial footing. Both Madeleine and Dr. Schulten-Baumer came into Isabell's life at the right time— it was almost magical, as if it was meant to be.

Talent alone is never enough; luck has to be added to the mix.

Isabell worked as a lawyer in a practice in Hamm, Germany, and also for the German department store chain Karstadt. This is where she met her future partner, former Karstadt CEO Wolfgang Urban.

*He is my greatest support, the most important person by my side…he gives me direction, helps me in many situations with his experience, and is the one I can hold on to. He asks the right questions and shows me quite plainly where I sugarcoat or where I am kidding myself, even though he is not a horse or dressage expert.*

Isabell's life became divided, thematically and geographically with her work and her horses, as she covered thousands of miles on crowded German highways. From Rheinberg to Mellendorf, from Mellendorf to Hamm, from Hamm to Mellendorf, from there to a show in Munich, Stuttgart, or Neumünster. Things could not go on as they were. She had to make a choice. Isabell decided to leave both her jobs as a lawyer and as store manager, and to instead start her own business as a professional rider and trainer. So far, her professional life had been the background music to her true passion, a sideshow. Now she turned her passion into her profession.

After this came a night when Isabell became the "head" of her family. She was sitting on the couch at home with her father as they discussed the family farm and her own professional goals, and he said, "Maybe you can buy a facility somewhere close by. So many farms are vacant now, that could be an option."

"Are you saying you don't want me at home anymore?" Isabell asked.

Heinrich Werth did not say much in reply, only, "Thank you, Isabell. That's enough."

The next morning, Heinrich told his wife, "Let's put our money where our mouths are. Let's write the farm over to Isabell. I don't want her to think that we don't want her here."

With that, the formalities were taken care of within a few weeks, and a fair solution was found for both Isabell and her sister, with clear conditions.

"When they 'close the lid on me,'" said Heinrich Werth, "I don't want them to have a falling out."

Isabell took over the family farm. It became her residence in the fall of 2003, and her sister lives in her own home on the property. With the support of Madeleine Winter-Schulze, Isabell expanded the facility and built a new house for herself and her family. Every tree, every shrub that she can see has been planted during her lifetime. She also planted hawthorn hedges throughout the property to help structure the space. She is now in charge of a competition barn, a training facility, a small horse breeding venture that her father runs, and an agricultural business, which produces some of the feed for her herd. Forty to fifty horses are in training on the farm, from the three-year-old newcomers to the Grand Prix competitors. Together with the broodmares, the foals, the boarders, and a herd of retirees happily grazing in the field, the facility accommodates around a hundred horses. Fourteen employees take care of the horses' well-being and their training. (Isabell very rarely accepts private students.) The veterinarian is on the grounds almost daily.

Technically, the business and the entire team revolve around one person and her system: Isabell. And she whirls around from morning till night.

Every morning, whenever Isabell is home, Brigitte—her mother—brings a glass of fresh-squeezed orange juice to the indoor arena. This is the opportunity for a quick exchange, regarding the farm.

Isabell asks from the saddle, "How are things going?"

If something is wrong or in question, mother and daughter discuss it over the arena wall. Nobody on the farm accepts long-lasting disagreements. Isabell left the belligerent part of her behind with Dr. Schulten-Baumer.

*When you live in the country, you can always go to town every now and then. If you live in the city and wish to get out to the country, it is more difficult. I have my island here. Everyone needs an island, especially when you are away as much as I am. You learn to appreciate "home" even more.*

Isabell and Wolfgang had a son, Frederik, in October 2009 when Isabell was forty years old. At the time, she had her life organized down to the most minute of details. She had a plan for every morning, and everything revolved around the horses. With a baby, it all changed. She had to learn to organize the horses around Frederik and make a drastic shift of importance in her mind from her four-legged family to her two-legged one.

*Frederik was absolutely planned. He is my greatest joy, my greatest love, and he has expanded my horizon in the most meaningful way. Nothing else is really important, as long as Frederik is happy and healthy.*

Often, Isabell feels bad because she is away from home so much, and Frederik developed an instinct early on to turn this to his advantage, seeking as much compensation from his mother as possible. Now, Isabell tries to choose competitions according to whether Frederik might enjoy them—for example, one with a petting zoo next to the showgrounds has a better chance of Isabell's participation than one with lots of stress and obligations, where Isabell has to pose for selfies instead of being with her son.

In many ways, Frederik's childhood has taken place on an idyllic island. His parents are intent on not turning him into a spoiled only child but instead teaching him the modest life of previous generations. The daily routine is due to careful decisions and planning. His world is more complicated and more organized than his mother's was. He, too, is surrounded by animals, but he is not stuck on the farm. He has already been on a plane many times. And best of all, somebody is always there to take care of him—both of his parents are home with him almost every night.

*When Frederik first came to the indoor arena, he always wanted to sit on my horse. Not on his cousin's pony, which was immediately offered to him. No, he wanted up on his mom's*

*horse—not to ride, but to be close to me. This was often impos-*
*sible because my horses were too wild. It bothered him, and he*
*complained. To him, it felt as if the horses took away his mother.*

Isabell's parents no longer take long trips. In the past, they would gather a cheerful crew from the local riding club, get on the bus or plane, and accompany Isabell to her bigger competitions. This started at the 1992 Olympic Games in Barcelona. The president of the local riding club arranged a bus for almost thirty people and a ski rack in the back for provisions (beer was obligatory). The cheering section from the Lower Rhine region crossed into France, laughing and chatting all the way to Spain, alcohol flowing freely. Each day, they trekked to the stadium as a boisterous fan club from their rental home in Barcelona. Four years later, at the Olympic Games in Atlanta, the loyal crew even got a house that was closer to the competition venue than the riders' lodgings! The Isabell Fan Tour visited Rome, Lipica, Gothenburg, and Jerez de la Frontera, and Isabell's parents made up for what they missed at home before, when responsibilities like animals needing to be fed and fields needing to be tended required the presence of their farmers.

Whenever Isabell returned home after a successful outing, a special celebration was in order. The riding club hosted glorious receptions, with more revelry and horses harnessed six-in-hand.

The Fan Tours only stopped traveling when, at the end of the World Equestrian Games in 2010, the president of the riding club suffered a heart attack. Fortunately, it did not have any serious consequences, and Isabell made sure he was safely transported home from Lexington, Kentucky, where the event was held—paramedics were waiting for him with a stretcher upon his arrival in Germany. The president of the club was part of her extended family, after all.

Today, the club structure has changed. Many of the younger generation of riders do not know Isabell personally. As a whole, the club life is no longer as central to the members as it once was.

And now Isabell's father Heinrich only drives as far as his own fields. He grabs the dogs and his grandson Frederik and hops on his four-wheeler. The acreage that he used to plow is now his playground. Maybe, while zipping about, his thoughts wander back to the time when he was still working the land according to the old traditions...or perhaps even further back, to the era that even he only knows from stories.

Heinrich Werth's grandfather bought the property in 1915. Industrialism dislodged him from his farm in Walsum, Germany, on the other side of the river Rhine. There was neither running water nor electricity on the farm—the well pump was operated manually. The family sat together at night by candlelight, but not for very long before their eyes started to close from fatigue. After all, they had to be up and running at four in the morning to milk.

"It's true, people back then worked very, very hard," muses Heinrich, "but they were not stressed."

Maybe, as he's driving around with his grandson, he remembers his childhood years, and the Second World War, when five of his uncles died on the battlefield and hungry townspeople came to the countryside to ask for food. The farm saw it all! American soldiers took up quarters there; you can even see bullet holes in the side of the main house, dating from this time.

But as Isabell's mother Brigitte points out, setting her coffee cup down with emphasis, "We will be sitting here all night if we keep talking about the past!"

# 2 GIGOLO

After Isabell had ridden the horse called Gigolo for the first time, she told him in spirit: Well, my friend, you will have to make a bit of an effort here, or else it will never happen between us.

Today, Isabell may find it difficult to imagine what would have become of her if Gigolo had not been on his best behavior that day. But, there was no danger it would not happen: Gigolo always gave her his very best.

She had already tried another horse at the same facility in Warendorf, Germany, shortly before her first ride on Gigolo. The horse's name was Whiskytime; he was a talented giant that she liked immediately. Gigolo was younger than Whiskytime, only six years old, and he had a blaze like a blurred watercolor. Isabell only got on him to avoid accusations that she had not considered all her options. She was supposed to decide on one of the available horses at the farm.

And now, there she was on Gigolo, with this "nothingness of a neck" in front of her.

*Beyond his withers, it went downhill for about eight inches, then a narrow, surprisingly long neck protruded upward, without any muscle. It felt as if I was sitting on the edge of a launch pad. Beautiful Gigolo? Not at all at that point. But then he started trotting, and he was completely different. That's when I knew: This is it. This is the horse and no other. There are very few horses out there where one second is enough and you just know he is meant to be yours. Gigolo's first trot step. The moment I first saw Bella Rose. My first look at Belantis. With these horses, it was exactly like this: one second. I rode, Gigolo trotted, and I said to myself, this is unbelievable. The athleticism, the sportiness, the carrying capacity, the impulsion—I had never experienced or felt anything like it.*

Isabell was nineteen then. She and Dr. Uwe Schulten-Baumer were visiting the doctor's son, once the best rider in his father's stable, who, having pursued his own career in medicine, had less and less time for his horses. Dr. Schulten-Baumer, Jr., had won a silver medal at the World Championships and a European Championship title, but this phase of his life was over, and he wanted to sell one of his horses. He had bought Gigolo as a five-year-old from the Düfer family, who rode the horse in Warendorf at the German Equestrian Federation (FN), the power center of the nation. However, the experts on-site had no idea what they had let go—Gigolo's talent went unnoticed. One of Germany's leading dressage experts at the time heard six months after that Dr. Schulten-Baumer had bought the horse for Isabell and even said: "Really? Did it have to be *that* one, of all horses?"

When Isabell teased the man about this years later, he admitted, "Don't tell anyone that Gigolo was up for sale in Warendorf and we didn't see his talent. That is pretty pathetic."

*I could literally feel it in my seat. Dr. Schulten-Baumer only had to look me in the eyes on that fateful day in 1989, and he knew it was the beginning of something big. He asked again if I really was sure. And I beamed at him and said without hesitating, "Yes, I am." It made me proud that, even back then, he already trusted my instincts so much. And that we easily agreed.*

And so it began: Gigolo, the chestnut Hanoverian with the long skinny neck, became the most successful competition horse in the history of modern equestrianism. His medal collection is legendary: Four times Olympic gold, twice silver. Four titles at the World Equestrian Games, eight at European Championships, and four German Championship titles. Gigolo beat the highly decorated Rembrandt, ridden by Germany's Nicole Uphoff, and put his stamp on an era, which, had international officials had their way, seemed to be reserved for the riders from the Netherlands.

And he shaped Isabell into the rider she would one day become.

*I learned from Gigolo what the "ideal" should feel like. He showed me what kind of synergy and interaction is possible with a horse that moves forward with passion, and the level of effortlessness that can be developed, even when performing at maximum difficulty. He taught me what determination and motivation are and that it is possible to ride a Grand Prix— the highest degree of difficulty—as if it were the most natural thing ever. The most difficult work was not really hard for him, because he derived such pleasure from it.*

*Gigolo's conformation became more harmonious over the years as his neck muscled up. But all of his life, he was less convincing as a still image than as an athlete in motion. That is what he was, through and through: An athlete. Gigolo preserved his strong character until his last breath. He was intelligent and had a great inner independence—he was never one to cuddle, but at the same time, he was determined to give it his utmost in the dressage ring, together with me. He was always alert, always burning for action, and always seemed to ask: "And? What are we doing next?" He did not have to rely on anyone else but did his own thing, as if it was his mission to take me along for the ride, and not vice versa. This attitude was so prevalent in his younger years that I could hardly channel his energy.*

Those who experienced Gigolo, boiling over with energy on the first day of a competition, could hardly believe that he would be able to show a dynamic-yet-relaxed Grand Prix one or two days later. He did not buck, he did not resist the tasks. He just became so hot, so charged up on energy, that he could hardly be controlled.

*Gigolo's eagerness to work and go forward was so overpowering that, at one point, he just didn't know which leg to move first. It seemed to me as if he was constantly urging me to "get going already"…it was always, "Come on, come on, let's go, let's go, let's go forward!" He was hyper-motivated. Ready to work through and through. Nothing interested him but the movements that he was about to perform.*

*Gigolo still had this spirit well into his twenties. Sometimes he was brought in from the field to have his mane neatened or to have a bath, and he would suddenly start to piaffe right in the aisle. He would look around as if to say: "Let's go! Start the music, please!"*

*It only became clear to me after a lot of experiences with other horses just how lucky I was to have had Gigolo. To be able to ride such a forward-thinking horse right at the beginning of my career was incredible. I never had to encourage him. My task was mainly to handle his vivacity without taking the fighting spirit out of him.*

It is one of the most important feats of riding dressage: To bring the horse, an animal always ready to flee, into an inner state where he can develop his full potential and yet does not lose his head. Nature plays a role here: When in a state of excitement, a horse performs the same types of movements that were eventually cultivated by the sport of dressage. That is the reason why, in best of cases, a world-class Grand Prix test resembles the metaphorical "ride on a razor blade." Gigolo and his rider were really well suited for each other—two offensive players, both always ready to risk everything.

The days of Gigolo were the times of new beginnings; Isabell did not know setbacks yet. Her career moved forward with rapid speed, and as strong and unclouded as her self-confidence was, she did not think about what might go wrong. She simply shrugged off falls from her young, wild horses and did not think about potential consequences. She did not yet have the responsibility of her own business, nor was she a parent. Back then, she did not think about whether it might be safer to longe an excited, barely controllable horse before riding so he could let off some steam. No...it was simply up, up, and away!

Isabell learned how to handle Gigolo's personality at shows. It did not work to drill him in an hour of warm up right before her class—he lost his freshness and motivation. It was better to work him in the morning to get some of the freshness out;

then, she only warmed him up for half an hour, and he brought all his joy of movement into the dressage ring.

> *One of my most cherished memories when I think about Gigolo is from the dressage stadium in Aachen. It was pouring and the sand ring was flooded. Deep puddles mirrored the cloudy sky, especially in those places where I had planned to ride my most tricky, most difficult movement during my Freestyle: the transition from extended canter to pirouette. Any other horse would perhaps have tried to avoid the puddles. But Gigolo said, "Yeah!" He was not to be deterred from his moment to perform, and he slammed through the water in canter with such fervor that water splashed everywhere. He did not have to "hold himself together" like some horses might have—he loved it.*
>
> *Gigolo loved water in every form. He taught all his stall neighbors at home how to dunk their hay into their water first, before munching it in delight. When he was not playing with water, he was constantly active in his stall, tinkering and pottering around. His door had to be secured with a special latch because he was so clever that he managed, again and again, to pry open the old bolt and escape.*

When Isabell first found Gigolo and he found her, on that life-changing day in Warendorf, she was far from thinking about success and medals. Her first goals were all about developing him for the sport of dressage. However, it can safely be assumed that Dr. Schulten-Baumer already had the podium in view. He thought big and had always wanted one thing only: major international success. Dr. Schulten-Baumer spared Gigolo, so eager to learn, all the steps that one usually takes with a young horse—all the youngster shows and championships. He was only interested in the High School movements, the maximum level of difficulty that is required at the very top of the international sport.

And Dr. Schulten-Baumer's plan paid off. Gigolo developed rapidly, competing in his first Grand Prix in 1990, at the age of seven. (Participation in the Grand Prix at that age would not be permitted according to today's regulations.) In 1991, at the age of eight, he won his first European Championship title. Isabell is particularly proud that he would eventually go to the Olympic Games ten years later, at the "old" age of seventeen, and win gold and silver. It shows that she and Dr. Schulten-Baumer did not wear him out with so much time in a high-performance sport. It also shows how tough Gigolo was. He only had to pause his career due to an injury once in his life.

Isabell's international career started with a thirteenth place at the European Championships in the Luxembourg resort town of Mondorf-les-Bains in 1989. She was aboard Weingart, her "schoolmaster" who was helping her learn to handle the most difficult tasks. Two years later, with Gigolo, she dashed gaily to their first great success. You could tell, from that moment on, she was a young woman who took on the world. No matter what happened, she would ride like she had nothing to lose.

*Back then I was coming from my family farm, with some local competition experience in riding from A to B. And suddenly, I could see the great wide world out there. That was just incredible for me. And that's exactly how I rode. I have always been competitive, but there was no pressure. I only wanted to show that I knew how to ride. Dr. Schulten-Baumer supported and pushed me and had a lot of fun doing it.*

The 1991 European Championships in Donaueschingen, Germany, offered a very special showdown: Two nice, young women smiled at each other—and then fought each other, tooth and nail. Twenty-four-year-old Nicole Uphoff came as the "established one," having been crowned Olympic Champion in 1988, and World Champion with Rembrandt, the elegant bay horse she now rode, just one year before. And Isabell Werth, age twenty-two, was the *parvenu* on young Gigolo. Both were quite unusual pictures in dressage, a sport that, until that moment, was considered something of a pastime for old rich folks who liked to fabricate secret intrigues, talk about each other badly behind the scenes, and outdo each other's presents to officials. A battle between two young up-and-comers? That was new. And full of piquancy: Nicole Uphoff, a former student of Dr. Schulten-Baumer, in a duel with Isabell Werth, his rising star.

Already the team competition, where the Germans won the gold medal (obligatory at the time), could hardly be recognized as being about a "team": Certainly, there were four pairs competing "together" for a medal. Besides Isabell and Nicole, there was the "mounted policeman," Klaus Balkenhol, with Goldstern, as well as Sven Rothenberger, aboard Andiamo. Yet, the Grand Prix came to a head as a duel between the two young ladies from the same team, who both looked as if they had just outgrown the "horse-girl" stage but fought for the lead as if they were lieutenants of the cavalry.

In the team competition, Nicole had to deal with the moods of her genius Rembrandt. He spooked at the television cameras, which, as would always be incomprehensible to him, moved when he passed them, and he jumped around skittishly. Isabell, on the other hand, carefree with her forward Gigolo, laid down an almost flawless test—only a little slip in the flying changes disrupted the perfect picture. She beat the champion by the fraction of eight points (back then, results were not converted to a percentage). Thus, the metaphorical gauntlet had been thrown down before the individual competition, taking place in the Grand Prix Special the following day.

Nicole vowed that she would get her nervous gelding under better control. Her expression darkened. She seemed to think about nothing else but her next performance and the question of how to derail Isabell's attack. Her concentration was apparent in her performance the next day: She regained control, focus, consistency, and elegance. Rembrandt did not have the chance to spook—there were only two tiny incidents—and when she left the ring, smiling, she knew: She had brought out the best in her horse.

As Nicole exited the arena, she met Isabell, who was on deck. "See ya," Nicole said to the younger woman.

The audience held its breath.

Isabell was sure that she could strike back. It was true that Nicole had taken every risk, had ridden all extensions to the maximum. "Riding forward" is what equestrian experts call it. So Isabell did the same, with no less nerve. She risked everything; the attack was on, and Gigolo fought for her and with her.

And Isabell won that duel, once again. It was her first individual title—European Champion. Meanwhile, Dr. Schulten-Baumer gleamed with the satisfaction that his new student had beaten his former student.

Nobody had anticipated that these two young, determined women in their elegant tailcoats, with their hair in tight buns under shiny top hats, would leave their mark on the competitive dressage world for many years to come. "Tough fights with soft hands"—this was the phrase that applied to the regular duels between Isabell and Nicole. And then, when the era of Rembrandt came to an end, the same was true for Isabell and Dutch rider Anky van Grunsven, with her elegant and highly talented horses, Bonfire and Salinero.

Thus, Isabell quickly learned how to win on the sport's biggest stage. Behind the scenes, however, traveling on the fancy dressage circuit, Isabell sometimes felt out of place—as if she had been transported into a strange world. The elite society of dressage riders, with a strict allocation of roles, long spoiled by consistent success since the last team defeat at the Olympic Games in Munich in 1972, was ruled and controlled by the great Liselott Linsenhoff. All the pieces of dressage came together at the Schafhof in Kronberg, Germany, the stable of this individual gold-medal winner of the Munich Games. Here, close to Frankfurt, numerous gold medals were aimed for and attained, and nobody questioned the successful system. The training practices of the industrial heiress were formative for the entire German dressage scene. Aachen resident Anton Fischer, a laundromat owner with white curls, served as a long-time Chef d'Equipe—essentially, Liselott's governor and master of ceremonies.

To everyone's surprise, it came naturally to Isabell to make her way in this world—her goal-oriented successes with such a talented young horse paved the way for her.

*Sometimes, I sat there at an expensive dinner and asked myself, somewhat at a loss, whether to use the cutlery from the inside out with every course or vice versa. All these things that were completely normal to everyone else present—how to stay in fancy hotels, how to deal with domestic staff, how to address people, how to behave at special functions, and how to make conversation—I had to pick up all of it. It was learning by doing. Dr. Schulten-Baumer introduced me "into society" and was by my side when the going got tough. And my, at the time, close friendship with Liselott Linsenhoff's daughter, Ann Kathrin, whom I had met in Mondorf as a teammate, helped me find my way around. All the while I sensed that not for all the money in the world could this way of life replace the warmth I had known in my parents' house.*

Isabell looked around...and composed herself in preparation to conquer a kingdom of which she was to be the queen very soon.

One year later in 1992, at the Olympic Games in Barcelona, Isabell and Dr. Schulten-Baumer were ready to pounce. Their plan was to spoil things for Nicole Uphoff and Rembrandt for the second time after the Europeans, but their Olympic premiere started off badly. Dr. Schulten-Baumer lost his temper so badly, right in the beginning, that he threatened to turn around and go back home. Coming up to the Games, he had expressed his concern several times that they might arrive and there would be no accreditation for him. "Accreditation" amounted to an ugly plastic card that identified someone as a member of the Olympic family. Without it, a person fell in the category of "absolute nobody."

The situation worsened when all others received the necessary ID cards, even those people from the German Equestrian Federation who had been declared "owners" of Gigolo or reserve horse Fabienne only to exhaust all possible access authorizations and get extra accreditations. It was only Dr. Schulten-Baumer whom Olympic staff members could not find in their computers. He was justifiably upset. He, of all people, the great "maestro," and the true owner of the horse said to be the hot favorite—Gigolo. He, who should be subject to the greatest respect in the industry, saw himself pushed back into oblivion.

Dr. Schulten-Baumer took this as a personal affront. He grabbed the barrier that he was not allowed to pass, unlike all the others with him, and threatened: "We are leaving!"

Even though his accreditation was found after some time, a negative tension had already spread. And then the accommodations were problematic. There was one house, an hour outside of Barcelona, where all the German dressage participants lived together: Riders, trainers, officials—a crowd that, naturally, was likely to hate each other in such a tense and uncomfortable situation. Everyone suffered from the heavy heat, especially those who were older. It was so hot in Barcelona that one day somebody actually fried an egg on a seat of the Olympic bleachers. And yet, the riders rode in tailcoats and top hats under the merciless sun.

To make matters worse, Mrs. Linsenhoff had hired a cook from the German Army in Warendorf who served the sweaty folks goulash with noodles in the middle of the day. George Theodorescu, the famous trainer and father of Olympian Monica Theodorescu and who later became the German national coach, commented with the attitude of a sophisticated bon vivant: "I only eat goulash when I am in Hungary. And I am never in Hungary."

For a moment, laughter relaxed the tense atmosphere. But all thought returned to how German dressage riders or their entourage should prepare for the arena when the most dangerous competition could be found amongst their own ranks...*and* when they were all forced to live together in a shared space.

*Nicole Uphoff was engaged to jumper rider Otto Becker at the time. The fact that Otto was also in Barcelona as part of the Olympic jumping team was everything but an advantage for the couple, as he had to live in different accommodations with his team. Hence, they hardly saw each other. Since I had the only room with a phone, I had to frequently accept Otto's phone calls, bring in Nicole, and leave my room to give their sweet talk appropriate space.*

*And even worse: Dr. Schulten-Baumer had to share a bathroom with Nicole Uphoff's parents, with whom he'd had a falling out years before. Within days, the underlying tensions became so overpowering that they eventually broke, and all of us, together, threw the Honorable Anton Fischer into the pool. You can blame it on cabin fever.*

It should be noted that the chicken-hearted Rembrandt and the overachiever Gigolo, whose nerves apparently worried everyone concerned, were as cool as cucumbers compared to the irritated humans in the Catalan villa!

The Grand Prix of the team medal competition saw the next episode of combat between Isabell and Nicole. Monica Theodorescu with Grunox was part of the team this time, alongside Klaus Balkenhol. She had to compete under especially difficult conditions: When she entered the stadium, the thermometer showed 104 degrees Fahrenheit.

Isabell and Nicole had their horses perfectly prepared. Rembrandt's fragile psyche had been wrapped in bubble wrap for days and just shortly before the performance, his rider "woke him up" with slightly more serious activities. Gigolo's nerves were also taken into account during the time leading up to competing. Isabell acted according to her own plan.

Ambitious and highly focused, both riders performed their tests, and neither of them blew it. Isabell even allowed herself to smile provocatively at the judges as she passed them on the short side. "So?" she seemed to say. "Do you dare to place me in front of the great Nicole again, like you did last year?"

Not this time. Nicole's lead only amounted to six points—a tiny fraction.

That the Germans won team gold did not surprise anyone, but an even greater cause awaited: the Olympic individual medals.

While Nicole let her Rembrandt shine at what many thought was the height of his career—so much so that the Swiss head judge Wolfgang Niggli claimed the performance brought tears to his eyes—Isabell's results with Gigolo dropped in the Grand Prix Special, and the Freestyle to music was not yet part of the Olympic program. The performance showed that while Isabell was not lacking the desire and ability to win, she still lacked the experience for such big moments.

Nicole reached the final halt in the heat of the arena with a crimson face. Her groom and fiance Otto Becker had to pour an entire bottle of water over her head as soon as she was out of the saddle. Isabell and Gigolo, on the other hand, were boiling over mentally. This manifested itself as mistakes in the ring. Many very atypical slipups happened. Gigolo got muddled in the flying changes, a pirouette failed...they "screwed up everything," according to Isabell. She had been flying high, participating in the Olympics at age twenty-three on her only-nine-year-old horse, team-gold-medal-winner in her first attempt with a brilliant performance—the world seemed to stand wide open for Isabell and Gigolo, the shooting stars of dressage. But then they did not shine as much during the finale as they could have, and, at first, the silver medal she won did not seem to be any comfort to Isabell.

The young German rider took away a new experience from Barcelona, which would be useful for coming shows and championships: She already knew how to win. She still had to learn how to lose. The magic of the first year had ended, and she was no longer walking the tightrope with a laugh—she had unexpectedly fallen off. To remain at the top, where the ride for gold medals took place, she needed more than easygoing overconfidence.

*I definitely learned the hard way. I would argue now that we were completely overambitious. I had to learn first what I needed to ride my tests just as optimally under pressure and that I must always meet the performance standards.*

Isabell's defeat in the Barcelona duel with Nicole upset her extremely. Not so much because she could not satisfy her personal ambition; she was mostly ashamed that she had disappointed Dr. Schulten-Baumer. He had done so much for her, and it had been possible to repeat the coup at the European Championships in Donaueschingen on a much grander scale at the Olympics, but she had messed it up. Isabell was quite hard on herself and came to the decision that she must grow from the experience. Perfection became the goal once and for all. It was as if dark clouds appeared over her, and she decided to work harder than ever.

In Barcelona, the German team won all obtainable medals: gold for the team and individual gold for Nicole, silver for Isabell, and bronze for Klaus Balkenhol with his feisty police horse Goldstern. Anton Fischer delivered the maximum that was possible to the German Equestrian Federation. Warendorf could let the champagne flow.

However, on the international dressage committees, officials were frowning. They racked their brains about how to break up the German dominance. Their reasons were sound: A sport in which the winning nation can be determined ahead of time and where competitors only have to fight internally for rankings is strongly suspected to be a minority program. It becomes the opposite of what the International Olympic

Committee means when it talks about "universality." It is also lacking the excitement that interests people outside the inner circle. The qualitatively superior continuation of a traditional culture is not enough for a sport to survive long-term, next to others such as tennis, cycling, or rugby. The "wow-effect" was missing. If the balance of power during competitions did not change, it was made clear to the Fédération Equestre Internationale (FEI), the continued existence of dressage in the Olympic program would, sooner or later, be at stake. As a result, this sport, the foundation of all equestrianism, would collapse into irrelevance.

So what was to be done? The emerging Dutch riders offered some competition but still needed a bit of propulsive power from the outside to be ready to attack the Germans. The entire sport had to be modernized, with possibly more latitude in the scoring system. A solution was found: a Freestyle to music.

Audiences wanted to see something like that, especially the non-horsey folk in front of the television: Beautiful horses "dancing" to saucy tunes, a little bit like pairs figure skating, with one partner in fur and the other in tails. Show and entertainment. For the traditionalists, music was thought to be unnecessary background noise in the dressage ring. This quiet sport, enjoyed by insiders in the early morning hours—where the jingling of bridles, the snorting of horses, and the chirping of birds in the trees was all you could hear—had turned into an ear-piercing opera or a disco. But, now the audience was able to tap its feet to the beat of the music, which was easier than noting petty comments about a not-perfectly-cadenced canter in the program. The Freestyle represented one step out into the world but also away from reliable scoring criteria based on a classical code of values: Performance with the aim to do the horse as much justice as possible and to maintain his health and long life. In retrospect, though, there is no doubt that with the implementation of the Freestyle and by riding on the wave of Dutch fan enthusiasm, the FEI ensured the survival of the Olympic dressage program and opened it to a lot more publicity worldwide.

*Dr. Schulten-Baumer and I did not argue against the changes outright. However, we were already afraid that medals would be awarded for just the Freestyle, without incorporating the scoring of the "classical" classes. Similar to what it is like in the Olympic individual ranking today, where you start again at zero after the team competition. After all, for the first time, the Freestyle opened the doors for non-equestrian criteria, such as artistic expression, choreography, and music. The clear comparison of athletic performance was blurred by effects—the components of technical difficulties have not yet been objectified by a transparent basic score, even today. In addition, the Freestyle made it possible to highlight the horse's strengths through repeated movements and a clever positioning of these movements in the arena, and to hide weaknesses, or even make them disappear behind the atmosphere created by the music.*

The result: Those who could handle music, atmosphere, and creative choreography now had a chance to position themselves against the dominant German dressage riders who had been, so far, untouchable in the saddle. And that is exactly what happened. More and more emphasis was placed on the Freestyle, and the Dutch riders, with Anky van Grunsven in the lead, waged a longstanding, resourceful, but also bitter attack against the competition from the country next door. They dragged more and more judges onto their side. The Dutch, one of the strongest equestrian nations in any case, developed into

Freestyle specialists, mainly within the World Cup, an event championed by Dutch dressage promoter Joep Bartels.

This meant that, from now on, Isabell not only had to be better than her competition, she also had to be so strong that the judges could not get past her, despite their tendency to want to break up old hierarchies.

These new duels, now between Isabell and Anky, two strong-willed riders—both highly talented, determined, and ready for anything—became symbolic of an entire era. These two, who grew as riders with each other's mutual competition, who each took a deep breath before entering the arena, who loaded up on adrenaline, and who gave each other nothing. These two, who goaded each other, who gained more brilliance every time they rode, ultimately became bitter rivals.

*I had to try to notch up my performance in order to compare to Anky, in order to be back in front. I had to be particularly creative.*

The result of Isabell's strategic considerations was a Freestyle the world had not seen before. This Freestyle's premiere took place at the European Championships in Mondorf in 1995, the place where she had her international debut six years earlier. The music played along lightly, playfully, similar to how Gigolo was supposed to be on his feet (as the result of hard work): "Just a Gigolo," combined with "Always Look on the Bright Side of Life." This Freestyle was an unprecedented sensation. The highlight of the performance actually deserved to go down in dressage history as the "Isabell Werth Triple." Never before had a rider shown such a series of difficult movements with her horse: Isabell rode in canter with full extension through the diagonal, to a certain point, where a switch flipped for Gigolo.

Instead of pushing forward with impulsion, he, all of a sudden, had to shorten significantly, bringing his hind legs far under his body to perform one-and-a-half pirouettes on his hind legs. This required absolute body control, so that the rhythm of the canter movement was never interrupted. It was like trying to fit a square peg into a round hole in the sport of riding. As if Usain Bolt, after a one-hundred meter sprint, had to keep running on the spot, without stopping his movement, and juggle balls at the same time.

And that was not all. Flying changes immediately followed the pirouettes, first every two strides and then tempi changes every stride. This did not just require strength and body control from the horse, but also enormous focus. Imagine Usain Bolt again, finished with his sprint and his juggling trick, now moving off into a tango. Would Bolt have been able to do it? Gigolo, the perfect athlete and acrobat was, and eventually, with practice, he was able to replicate it very casually. He gave such challenges more than his all. Just like his rider.

When the audience in Mondorf saw Isabell's Freestyle, some actually sat with their mouths open in amazement. The leading Swedish judge at the time, Eric Lette, pulled out maximum marks and could hardly compose himself. The element of surprise had upstaged all politics. Isabell had parried the Dutch attack for the time being.

The crowd had armed themselves with "Oranje" (the nickname for national sports teams from the Netherlands) hats, jackets, and flags—Dutch colors—as well as a large dose of fanaticism. The attempt had begun to turn the "posh sport of dressage" into a sideshow of German-Dutch rivalry that, traditionally, was enacted in the soccer stadium.

There was a simple reason that Isabell did not have to suffer more from the Dutch front at the Olympic Games in

Atlanta one year later. You see, the German team was mainly preoccupied with itself. First, Nicole Uphoff enforced her right to compete as the defending Olympic Champion with the help of a preliminary injunction and followed the team with Rembrandt, who was already seventeen years old. It turned out that the genius bay horse was no longer fit enough for the demands of the arena, and she had to withdraw before the finale, and before the vets did it for her. In addition, there was unease within the team. Martin Schaudt took Durgo to Atlanta, a highly gifted horse with a traumatic past. His previous owners had been unable to manage him and he'd been taken to the slaughterhouse at the age of five, avoiding the "skinner" only because of a mistake. Durgo remained a difficult horse, which, ultimately, was a lucky break for Schaudt. Nobody wanted to buy the talented mover from him, so he inevitably turned into a championship rider himself! But he was the "new kid," an outsider without a lobby, and he was considered a longshot. So, right up until the last moment, traveling reserve rider Nadine Capellmann tried to replace him and make it onto the team herself. But it was to no avail.

The constant comparison put the young man and his tricky horse under immense performance pressure before they even rode for scores. Schaudt felt picked on, sat on a tack box, and whined that he wanted to go home to the Alps. And all of this happened even though he and Nadine generally got along well and later even dated for a while. Isabell tried to observe these developments and their implications from a distance.

*For me, talking with Monica Theodorescu over a glass of beer on the porch of our hotel every night was highly relaxing and entertaining at the same time.*

Thus, domestic bliss went out the window once again among the Germans, who had decided to cohabitate once more, despite the stressful and unhappy experiences of Barcelona. This time, they took up lodgings on a farm. Balkenhol was part of the team once again. But even though he was wearing his police uniform, he could not install order.

Cabin fever was predestined to set in again, and the then seventy-two-year-old Chef d'Equipe Anton Fischer was, once again, its victim. He desperately tried to calm down his crew. They, however, released bugs in his room, drank his champagne, and refilled the bottles with water. In Atlanta, there was hardly a break to focus on one's own performance. But this time, Isabell was not to be flustered. She knew she must remain composed. It was obvious that any tension in her transferred to Gigolo. He did not have a clue what everyone was so upset about, but he tended to be borderline hysteric every now and then. Therefore, Dr. Schulten-Baumer and Isabell rented rooms in a motel close to the horse park entrance for the duration of the competition and did their own thing.

By now, Gigolo had reached the peak of his potential. He was thirteen years old and had been around the block. He performed the movements effortlessly, his body was still full of spring and elasticity, and he was full of energy in his very best moments. He was also at his prettiest. His neck appeared round, now equipped with firm muscles. Nothing prevented him from fully developing his power; he was at his best physical state. His training had, more and more, enabled him to use his own body optimally. His flexibility, carriage, and balance were worthy of a top human gymnast. Experts might even say that such a horse, fully working through his body with optimally molded musculature, could find the ideal peak of physical expression.

And of course, Gigolo had also developed mentally. He now understood exactly when it counted most, which is when he always gave it one hundred percent.

And yet, the entire Atlanta adventure started off similar to Barcelona.

Isabell and Gigolo turned in a fantastic Grand Prix for the team, earning the Germans the expected gold medal once again. But then their Grand Prix Special was full of mistakes. Isabell lost her lead to Anky van Grunsven on the bay gelding Bonfire, giving all of the Netherlands new hope. Had the time finally come? Would the "Oranje" be able to wrench individual gold away from the Germans? There was a good chance, after all, as only the Dutch specialty was still to be ridden—the Freestyle, specifically included in the program to strengthen the Dutch and to make the dominant Germans vulnerable.

The riders had two days off before the finale; two days where Isabell ran around with big question marks in her eyes. What now? She dreaded the psychological effect the results so far would likely have on the five judges. They had seen it clearly: The favorite was struggling. This could change their inner perspective. They would wait for and watch for Isabell's mistakes in the Freestyle and might even see just how they would juggle decisive points to make way for a sensation and finally award the gold medal to Anky.

*I found Bonfire fascinating. He might not have been the ultimate beauty, but his movement was spectacular. He had extreme shoulder freedom. And he was an incredibly honest, athletic horse: He had a lot to offer—besides the walk, maybe—and he did not have to be kept in such a state of tension as Anky's future horse, Salinero. Those two were real opponents for Gigolo and myself. And he helped shape an era.*

Isabell and Dr. Schulten-Baumer went into tunnel-vision mode. In Atlanta, only the two of them and Gigolo existed. And when the day finally came, only one thing was important:

Attack.

*I said to myself, We will fight and turn everything around. And it worked. You have these moments when you enter the arena and you are carried by the atmosphere. You feel that something very special is happening around you. And that Freestyle, in those Games, it carried me—everything was perfect, from A to Z. The stadium was full, the atmosphere electrifying, and I suddenly started to enjoy every second of it.*

Isabell's astounding performance in Atlanta can still be watched online. There was no moment in her program when one could breathe; one highlight followed another. Down the centerline, the Freestyle began with a highly difficult movement, the passage, immediately followed by the piaffe, and, during the piaffe, Gigolo turned into a pirouette. It was a movement as rich as a three-tier cake. Naturally, the canter work also included the Isabell Werth Triple. It was an extravaganza from beginning to end, and all the elements were executed perfectly, seamlessly. A golden Freestyle. What else?

After Isabell had saluted and left the arena through a lane of enthusiastically applauding people, after Gigolo had received the obligatory sugar cube from Dr. Schulten-Baumer, after Isabell had dismounted and was surrounded by people, only then did she react, as if from far away. And after she had finally stepped up on the podium during the prize-giving ceremony, after she had received the gold medal, when the German national anthem was playing, then she started to cry. Entire streams, rivers of tears—she could not hold back.

*All the pressure of previous years and days dispersed with those tears. I still struggled with the disappointment that I could not deliver the triumph that Dr. Schulten-Baumer had longed for four years earlier. And now, I had made up for this failure. Our great dream of winning an individual Olympic gold medal had come true! The goal had been accomplished. What a relief! I had been riding for Dr. Schulten-Baumer for ten years, and I felt I had finally proven worthy of the role that he had in mind for me. I cried and cried; I cried the awful tension away, the exhausting days, the daily stress of practicing perfection.*

And with every tear, something else seemed to become ever more tangible: that the pain of the next failure was already at the doorstep of the grand triumph Isabell was just now celebrating on the podium in Atlanta. The bond and the harmony that had prevailed between her and Dr. Schulten-Baumer during the past days also gave her an inkling of the potential frustration to come. And, of course, she knew even during the moment of her greatest success that the Dutch would not give up. Their weakness, not to be able to demonstrate their team's potential to its fullest during championships, distorted the picture. Someday, as much was certain, they would succeed. But Isabell and Gigolo would make sure they fought in vain for a long time. They had to be patient until the very last act of the drama.

The animosities between teams became more and more disturbing; aggression clouded championships. It reached a point where the aggression would have been too much in a football game, let alone in the conservative world of dressage competition. There was a time when Isabell went to pick up her detailed result sheets at the show office after her win at the 1997 European Championships in Verden, Germany, but they were missing. Every rider had a right to these result sheets before scores became available digitally. Isabell's missing results reappeared in a Dutch equestrian journal, annotated with paranoid comments about the scandalously and allegedly "biased" scoring. Isabell was then subjected to boos from the crowd at Dutch competitions for the rest of the year. Agitated fans shouted questions about the "German judging conspiracy." She was made aware of any small weakness when it was highlighted by the press in an overblown fashion: Gigolo had started to occasionally wiggle with his hind leg in the piaffe. He was swishing his tail during the test. Petitions against individual members of the ground jury were collected.

Isabell may love competitive opposition, but she needs a harmonic social environment and found these experiences very unpleasant. They took the joy out of her beloved sport. She complained that she now had to justify every good performance. She became more and more thin-skinned, while inwardly clenching her fist at the same time.

Isabell's morale hit rock bottom during the 1998 World Equestrian Games in Rome. Isabell's usual smile disappeared, and Anky van Grunsven's face froze in contempt. Asked about Isabell's scores, the Dutch rider said snarkily, "I really don't care, but it is bad for the sport."

The tension that both riders were under was appalling. Their coaches positioned themselves on either sideline of the dressage ring; just their looks meant business. The two men also came across as a clash of cultures: On the one hand, there was the conservative Dr. Schulten-Baumer, no longer so young, in a suit and tie. On the other hand, there was Sjef Janssen, a former cyclist with a blonde rockstar hairdo, whom Anky was to marry later in Las Vegas.

Busloads of Dutch fans poured into the stadium and stirred up opinion against their favorite's German rival. And indeed:

When Anky's score was announced after her Freestyle, Isabell had withdrawn to the barn to not have to witness the hatred in person. She knew, when boos and hisses echoed across to where she stood with the horses, out of the spotlight, that she had become the new World Champion. It was a poisoned victory, though, as she had to defend herself against nasty allegations from now on. From a nationalist standpoint, this might have been the darkest day in dressage sport ever. Even when Isabell and Gigolo entered the arena for the victory ceremony, they were exposed to humiliating hoots and slurs. Her sport had always been a question of mind over matter for her, but now it took a turn for the worse. It took all her willpower to be able to even feel a little bit pleased about her success.

*I have always been driven by the competition, the positive fight for the best performance. I find that fascinating, and I get a thrill out of it—to be on par with the best in the world. But during that time competing against Anky, everything was so heated up and nationalistic. It seemed as if I had to fight against a wall of orange in every arena. I even heard the word "Nazi" on more than one occasion.*

When Isabell won a Freestyle over Bonfire at the show in Geneva with Amaretto, the young horse who was to be Gigolo's successor, things got out of hand. Anky lost her composure in the foyer of the press conference and snapped at Isabell. It became clear to Isabell that Anky believed Isabell had only won because she called up the judges regularly and worked to influence them.

"What do you want from me?" Isabell asked. Anky just huffed.

The truth was, while Isabell was now supposed to justify her success all the time, Anky was also under immense pressure as the figurehead of Dutch paranoia. So much for "horse-girl idyll"…the tension got to both of them. This was no longer about having fun.

Isabell's aim was to not be drawn into a bad movie by Anky's fan club, entitled: "Two Drama Queens in Tails." That night, the Swiss show jumper Willi Melliger, who passed away in 2018, came to Isabell and said something to her that sounded a lot like Clint Eastwood, and which she recalls clearly to this day: "Punish your enemies through victories."

*Willi Melliger's advice connected me even more to Gigolo, the horse that gave me his all and carried me to my triumph. I owed it to him to defend his honor against any allegations.*

The truth was, Gigolo was always a better horse than Bonfire with regard to quality. Bonfire was an extremely elegant bay with exceptional potential for the higher movements, specifically passage and piaffe, which are crucial movements in determining whether a horse can become a star or not. But Bonfire had serious problems with the walk. He was lacking class in one of the three basic gaits. His Dutch rider, indeed, managed to compensate for her horse's major weaknesses with a fireworks display of accentuated movements that wowed the audience and the judges. Gigolo, in the meantime, remained a model example for clean and serious performance. Back then, a considerate debate about dressage fundamentals and the contrast between the two horses might have done the sport good. But it was not possible: Two irreconcilable sides stood opposite each other, and the riders' relationship only began to relax a little when Gigolo and Bonfire eventually ended their careers.

But that comes later.

It was 1999 when Anky van Grunsven left the German elite behind and became the European Champion in Arnheim, the Netherlands. However, this feat was accomplished without Isabell's challenge. The German rider followed the competition in jeans and t-shirt from the bleachers, for her situation had rapidly changed. She was no longer invulnerable. On the contrary: She had to realize how swiftly luck can sometimes turn the other way.

*I'd often thought it, that unhappy possibility at the back of my mind. It was all going too well. At some point I had to expect the bubble to burst. But I got a tragedy.*

First, her next Olympic hope, Amaretto, died painfully, during a severe colic episode.

Then Gigolo hurt himself.

Isabell did not quit without a fight and started in Arnheim with her reserve horse, Antony. But when he had a fever before the Freestyle, she had to withdraw. Just to be on the safe side, the organizers prepared new music to play during the awards presentation: the Dutch national anthem.

Isabell, her European Championship title lost, sighed and expressed the hope that, surely, her bad luck had to be over. A little bit of dark humor rang in her words, since Gigolo stood in his stall with a tendon injury, and no one knew if he was to ever fully recover at sixteen years old.

And the worst thing? Secretly, she was consumed by feelings of guilt.

*The question of whether I could have prevented Gigolo's injury, or at least the full extent of it, tormented me. I saw the images of the show in Aachen go by in my mind, again and again, of this fatal Saturday in June 1999, when I tacked up Gigolo for the Grand Prix Special. I clearly felt that something was wrong during the warm-up, and I said to Dr. Schulten-Baumer, who stood on the sideline of the warm-up ring: "Something is not right." But he refused to accept this. "You always have an excuse," he complained to me. "It's because your hand is not quiet, just ride correctly for once." So, I sucked it up and entered the arena, rode the customary loop around the ring, and once again, I had the feeling that Gigolo had taken a wrong step somehow. But I did not follow my gut feeling. Instead, as usual, I did what Dr. Schulten-Baumer told me to do.*

*During the test, Gigolo's conditioned worsened. We had closed our eyes before the truth out of sheer ambition. I had too willingly obeyed to walk the wrong route. I will forever blame myself that I did not object more strongly in that moment and have it my way. I am responsible. I am the reason Gigolo's initial injury got worse and the consequences became severe.*

Gigolo moved through the difficult test with his injury, and people with a sharp eye saw that he was lame. Out of habit, the judges still saw him in fifth place, even though they should have rung the bell to end such a performance early. Experts, depending on which side they were on, were either horrified, or knowingly nudged each other with their elbows. Journalists worked on wording that represented the shocking situation appropriately. Isabell's parents were full of sympathy for their daughter.

*It was an absolutely shitty feeling. A disaster.*

After the test, the veterinarian diagnosed a "beginning lameness" in Gigolo's front right leg. The leg was swollen and tender.

Gigolo, Isabell's loyal companion, suffered from a suspensory ligament injury. The recovery of such an injury takes a long time, especially if the horse is already sixteen. In the nine years of his exceptional career, Gigolo had not only always been motivated, but he had also been very tough. Aachen was his first serious injury.

Coincidence imposed itself here: It was Gigolo who bound Dr. Schulten-Baumer and his young neighbor together in 1989, the day of their first meeting, to become an unbeatable team. And it was Gigolo who also most clearly represented the ruin of their relationship. The argument in the barn, following the ruinous test, could not be ignored.

*I really want to emphasize here that I don't want to shift the responsibility to Dr. Schulten-Baumer. I sat on Gigolo, and I was the one who had the power to act differently. I was almost thirty years old. The times of blind obedience were definitely over.*

Gigolo needed six months to recover. He missed the European Championships, but the 2000 Olympic Games in Sydney lay ahead.

It was almost a miracle that Isabell managed to qualify with Gigolo for the top event of her sport once again: A seventeen-year-old horse that had already achieved so much and was coming back from serious injury was still capable of such impressive performances. It seemed as if fate finally treated her kindly again. Originally, poor Amaretto was intended to be brought along for Sydney, but now Gigolo filled in for Isabell once more. An important part of the process, these Games helped finally heal the sore point that the events of Aachen had left behind. The bitter moment when Isabell had not heeded her own instincts, resulting in Gigolo's injury, had not, in fact, ended his career as so many feared. Gigolo was still in the game—a little bit older and richer, having survived one more painful experience, but, as always, full of drive.

And despite Anky van Grunsven being the hot favorite once again, and even though she had saddled Bonfire one more time, also now seventeen years old, the excitement was not as prominent as it used to be. Some Dutch fans had still packed their Oranje hats for Australia, but the two sides no longer went crazy, attacking each other. Just like the two aging horses, the nationalist sentiments also became a little more mellow.

Gigolo did not reach his best form possible in the Special.

*The shoeing was to blame. Since the horses had to start their quarantine weeks before the Games, due to the strict Australian regulations, Gigolo had to have a farrier appointment. He had very thin hoof walls, which is why our farrier at home made sure not to take off a lot of hoof horn. He also made an effort to make the hot shoeing process as short as possible, so as not to lose more unnecessary hoof matter. Our farrier in Sydney didn't know Gigolo that well. This is by no means an accusation, but it took Gigolo a little while before he was his usual self. Of all the tests, he showed his weakest performance in the Grand Prix Special. The point is, it wasn't because he and I were suffering under the same kind of pressure we had in Barcelona and Atlanta. And also, most importantly, it wasn't because his tendon was bothering him; it was a temporary problem that eventually solved itself.*

*I enjoyed our Freestyle, knowing it was Gigolo's farewell performance on the big stage. He didn't make any mistakes, but the fire inside him did not burn as it once did. He was the most beautiful at the height of his career. The sparkle and the charisma of younger years are naturally lost a little with*

*time, and performance becomes more about solidity and expe-
rience—which, by the way, doesn't have to be a bad thing.
Gigolo delivered a brilliant performance in Sydney. But I still
felt it very clearly: His time had come.*

For the first time, the duel between the four-legged seniors
fell to Bonfire. Just this once, Anky passed Isabell without
controversy. The judges attested Gigolo delivered a flawless
performance, but Bonfire was truly dancing. Isabell's performance was a model example, fit for a book about correct
dressage riding, but it was not enough to keep the competition at bay this time. Bonfire sparkled with star-appeal,
once more lifting his legs like a circus horse to the Neil Diamond's hit "Song Sung Blue," and the judges pulled out a world
record score.

On that day, Isabell also had reasons to cry on the winner's
podium—this time with silver around her neck, listening to
the Dutch national anthem.

"It wasn't always easy," she said after the ceremony as she
thought about all the booing she'd had to endure while she was
winning gold medals and titles that others felt should have
been won by the Dutch riders.

Whether silver or gold, though, her success in Sydney was
a small extra, as it settled the matter: Gigolo was now the most
successful dressage horse in history. And the great Bonfire could
finally leave with a gold medal as both horses went toward their
retirement. For the moment, the fierce German-Dutch head-to-
head had come to an end—albeit "to be continued."

Isabell had to, yet again, defy a lack of peace within her
own camp in Sydney. The atmosphere on the German team
was one of jealousy and animosity. The other female riders on
the team—Ulla Salzgeber with Rusty, Nadine Capellmann with

Farbenfroh, and Alexandra Simons-de Ridder with Chacomo—
did not feel it necessary to watch the rides of their teammates.
Anton Fischer, by now seventy-five years old, again tried his
best to conciliate, but it is fair to say that never before or after
has an Olympic team reacted to winning a team gold medal
with such grumpy looks on their faces as the German dressage
team did in Sydney.

Those on the outside feared that something terrible had
happened, about which nobody wanted to talk, but this was not
the case. The cause of the rift was that one rider of the four-
some had to give up the individual competition. They were
all qualified, but only three riders per nation were allowed to
start. Isabell was the strongest rider; Nadine Capellmann, with
the colorful chestnut Farbenfroh, was second best. Ulla Salzgeber—not known as the life of the party in any case—prevailed
over her rival Alexandra Simons-de Ridder, evoking bitterness
on Alexandra's part as both had, somewhat bewilderingly,
achieved the same score. The fact they were both blessed with
wonderful horses—one with the large, imposing Rusty, the
other one with the impressively passaging Chacomo—was not
enough to help either find peace in the process.

In the end, the music stopped playing during Ulla's Freestyle. The black-haired amazon fought grimly on and came
third after Anky and Isabell; the rest of the team acknowledged the result with a bleak nod.

In comparison with the German intra-squad strife,
Isabell's relationship with Anky van Grunsven and her sup-
porters became more relaxed over the years. Initially, both
women were unable to separate business from emotions.
Anky's trainer, Sjef Janssen, was able to, though. A scrupu-
lous, clever guy, always fighting for his advantage, he had
been hardened through his career in cycling. Ultimately, all

three of them worked together in changing the economics of the sport of dressage. They lobbied to help it become more professional and no longer only a hobby for rich people who managed to make a name for themselves in the top level of the sport with the help of their bank account. Neither Isabell nor Anky were from classic, rich dressage families, and they wanted to ensure that people like them were enabled to make an independent living through the sport, more specifically, as riders in the arena and not as assistants of a more privileged sector of society. This meant that, in general, higher prize money had to be allocated at dressage competitions, so that athletes did not only have to spend money, but were also able to win money with a good performance. In fact, the standard of today's prize money in Europe is not least owed to the initiative of this once hostile trio, which made an attempt to democratize their discipline at least a little. After all, one assumes, at least theoretically, a level playing field for sports that culminate at the Olympic Games. Isabell, Anky, and Sjef began to turn dressage riding from an expensive hobby for a few high-flyers into a professional sport, and they led the way as examples.

Gigolo, who had bent over backward for Isabell for ten years, received a grand goodbye at his retirement celebration. Everything that is proven to make an audience cry on such occasions was summoned at the indoor show in Stuttgart, Germany: A lightshow, then lights off, and the four-legged hero in the ring, treating his fans to one last dance in the arena, his Freestyle music played live by an orchestra. Gigolo showed that he was in great shape; he was not "limping toward retirement" in any way. Thomas Bach, later the president of the International Olympic Committee, gave a a wonderful speech about Isabell's heroic horse, and wheelbarrows full of oats and carrots were brought in as a symbol that he would now be able to stuff himself as much as his heart pleased!

Isabell was one hundred percent at peace with herself and her horse. No long farewell tour was necessary. It was the end of November, and her journey with this chestnut, so full of character, had come to an end.

The choreography that Isabell developed for Gigolo is still the foundation of her performances today. In those days, her Freestyles included the most difficult movements at all possible within the rules. This has not changed. However, the competition has also learned something, and none of her risky combinations, which once took the international audience's breath away, is any longer exclusively hers.

Few noticed that the first three Freestyles Isabell rode with Weihegold almost exactly followed the template for Gigolo's Freestyle, just to new music, which she had had put together for her performance at the World Equestrian Games in Rome. However, never again has a horse been able to finish an exact copy of Gigolo's choreography and timing. This serves to show the movement this horse was capable of, and the enormous ground coverage he produced with his outstanding gaits and impulsion.

Isabell sometimes dreams that she could start over with this horse, with the knowledge she has today. Imagine what kind of performances they would be capable of!

Back home in Rheinberg, Gigolo was ridden by a girl at the farm for a while. He had to be "trained down." After a few months, he was brought to Mellendorf, close to Hanover, where Isabell now kept and trained her horses. She sat on the old gentleman's back a few times after, as at first, they alternated between riding him and turning him out. After two hours of turnout the old campaigner had usually had enough and wanted to come in and work.

*But eventually the day came when I brought Gigolo in from the field to ride him, and he had decided that it was time. He was calling to his friends in the field and indicated in no uncertain terms: Take me back outside to my buddies. Gigolo had finally fully retired on his own terms.*

*When I drove onto the property and saw him standing in the field, together with other retirees, Antony and Fabienne, I was happy. I laughed and said to myself: Just look, twenty gold medals, running around a pasture! What an era in my life. That era came to a close with the end of Gigolo's career. It was a great feeling.*

Gigolo reached the grand old age of twenty-six years. He incurred the worst injury of his life out in his retirement field, when he was about twenty-three. A group of young horses had gone through the fence at night; they probably chased him, and he fell. He was in a miserable condition the next morning and in a great deal of pain, standing only on three legs. It turned out that he had injured a nerve, and from that day until his last, he was troubled by it.

Isabell was by his side, three years later, when she had to say goodbye. She needed a long time to recover from the loss. If the former athletic "wonder horse" had not been provoked by youth, he surely would have made it to thirty.

# 3   THE DOCTOR

Dr. Uwe Schulten-Baumer—known by many as simply "The Doctor"—could be easily recognized from behind due to his characteristically round head and distinctive ears. On top you might find a borsalino of soft felt or, in the summer, a breathable Panama straw hat. At shows, he often wore a trench coat, with the belt pulled tightly around his classic belly and the pant legs of a suit, tailored at one of the finest addresses in Düsseldorf, peeking from underneath. On his feet: expensive, correctly polished leather shoes, with a few sandy traces—at most—from the outdoor arena. In one hand: a large umbrella or maybe a folding chair for tedious training rounds. He stood, or sat, on the side of the training arena and intently watched Isabell ride. When she finished and rode on a long rein, he might turn around, at which point one could see a flash of his silk tie from the luxury brand Hermès under his shirt collar. He collected these ties; he owned dozens. For him, correct appearance was a must. He wanted to be perceived as an accomplished gentleman and was never lacking the appropriate outfit.

Friends, said Dr. Uwe Schulten-Baumer sometimes, he did not need. He was hardly on a first-name basis with anyone.

It was foreign to him to confide in another person. This showed in the smile that he wore for the general public. At first sight this smile might almost seem distanced in a shy way. On second look, it was only distan*cing*. Almost wary. It would seem he considered each potential interaction before it happened: Could this person engage with him in a serious conversation about horses? No, likely not. Did this person at least show the necessary respect that a gentleman like The Doctor deserved? Did this individual honor The Doctor's social standing and his success? Did the person know his schooling of Nicole Uphoff and Rembrandt had revolutionized dressage riding? That he had been the initiator and manager of the greatest career ever known in the sport of dressage for years— that of Isabell Werth? Also unlikely.

Those who looked deep into his universal smile, recognized the danger lurking behind it. The Doctor was incredibly sensitive; he was a person who could snap for any minor reason—especially if he felt that somebody who was clearly inferior to him met him boldly at eye level...and it was worse if the person dared pat him "pal-like" on the shoulder. Or, if somebody referred to him as Isabell's "trainer," even though he was far more than that—mentor, patron, master. In those moments, it was best to rely on his formal politeness, and then to disappear quickly.

Life experience teaches us that those who snap quickly are also quick-tempered. That was the case with The Doctor. Rumor had it that he always traveled with two identically packed suitcases, so that he could leave immediately should the need arise. It would have been very much like him to be prepared for such an event. But the truth, in the end, was different. He may have often threatened to leave—but he always stayed.

The Doctor could be a charming man, sometimes almost coy, and he was a first-rate connoisseur of horses who could speak about the subject that had dominated his life in a wonderfully clear and precise diction, which demonstrated his respect for the horse. He was also choleric, with fits of rage that often provoked resistance in those people closest to him.

And Isabell was particularly close to him.

*The Doctor held an incredible fascination for me. From the first day, I had the feeling that his usual distance, which he maintained with most people, didn't apply to me. The chemistry between us was just right. I looked forward to riding with him every day. I soaked up everything he taught me and enjoyed my time with him immensely. At shows, in the warm-up ring, I watched all the riders at that time with wide eyes. I might bring those lessons learned in the warm-up ring home with me and try them out on Monday mornings, and The Doctor would laugh and say: "So, what is it that you learned this weekend?" You steal a third of your riding skills with your eyes, was one of his conclusions. Dr. Schulten-Baumer shaped and facilitated my entire athletic and professional career. I have since progressed, of course, but he laid the foundation. We had a great fundamental trust in each other and a deep emotional connection. I had the same passion he had in me; I think he realized a bit of him ran through me. When I think about The Doctor today, it is only with a feeling of great warmth and gratitude.*

Dr. Schulten-Baumer must have had an eye on the young rider Isabell was becoming for a long time before he, in a sense, won her over to pursue his own ambitions. She and his youngest daughter, Verena, went to the same school for a while. Both girls were members of the same riding club and participated in the German riding examinations together. There is even a photo of the two of them, Isabell on Funny, her pony, and Verena on Wisby, a big veteran schoolmaster. Tiny horse and big, stolid veteran stand next to each other in the picture, like ambassadors from two different equestrian worlds; they had just competed against each other in a class and Isabell, the girl from the metaphorical "ground floor," had won against Verena, the girl from the floor above.

*Compared to what The Doctor represented to me back then, I felt like a "country girl." When he and his family arrived at the riding club's indoor arena on Sunday mornings, I stood curiously on the side and watched how this man, with his equestrian-world panache, trained his oldest daughter, Alexa, who rode his horses at the classiest shows during those years. I saw the level at which he was teaching her and tried to learn everything that he offered, simply by watching. There were rumors in the neighborhood about how their training sessions often took place with raised voices. I would later experience this first-hand—but I also helped initiate those interactions, of course.*

Yelling was the norm in any arena back then. The harsh tone of the cavalry was still part of the general repertoire of riding education in the seventies and eighties. In general, it is quite astonishing how a lot of people were treated back then at their lesson barns and home arenas. They had to pay to basically be hassled like many grooms were—something that would most likely not be tolerated today. The "old-world" view of trainers, who could afford to "have a go" at their students and "dress them down" when they did not follow instructions, still prevailed. The greatest riding masters of all time were understood to have conducted themselves that way; The Doctor's teachers lashed out at him whenever they felt like it, for example. The times were still true to the motto: "Shut up and ride." If somebody tried to say that his or her horse was not feeling quite right on a particular day, even if it was mentioned hesitantly, the trainer would, more often than not, tear into the student with scorn.

*The tough life of a "protégé" didn't scare me. Rather, I perceived it to be an honor if I was yelled at. It showed that somebody was actively paying attention to me. Nothing of the sort would have lessened my unconditional thirst for knowledge and my enthusiasm for horses. On the contrary, I was mesmerized listening to and watching The Doctor, and through him I experienced a completely different quality of riding. And I wanted to be able to do the same thing.*

When she was a teenager, the course that Isabell wanted to use to prepare for her riding badge exam (as they have in Germany) was held by a former soldier—a retired colonel, who directed the children in the arena like soldiers during drills at the army barracks.

"Ride...march!"

"Ride..turrrrrn right!"

Isabell rode Funny's successor then—a smallish, formerly retired horse called Abendwind (Evening Wind) that her father Heinrich had brought back to work for his daughter. Abendwind, known around the barn as Sammy, was an experienced schoolmaster—the type that some call a "professor," because he fancies that he is smarter than everyone else. Especially humans.

*When our trainer instructed everyone to pick up the canter—"Ride…canter-march!"—he only had to start saying the syllable, "Can…" and Sammy knew what he was supposed to do. However, he was not suited to go last in a group. When it came his turn to canter, he started to buck, unless he was in the lead. And he did this so reliably that he bucked during the "audition" for the riding course, as soon as the colonel had called out "Can…" Sammy's bucking was so impressive the old officer kicked us out. Not good enough.*

*That's how my relationship with Dr. Uwe Schulten-Baumer began. His first wife saw what happened with the Colonel and decided I should take lessons from her husband at the same time as the course. And so, I eventually took the exam…with the best dressage score.*

This inner grit and ability to come back and fight when down is innate to every true athlete. The Isabell Werth "punch," which the entire equestrian world got to know later, began to show up during these early years. The Doctor called her parents and asked whether she could come and ride with him more often. They declined, at first, without informing their daughter about the offer. Their wish for Isabell was to grow up in a harmonious environment and decide for herself about serious training when she turned eighteen.

But Isabell already knew very well what she wanted.

Isabell was seventeen in December 1986 when she celebrated New Year's Eve at the Scheepers Family Farm located in Rheinberg, very close to the seventies-style white villa where Dr. Schulten-Baumer resided with his family.

*That is where the fatal party happened. Where it all began.*

The Doctor was also there. He took the opportunity and talked to Isabell, telling her he was in a bit of a spot as his usual rider was in the hospital and now his horses did not have enough exercise—he was looking for help. Isabell went to his stable the next day. And, when Dr. Schulten-Baumer's rider had recovered, The Doctor still wanted Isabell to ride for him and asked if she would continue. She had hoped for this offer and agreed immediately.

*It was as if a door opened for me into a world that, thus far, I had only known from television. I listened to him, in awe, deeply impressed, and wide-eyed. I saw him to be a sort of guru, and believed, finally, I had found a teacher worth following.*

It must have already been clear to The Doctor how much potential was in the new relationship with the young rider: He, with his passion, his knowledge, and his financial means, and she, with her unique feel for the inner state of horses, her irrepressible ambition, and her immense courage.

The first horse he gave her to ride was one that nobody enjoyed.

*Posilippo was a large chestnut that everybody was scared of. He was not really mean, but very sassy, unruly, and he had a buck in him.*

Posilippo was fresh, as horse people say. He soaked up energy and released it in a way that regularly sent riders to the ground. But not Isabell. Back when she had been in the hospital, at seven years old, she had not sworn for no reason to show her sassy gray mare, at the next opportunity, that her rider was not one to give up so easily. She had not been catapulted from her mount, cleaned the dirt off her breeches, and got back in the saddle, sometimes even multiple times during the day, in vain. Allowing fear to take hold was never an option for her. Posilippo? He was business as usual. She thought it normal to ride such a bucking freak. She rode him with total devotion and focus, and the more she committed herself, the more horses The Doctor gave to her to ride, especially, as his children—his son Uwe, a successful doctor, and his daughter Alexa—withdrew more and more from the competition circuit. Isabell was able to learn from their experienced horses. She took over the ride on the mare Fabienne, among others, who was to carry her to the World Cup victory in Gothenburg, Sweden, in 1992.

*I was deeply happy and grateful that I was allowed to ride all these horses, and it would have never occurred to me that I was doing The Doctor a favor. I only figured out later that while I may have made my dreams come true with his help, he also realized his dreams with me. The mutual passion for horses and success bound us tightly together over the years.*

Uwe Schulten-Baumer was a self-made man—a farmer's son, born on January 14, 1926, in Kettwig, Germany. Horses fascinated him from an early age. As a child, he helped to brush, feed, and water the horses at a nearby barn and received his first riding lessons in return. Dr. Schulten-Baumer did his military service with the marines, going to a cadet school where he was allowed to ride the horses at the commander's headquarters on the weekends. He had to serve for six months during the Second World War and was stationed on the cruiser Nürnberg in the Baltic Sea. He completed a commercial apprenticeship after the war, then went back to complete high school, studied economy in Würzburg and Bonn, and wrote his doctoral thesis on the cement industry. He found employment at the Raw Iron Association, became a board member, and eventually, a director.

His job was challenging, and he had to travel often. But it seemed as if all his life, all of that was just a means to an end, so that he could follow his passion for horses. The "blind passion," as he called it. He acquired his outstanding skills in training and schooling horses himself, simply by being a meticulous observer and by dealing with the best teachers of his time. Fritz Tempelmann, for example, and Major General Albert Stecken. Dr. Schulten-Baumer never completed a classical professional rider apprenticeship of his own. He was a highly specialized autodidact, who never stopped to continue his education.

*He regularly met with Major Stecken over dinner to philosophize about the schooling of horses. It bothers me when things that such experts continuously developed over time and through intensive discussion and passionate exchange are judged so carelessly today.*

It is said that The Doctor was an excellent jumper rider and even dared tackle the then still extremely massive Parcours des Concours Hippique International Officiel, short CHIO, in Aachen, with his erratic mare Senta. He was also inspired by Olympic show-jumping winner Alwin Schockemöhle. Those who saw him ride speak respectfully of his time in the jumping saddle. Later he focused on dressage, and of course, very soon, he no longer had time to make a name for himself on the back of a horse. He let others ride for him: first his children (especially his son Uwe and his daughter Alexa); then Isabell.

*When Dr. Schulten-Baumer came home from a business trip to Switzerland or Brazil, the entire household and barn staff remained in a tense silence. Everyone listened for the next sound as he went to the mailbox, took his letters, and closed it again. If he slammed it shut, everyone in the house and in the arena cringed. Uh-oh. In a bad mood. Sometimes, three horses would still be ridden until late in the evening—his chance to relax and recharge his batteries. His lifeline.*

*The horses were always on his mind, twenty-four hours a day. He never stopped thinking about them, about their general character traits and particularities and needs. And about which methods might make them successful? That, too. All his life he didn't seek out a horse's weakness but his potential. To focus on that…that was the source of his happiness. That, and to discover talented horses.*

*The Doctor loved shopping at horse auctions. There was hardly an auction in Verden, the heart of Hanoverian breeding, that he did not visit. Very often, we didn't even try the horses that he was interested in. If we did try them, we always rode several horses to throw others off our track, since he was always worried that otherwise the bidding for a horse would go too high. He always went to the auction before the presentation of the sale horses, sat down (sometimes we sat there together), and observed every single prospect. How intently he looked at them! How meticulously he applied his standards! I listened and learned. A day like that was like a study trip for me. Back then, the breeding association auctions still offered the top horses for their respective age groups. Today, the best prices are already fetched beforehand.*

*The most important question for The Doctor was: What were the horse's gaits like? He immediately lost interest in a horse without convincing movement in walk, trot, and canter.*

*What was the horse's rideability like? Was he motivated to perform or did he sabotage the rider's efforts? He noted his comments in small print in his auction catalog, and he did this to not just consider potential purchases, but to school his eye for horses. He compared them and continued to educate himself that way. The Doctor was famous for recognizing the potential of a young horse. In his mind, he was already developing options for schooling sessions. Lacking ideal conformation? That could be improved through specific muscle training. Nervousness, resistance, a wild temperament? That was just fine for me as a rider—plus, The Doctor was always confident that we would find and fix the reason for any problems.*

*It was fifty-fifty when he went to an auction. He always said beforehand that he didn't really need another horse, that he already had so many that cost him a lot of money. But back at home or the barn, we would keep checking the time all the while he was gone, waiting for the phone to ring and for him to say, "Get a stall ready; I bought one."*

*The drama at an auction invigorated Dr. Schulten-Baumer like a player at the roulette table, and he enjoyed the thrill even when he was older. When he was looking at horses, he determined, long before the bidding started, which one was worth considering. He envisioned where this horse would stand in five years when under his tutelage. He was, in a way, "infected" as soon as the auction started and the horses were led into the arena with the first offers coming on the table. He could never get enough. He had to bid.*

*The Doctor had long ago agreed on a secret signal system with the auctioneers—a way to deceive potential copycats. He never gave a simple hand sign to bid, and he did not wave his catalog. He also always confided in the auctioneer beforehand, letting him know which horse he was interested in…*

then, all he had to do was make eye contact with him in the decisive moment. Then, it would be enough if The Doctor discreetly touched the glasses that were usually dangling from a small strap in front of his chest. Sometimes others caught on and there was trouble. But mostly, he arrived home quivering with energy…and had bought a horse.

Then we would try the horse, and when we both realized that he had made a good purchase, that the hope for a grand future was valid, that I would take on the new challenge with pleasure, that I was ecstatic with the possibilities, then both of us were overjoyed. "Thank God," he would say. "I am glad. I did buy the right one."

Afterward, he would still sleep miserably as doubts haunted him at night, and he still wondered if he had made a mistake. Did he see the horse right? Did he judge the horse's potential correctly? I mean, he couldn't afford to spend fifty thousand deutsche mark on a young horse "just to try" like the many uber-rich in the dressage scene could. He didn't play in that league. He had to hit the mark with his decisions, or he compromised everything. The fear that the money wouldn't last had haunted him ever since childhood. It followed him into his pensive nights. Could he have been wrong about the horse? This could go on for weeks. He, of course, decided each night to call me immediately the next morning.

He never took anything lightly. He never said that a horse was good for nothing, or that we couldn't keep him, or we would just buy another one. He said, "We have the horse now, and if we have a problem with him, we have to solve it." He said, "We have to find the key to every horse." This sentence has become second nature to me. We engaged with each horse, thought about solutions, and that was why he had sleepless nights sometimes…much like the ones I have today.

*Finding the key: That is the foundation of the method The Doctor taught me. I have acted according to this belief until today: Principally, every horse is without faults. Whatever the perceived problem, the rider has to find a way to bring the horse's strength to its full potential. The rider has to form the horse and pave its way.*

*However, sometimes, it didn't all work out as we would like it to. For example, when Dr. Schulten-Baumer bought Richard Kimble. He was an elegant, long-legged, bay four-year-old with a broad blaze that The Doctor spontaneously bought at an auction in Westphalia—and was a little bit surprised that he had been able to buy him for such a good price. The reason became clear when he got the horse home: Richard Kimble stuck his tongue out, a sign of resistance to the rein aids, and technically, a deal breaker. If we couldn't solve the problem quickly, the money he spent would have, indeed, been lost. Dr. Schulten-Baumer called me between classes at my university: "You have to come right away," he insisted. So I did...and we discovered quickly that the horse had been disciplined in an inappropriate manner, likely during his time at the auction. He had probably resisted the reins, and as a consequence, the handlers had tightened his noseband more and more. I rode him with a very loose noseband for a few weeks—and his tongue stayed in.*

Richard Kimble developed as they hoped and was one of the horses that Isabell took with her when she moved from Dr. Schulten-Baumer's facility. Unfortunately, he injured himself when he was eight and had to be retired from competition. Wondering what might have been doesn't help in a case like this. It was simply fate. The horse has been enjoying his early retirement in a field at Isabell's ever since.

*The Doctor always risked a lot. He invested all his assets in his equestrian facility and horses. He never said he would rather buy real estate or play the market. He invested in horses despite knowing very well that any one of them could lie dead in the barn tomorrow.*

The reasons why Dr. Schulten-Baumer decided, shortly before Isabell came to him, to take a student at his facility—the eventual Olympic gold medalist Nicole Uphoff—remain unclear. He would have generally been reluctant to do so. He preferred to manage his own equine projects and not act as a trainer for other people. Although he always stood ostensibly on the sidelines, he saw himself as the center of his equestrian business. It is possible that he was fascinated by the challenge that Nicole's horse, Rembrandt, posed. He was a particularly pretty, rangy bay, and he had already given two trainers a tough time when he came to The Doctor. The Westphalian's movement, his impulsion, and his star-quality was recognized by everyone. And he was very quick and eager to learn. Everybody looked up when he floated through the arena in an extended trot, with his ears pricked forward. He performed piaffe like a metronome; his flying changes were rhythmic and dead-straight. Rembrandt could do anything. But he left a trail of failed trainers behind him: Klaus Balkenhol had given up. Fritz Tempelmann, with whom Dr. Schulten-Baumer had engaged in a horsemanship and equitation discussion for years, had broken a leg falling off Rembrandt. The horse just could not be brought under complete control, which was somewhat ironic in the sport of dressage, where every little hair has to be in perfect place.

Rembrandt frequently burned up his excess energy by startling at imaginary dangers. The rustle of fall leaves became a horrific experience, a flower pot could easily turn into a monster, and a faraway umbrella was a terrifying threat. Rembrandt jumped up and down and tried to honor his destiny as an animal of flight—he just wanted to get away and was not easily calmed once frightened. This got so bad that Rembrandt could no longer be ridden in competition.

This case appealed to The Doctor. Nicole Uphoff, twenty at the time, sat helplessly on her horse and did not know what to do. But Dr. Schulten-Baumer knew. He immediately recognized the disaster: When Rembrandt ran away from something, he was punished. As a consequence, it got worse every time he ran away—after all, he was now not only afraid of the diverse phantoms, but also of the subsequent punishment. Thus, The Doctor's main recommendation was to pat the horse's neck reassuringly whenever an object appeared where he might spook and to lengthen the reins so that he had the opportunity to look thoroughly at the cause of his fear. Although the problem never fully ceased to be an issue—Rembrandt even spooked considerably during his Olympic triumph in Seoul in 1988—eventually, the genius in him got the better of his weaknesses.

Dr. Schulten-Baumer dedicated himself to Nicole and Rembrandt, working with them with great patience, much commitment, and meticulously detailed work. To be fair to the horse, as well as the rider (she was then basically just a talented amateur), he adjusted his complete way of training, turned his back on classical methods, and began to develop exercises from Rembrandt's natural flow of movement. He let Nicole ride thousands of transitions from one movement into the next. He used Rembrandt's natural suppleness and encouraged his back to stretch, and finally, swing, through a deep position of the horse's neck—at times extremely deep.

This allowed Nicole to have better control. The success was an unparalleled surprise coup in Lausanne in 1987, where Nicole beat the then Olympic Games favorite Christine Stückelberger from Switzerland, who asked, alarmed: "Who is this girl?" A hopeless case that had left many frustrated trainers in its wake had turned into a worldwide sensation.

The effortlessness with which Nicole Uphoff directed her horse—quietly, with soft hands and almost invisible aids—changed the entire image of dressage. Rembrandt's beautiful transitions, especially from passage to piaffe, became legendary. Critics today would possibly be bothered by his piaffes. In fact, he did not take up as much weight with the hindquarters as he should have. He did not step underneath himself enough with his hind legs. But at the Olympic Games in Seoul, the judges calmly overlooked this out of sheer enthusiasm about this new era of elegance, and they awarded her the gold medal.

Isabell, the new "hatchling" at the barn, learned as much from Nicole as she could.

*But...we were not friends. At times, I found Nicole's capricious nature irritating. Sometimes, she didn't even seem to notice that I was there. Others times, she greeted me cheerfully. We rode together in Dr. Schulten-Baumer's indoor many times while The Doctor argued loudly with his daughter Alexa. Flushed with discomfort at such moments, we kept our heads down and kept riding.*

When Nicole Uphoff and Rembrandt became the Olympic Champions in the fall of 1988, Uwe Schulten-Baumer was no longer her trainer. In April of that year, a fight occurred that showed what The Doctor could be like: highly sensitive, proud, and not to be bribed. From his perspective, Nicole Uphoff's mother had dared to do the unthinkable and had not shown the appropriate respect. Her daughter's reserve horse, Askan, was lame. An argument ensued, and she bluntly blamed The Doctor for the horse's lameness. Many others would have simply accepted the woman's behavior, with one eye on the great success that was visible on the horizon. Not so The Doctor. Top medal favorite, shooting star, winning combination or not—he could not live with such disregard for all his effort. He showed Mother Uphoff the door. "Tomorrow, I do not want to see any of your horses here anymore. Goodbye," he said. And that was it.

Nicole Uphoff won Olympic gold in 1988 and again in Barcelona in 1992, and she did so without the man who had laid the foundation for everything. In the meantime, The Doctor turned all his energy toward his new favorite student: Isabell. He swore himself to the task of developing a new winner, now more than ever. And his chosen rider did not have to be asked twice. One year after Nicole left his barn, Isabell became the European Champion aboard Weingart, a representative of an "old school" type of horse—the type that had to work hard to school the movements. Two years later, she would beat the great diva herself, topping Nicole and Rembrandt in the Grand Prix Special at the European Championships in Donaueschingen, Germany, this time with Gigolo. The Doctor was thrilled. He had officially arrived where he had always seen himself: at the very top. And Isabell had surpassed her own dreams. This was likely the best phase of their relationship: The master and his muse. The Doctor steered the Honda minibike with Isabell behind him, and together they rattled across the castle grounds in Donaueschingen, at a speed that blew the start lists out of the spectators' hands when they passed by. Isabell's laughter rang in bursts across the showgrounds. She was twenty-two, had made all her dreams come true, and was alight with happy energy. Her teacher, patron, and sponsor—forty-three years her senior—had prevailed, had thawed his smile, and both reveled in life, the horses, and their success as they celebrated with a drive in the sunshine. At that moment, they became an inseparable duo. If once Isabell was not close to him, The Doctor asked nervously where she was. She never stayed away for long.

*We were mutually grateful. I, of course, was at first more indebted to him than he was to me. But, at the end of the day, it was a symbiosis. Our relationship was accompanied by a lot of warmth. I can imagine that I may have been the only person in all those years with whom he really felt comfortable and at home. At least for a certain period of time, before our own conflict started. Somehow, I think, I was the person through which he completely realized himself. He protected me in a way and took care of me.*

And what was this conflict? Donaueschingen was only the beginning of a great story of success that is mainly connected with the athletically charmed Gigolo. But the first signs of discord already lurked behind the sunny picture, although they were perhaps initially imperceptible. Isabell was glad and grateful that she was allowed to ride the superb horses owned by one of the most renowned dressage experts. Out of sheer awe, she would not have suggested that he should pay her in any way for her time. Dr. Schulten-Baumer paid a professional rider to train his horses at home, but he never even considered sending "an employee" to show his horses. His employee would, of course, have liked to eventually harvest the fruit of her labor, but The Doctor did not believe in the idea that one's staff had to be motivated to continue to do their jobs every once in a while. Why should he pay for his employees to make a name for themselves and have fun? He also thought that it would only confuse his horses to have multiple people competing them.

*Very soon I was riding more horses than Dr. Schulten-Baumer's professional rider. And I did it with eagerness and without calculation. The success was what was important to me—I had tasted blood and wanted more of it. During this time, the German Sports Aid Foundation was an important support for me, because the costs do add up due to the many trips. I had to fund those myself, and after all, I was still in school. We lived in hotels during competitions, mostly higher end—it had to be the Hilton, Sheraton, Mövenpick. I would have preferred a less pricy bed and breakfast! My parents often had to help me out.*

Isabell never worked for The Doctor; she was never paid for her riding. That made the funding of the entire business difficult in the beginning. Isabell's mother drove the horses to shows in the trailer during the first years—Rheinberg to Stuttgart, and back. But then she became nervous about the responsibility of trailering Gigolo as his value increased—*especially* when she heard that millions of dollars had been offered for the horse! So then, a professional shipper had to be paid, and the question of funding this new expense was a sensitive topic between The Doctor and Isabell, up until the end.

*It was not really a walk in the park, this arrangement. Hardly anyone does anything like this anymore; everybody asks, "What do I get in return?"*

In the beginning, Isabell did not even have a share in the earnings from the occasional horse sale, even though it was her unpaid training that had increased the value of the horse that was sold. She only received commissions later. Initially, The Doctor was of the opinion that all income generated by his horses was due to him, since he bore the full risk and the costs associated with the purchase, care, and upkeep of the horses. He was always worried that he was somehow being cheated. It took time before they found a fair solution that included Isabell, who received half the sponsorship income and a commission for any horse sales, yet the prize money remained with The Doctor. Over time, Dr. Schulten-Baumer did come to realize that she played a substantial role in adding value to his competition barn.

The fear of loss connected to the horses was, of course, very real. When The Doctor lost two horses within a short time—one with a broken hip, the other one through an illness—he was actually about to give up his facility. If it had not been for one of his friends, Herwart von der Decken, then manager of the Association for the Promotion of Hanoverian Horses in Equestrian Sport (FRH) and president of the Hanoverian Breeding Association, Dr. Schulten-Baumer might have very possibly thrown in the towel. But as it was, his supporter from Hanover rustled up the means to buy a new horse. This horse was Antony, the dark bay gelding that would be a backup for Gigolo, and with whom Isabell became the European Team Champion in 1999 and 2001. (Antony lived on to the old age of twenty-seven.) The crisis at the Schulten-Baumer barn passed, and with time, the number of horses in the barn grew. They had started with six stalls, and one by one, the number increased to twenty-five.

It was not just the risk alone that worried The Doctor. It was his fear of suddenly falling into poverty, which he'd had since childhood and which never let go. It was what drove him—and ultimately, it would be his downfall. His parents sold the family farm when he was still a boy, perhaps because they lost money through poor investments. His mother's despair, when faced with the dramatic loss, hit young Uwe hard. He still talked about it as an elderly man and the devastating effects the trauma had on his life, saying, "I know what it means to lose everything overnight." He seemed to have sworn to himself as a child that he would never lose his financial independence. That he would "make good" from within himself. But, all his life, he was part of an environment in which many people were considerably richer than he. This was the dressage world, a place where many people traditionally only saw one purpose: to outdo their rivals with more expensive horse purchases. And it was also the environment where a well-off person would feel poor. Those who were not super-rich could only assert themselves by pursuing markedly clever strategies.

Technically, there are only two options if one wants to succeed in upper-level equestrian sport. Either you must offer your talents in the marketplace, which can mean standing in the arena in the rain, teaching the pubescent daughters of millionaires, but receiving an opulent fee to do so—and sometimes, an almost royal commission related to horse sales. That person can live well...as a servant of the rich. Or, you replace money with genius, buy horses at auctions rather inexpensively and then turn them into first-class performers that will bring glory due to your own excellent skills and those of a highly talented rider. With the latter, Dr. Schulten-Baumer could satisfy his aspirations to be a successful dressage trainer, while remaining a master, and not a servant. However, his system left little room for error. He feared downfall all his life.

*He developed tremendous ambition to obtain prosperity and recognition. That was his motivation. In the beginning, after the war, he might have felt a bit lost. Not equal. He earned the respect of others through success and effort, independence, and reputation.*

Right at the beginning of Isabell's career, in 1990, The Doctor had to counter a massive attack from the ambitious millionaire front. He did not own Gigolo then, but Isabell already rode him competitively, and the horse participated in his first international competition at the very highest level: the Grand Prix in s'-Hertogenbosch, the Netherlands, which was part of the World Cup Finals. The Doctor had agreed to a deal for the horse with his son but it was not yet closed. The situation was still fragile, and the competition's spies already sat ringside and made plans to commit sabotage.

After Isabell came in third with the immature seven-year-old, and everyone had seen what the chestnut with the plain neck was really made of, founder and owner of the mail-order company Neckermann AG Josef Neckermann began to put pressure on Dr. Schulten-Baumer. The headstrong elderly gentleman from Frankfurt, an icon of dressage sport, had not been actively riding for a long time. However, he was still involved in the circuit, sponsoring rising star Sven Rothenberger, son of an industrialist from Bad Homburg. He was always looking for horses for his protégé and negotiated their purchase again and again. Now he set his sights on Gigolo. Neckermann and Schulten-Baumer started persistent negotiations.

The phone rang many times—not just The Doctor's, but also at the Werth's farm in Rheinberg. The Rothenberger family wanted to persuade Isabell's parents to use their influence to make the deal. Finally, The Doctor determinedly took Josef

Neckermann aside and asked him not to ruin his deal and buy the horse "out from under" Isabell, as is often said in equestrian circles. He and his son had agreed on an adequate but not extravagant price, which Neckermann could easily multiply many times over. The Frankfurt businessman did not give up his efforts in the face of The Doctor's request, but instead got angry. The Doctor, on the other hand, started to panic. After all, he did not want to cheat his son, who had promised not to sell the horse to a third party, out of so much money.

In this moment, Dr. Schulten-Baumer not only defended Isabell's career, but his entire system and his own reputation. And he won. Looking for help, he turned to his friend von der Decken, who suspected Isabell and Gigolo would be excellent advertising for Hanoverian breeding in the near future. And he took care that they stayed together. The FRH took on half the sales price of 160,000 Deutschmark (about $93,000). This was the cost of Gigolo—at least, that is the number Isabell remembers. In hindsight, this was a really reasonable price, considering what a dressage prospect costs today. And it did not reflect the fact that Gigolo had won almost a million Deutschmark in prize money, and done so in dressage, where remuneration is low compared to jumping.

*It was a life lesson: The sport may apppear to be all elegance and class, but do not ever be too trusting or naïve, even for just one moment. The smart strategist has to think ahead in many steps to not be overpowered by the competition. The joy when something goes well for you cannot make you lower your guard. When I consider what would have not happened, had The Doctor failed to find a solution back then, it has made me vigilant in my own dealings now and sharpened my senses. This is part of the knowledge that he has passed on. I would not have managed my first steps with my independent business without a healthy dose of distrust.*

While The Doctor's barn was considered a hobby, today Isabell runs a small, professional business. She pays for the hotel and the travel expenses for all her employees who accompany her to shows. The business has to net enough to cover that, but the arrangement is more comfortable than it was with The Doctor back then. His belief that everything was too expensive and that everyone was only after his money poisoned his relationships. Every expense was assessed and reassessed intensively. At the same time, he put himself in a quandary: He invested all his money in horses, whose fragility, in turn, made him break out in a cold sweat. Imminent vet bills gave him nightmares. More dark clouds appeared on the horizon. Jealousy and bitterness charged the atmosphere behind the snow-white walls of his facility with increasing negative energy.

*In my opinion, The Doctor did not manage to organize his life, and because of this, controversial, self-created problems tore at him. His ego was stronger than any diplomacy. He was a person who could stand living in discord.*

When Isabell started riding his horses, The Doctor had just separated from his first wife—Uwe's, Alexa's, and Verena's mother. There was a second Mrs. Schulten-Baumer, coincidentally Isabell's elementary school teacher, who used to live in the neighborhood. She brought her daughter Ellen from her first marriage into the relationship. Ellen also turned into an ambitious rider.

At first, Isabell and Ellen did not have any problems with each other. On the contrary, they got along well. The distribution of roles was uncomplicated: Isabell was the strong, successful rider with the growing trophy collection. And Ellen, eleven years her junior, benefited from a professional role model and took the path toward the upper level dressage competition in Isabell's wake. Ellen was only sixteen when Isabell became the Olympic Champion on Gigolo in Atlanta in 1996. But the older she got, the more difficulties arose. Isabell was increasingly perceived as competition in the barn. After all, she was only the neighbor's child; Ellen, however, was the daughter of the house. Technically, it would seem like it should have been The Doctor's task to clear the air, but he did not do it. Torn between the two parties, he could not bring himself to establish clear rules. He was afraid of the conflict and so avoided it.

*There came a time when Ellen took over the dominant position in the barn. The Doctor even stirred up the competitiveness between us. He believed it would spur us on to even greater performances.*

Ellen achieved her first successes, distinguishing herself at the junior championships, and brought home international medals, although Isabell's performances were considerably superior. In the same year that Ellen Schulten-Baumer became the Young Rider European Champion, Isabell won two World Championship titles in Rome. So, who was the better rider? Who had to be respected more, loved more, and protected more? Who had the right to the better horse, the more intensive support, the undivided attention? It is not hard to see that Isabell's answers to these questions would differ from those of Ellen and her mother. The Doctor's ego began to spin in circles when faced with this conflict. Isabell no longer fit as well into the pattern of his needs. And his family pulled on him.

*And again, the conflict escalated around the issue of money. The Doctor and I still agreed on one subject: Where the horses, their training steps, and their special needs were concerned, the energy between us flowed as always. The long-standing, emotional unison continuously saw us through family-related problems and his authoritative games. I was still fascinated by his clarity when dealing with horses, by his foresight and his meticulousness. I appreciated the way he demanded respect for the horse from everyone in the barn. Everything had to be clean and neat, the tack room tidy, the stalls clean, the aisle swept. And nobody was allowed to call a horse a "nag" or worse. But in the arena, we fought more frequently and fiercely.*

*Eventually, not a day passed where we did not yell at each other. I would shout that this time, this was definitely it, and I'd try to leave. He would follow me and ask me to come back. But then he reliably worked himself up again about how much everything cost. I suggested several different business models for financing a competition barn on a, in my opinion, more equitable foundation. But we did not reach a consensus.*

*Despite all my respect, gratitude, and appreciation for him, I have to say: The Doctor caused all his problems himself. He lived by his ego during his best years, regardless of other people's souls. And eventually, he had to pay.*

Until now, Isabell had taken The Doctor for what he was. She had endured his perfectionism. The moments when she came out of a test, beaming and proud, and he, before anything else, had to release pressure by confronting her with her mistakes. Despite her victory, not everything had gone to his satisfaction. He regularly criticized the smallest detail. Other people noticed and noted to her that perhaps it wasn't right, but Isabell did not complain. She just swallowed the tears of disappointment. Why did he not acknowledge her efforts? He justified his dissatisfied comments by saying that he had to provide an objective critique of her performance. Only offering a few friendly compliments would just water her down.

*I endured it, because I knew: This is high-performance sport, not a walk in the park. Whoever does not bring the necessary toughness will not be successful.*

She also withstood his idiosyncrasies, his demand to always have her available, his unfairness, and the fact that he had made her success a part of his own. His superstition was legendary: He wanted to turn around immediately when a cat crossed the street, or if two traffic lights turned red back to back. It went so far that he wouldn't allow Isabell's mother to watch her daughter ride; he claimed she was bad luck. He even sent her away once when he noticed she was standing behind a post, trying to sneak a look at Gigolo.

Their love for horses was strong enough to bind Isabell and Dr. Schulten-Baumer beyond all constraints. And Isabell knew well that he could not only yell at her, but also sometimes cry like a child when they had made real progress. When it felt like nothing was working anymore, her stable home life helped her through the crises. She could always escape to her parents and soak up the harmony that she was missing at The Doctor's.

But the day came when the constant bickering became too much. The Doctor changed the roles of those in his barn, and again, the fight was about money. When Madeleine Winter-Schulze—herself a very successful dressage rider on her way to becoming one of the biggest names in German equestrianism—appeared, it seemed as if the dissonance at the farm took on a new tone. First, Madeleine bought herself a horse: Aurelius, with whom she did not get along well. Then she bought Satchmo and Richard Kimble, the two five-year-olds that stood for Isabell's future. And later Apache, and then Antony, even though, at that point, he was on his way to retirement. She purchased the horses under the stipulation that The Doctor would continue to support Isabell as their rider. He assumed that this was the solution to his problems: Earning enough money by selling the horses to secure the future of the show barn, to fulfill his family's demands, and to calm his inner anxieties. He would be able to keep the horses at his facility and continue to drive their training forward. And he could still continue to profit from Isabell's outstanding equestrian abilities, which gave him the prestige he desired. Yet he had it all with less of a risk.

But his plan did not work out. Since Isabell was no longer riding The Doctor's horses, but Madeleine's, he had lost power over her. He had lost unrestricted access to her. He had waived his beloved ownership, and the self-constructed role as "the master" no longer functioned as it used to. Sponsor, patron, teacher—that was yesterday.

*I felt that selling the horses to Madeleine was the beginning of the end. The sense of basic trust we had faded away and with it, the illusion that we had formed an inseparable companionship. Back then, I wouldn't have guessed that this painful ending was to turn into the second lucky chance of my life.*

Isabell decided to cease cooperation with The Doctor in the beginning of 2001 after sixteen years together. She moved out of his facility in the fall. He was seventy-five years old and would learn very soon that the most successful chapter of his career as a dressage trainer was over. She was thirty-one and started a new life without him.

Isabell chose the timing carefully: She only left after Gigolo had been retired. She had ridden him in the Olympic Games in Sydney just one year previously and had won gold with the team, as well as individual silver. In November of the same year, he had been given a festive and tearful farewell at a show in Stuttgart. The Doctor thought it too early; he would have liked to have kept the horse in the ring a little longer. Maybe because he knew what was coming.

*I couldn't bear the idea that anybody else could ride Gigolo. As long as Gigolo was still competing, I felt committed to him, as well as to The Doctor. After we had retired him, I started planning my own goodbye. We managed another year together with great difficulty. Then, it was finally over.*

Although the threat of their separation had hung in the air for a long time, The Doctor did not expect that Isabell was really serious. Not until the very end, at least. He thought it impossible that she could liberate herself from his influence. He believed that she would establish herself as a lawyer and reduce the amount she rode instead of continuing in her sport independently.

*Today, I don't understand how I tolerated all of it. And yet, I would do it all over again. He only realized what he had lost when I was gone. At first, he still had hopes to replicate with Ellen what he had achieved with me. He had thrown all emotions overboard and wanted to do it again. But you can't just repeat something like that at will. We had a symbiosis, and that doesn't happen very often.*

*I can hardly remember the hours when I was packing my things. I felt numb walking through the barn and collecting my stuff. I left a lot of things behind that were a daily part of me for sixteen years. I mainly took things that belonged to the three horses that moved with me in the end. I pointed at items... "Take it," he said. Surreal moments. I have blocked out most of the images. But I still remember the pain. And that The Doctor wanted to keep the little Honda minibike that we had loved to cruise around on together at shows. I left it to him; I was moved that he clung on to that memento of our best times. A little later at a show, I saw Ellen driving around with the scooter and it stung. I assume that it was his way to punish me for my autonomy. He knew how he could stab me in the heart.*

Isabell and Dr. Schulten-Baumer needed at least two years before they were able to face each other more or less calmly. Isabell boarded her horses at Mr. and Mrs. Winter-Schulze facility in Mellendorf for two years and was supported by new trainers. The Doctor was now on the road with his stepdaughter, who really was the "number one" in the barn now and had to withstand the pressure that came with it. But it was not a happy collaboration.

Six years after Isabell's separation from the Schulten-Baumer stables, Isabell and Ellen even rode on the same team—they won team silver at the European Championships in Turin in 2007. Two years later, Ellen was also part of the bronze-medal team in Windsor, England. After that, her international appearances quickly came to an end. A great career failed to materialize. She was no Isabell.

*I had to learn to go on alone. Initially, I felt as if I had a limb amputated. Numerous times, I thought I was hearing his voice in the arena. Again and again, I waited to hear which instructions he would give me now. I was looking for him and yet also felt free as a bird. The cocoon had gone, the protective cloak that his authority had given me—but also the metaphorical cage whose limits had oriented me thus far. I had come to him as a girl, had learned everything from him, and now my strong partner was missing. For years, I was unconsciously waiting for a voice from the outside that did not come. No other trainer could replace The Doctor. He had set an example in what was important to me.*

*A process of internalization began. I had to integrate everything that he had taught me in terms of fundamental knowledge into my own, independent thinking and my own actions. I literally had to manage alone to make my work-style work. And it took me a long time. I only knew five years later, when I had won the World Championship title with Satchmo in Aachen, that I had found my own way.*

*I wish I could still exchange views with him today, since he followed my progress with joy and pride until the end. Our contact improved over the years. It even became possible that I could ask him for advice; for example, when Madeleine and I had just bought Don Johnson, I started pondering after the purchase as The Doctor had done so many times before: What if I made a mistake? This horse was truly not a model exhibit for the sport of dressage. His neck was set unfavourably (his lower neck strongly pronounced). In addition, his body had a downhill tendency with his croup higher than his shoulders. He was the complete opposite of what is wanted in dressage, where the horse technically needs to "sit" on his hindquarters in the most important movements to be able to open up and "free" the front end. And his character: wild, sassy, skittish at times, and boyishly charming, cuddly, and cooperative when he was in the mood. I asked The Doctor: "What do you think,*

*can we sort out the physical deficits?" He replied that if the
horse had phenomenal gaits and was elastic, then you had the
chance to form him. It gave me the confidence to say, "Yes,
we will tackle 'Project Johnny.'"*

Isabell and Don Johnson finished second at the German
Championships in 2013 and were nominated for the European
Championships. He was eleven, and Isabell seemed to have
accomplished the most important steps: He had built up so
much muscle through meticulous training that a significant
difference in his silhouette was visible. The strength he had
developed enabled him to carry himself elegantly. She told
journalists at that time that he was slowly arriving in his own
body, and she could finally bring out his full potential. Don
Johnson developed into one of the pillars of her barn, her
"number two" behind Weihegold. He has won and still wins
World Cup freestyles and other important competitions. The
only thing that hasn't really changed is his character.

Ten years had passed when the Doctor offered Isabell Laurenti, one of his own promising youngsters. A monumental
Oldenburg but a chicken at heart, the horse was just right for
Isabell's sensitivity. At The Doctor's, nobody had any use for
Laurenti, and he wanted to "get rid of him"—figuratively speaking. Of course, he believed in the horse's future in dressage,
but he had to bring Laurenti to Isabell's since the situation
would have been too delicate if he kept Laurenti at his place.

Isabell found that The Doctor's good horse sense had functioned as well as ever, Madeleine bought Laurenti, and Isabell
told him: "You can always bring that type of horse to us."

But the more years passed and the less Dr. Schulten-Baumer
got along with his stepdaughter, the more he was surrounded
by loneliness. His brilliance withered. At one point, he told

Isabell that it was the biggest mistake of his life to sell those horses to Madeleine. But it was too late; it could not be undone. His fear of loss caused him to give up the greatest gift that life had ever given him. Falling caused by the fear of falling.

One day, The Doctor called Isabell and said that he had, once more, bought a horse for her. He had gone to the auction in Verden like he used to and felt as if he had been carried back in time. He wore his elegant clothes as was his habit, placed his bid from the background as always, and said at the end: "This one is for Isabell." He came to visit her, bringing the little set of a plate and cups that a buyer receives at Hanoverian auctions as a parting gift. He told her about the horse—and then said she had to go and pay for him.

Luckily, Isabell managed to annul the deal he had made in her name without a fuss.

Everyone who saw Dr. Schulten-Baumer at a show in his final days was heartbroken for him. He wandered the grounds, emaciated, sick, and lonely, as if looking for his former self. His white collar and his watch seemed too big for him; the famous hat slid down to his ears. Those who talked to him took care not to let him know how far he was removed from the world he once dominated. It often seemed as if he wanted to ask, as he had in his heyday, "Where is Isabell?" knowing he'd find her back at his side immediately.

Dr. Uwe Schulten-Baumer died on October 28, 2014, at the age of eighty-eight.

With laughter, Isabell sometimes tells others about the picture The Doctor used to present, from time to time, when she arrived back at the barn at night after a show with the trailer. He would step out the front door, always bent on composure, wearing a bathrobe over a white shirt and tie... and below his three-quarter-length underpants showed (also apparently tailor-made for him) above his socks and slippers. A sight to behold.

The Doctor gave Isabell life lessons. A foundation. It was something much more valuable than a degree. She grew up during the sixteen years she spent with him. And she will probably never finish contemplating his life and their time together.

# 4 ROLLKUR

At this point in this book, it is time for a digression from Isabell's story to allow for a discussion of the fundamental principles of riding. The question of what is the best, most correct way to school a horse has occupied mankind ever since the horse was first mounted. It is impossible to provide a simple answer to this question, as the topic is highly complex. Every horse is different; therefore, ready-made templates do not exist. Naturally, generations of experts, having been profoundly involved with the education of horses, have developed a foundation regardless—one that is presumably applicable to all equines. The origins of these equestrian teachings, passed on by prominent authorities, can be found in the military. The horse has been an important partner of man in times of war for thousands of years, and the union between rider and horse was fundamental. It made the difference between life and death. Although today this union only makes a difference between success and failure in the dressage ring, that legacy of military partnership remains firmly in place as the foundation of equestrianism.

The first equestrian treatise in history is estimated to have emerged around 365 BC. Its author was Xenophon of Athens, one of the prominent all-round talents of his time: a politician, writer, military commander, and a disciple of Socrates, making a significant contribution to the history of philosophy. Xenophon is still cited as the "crown witness" when it comes to hippological studies, where the correct training of horses is the focus. Much of Xenophon's knowledge, articulated in clear and exact language about horsemanship is absolutely timeless. The objectives of his military-influenced teachings rarely differ from what is required of today's civilian equestrian life.

Isabell continues to read Xenophon's texts with enthusiasm and is, time and again, impressed by the profundity with which people have engaged with horses since antiquity. This is particularly remarkable since, in those days, horses were specialized in entirely different things than those of the Haute Ècole.

*I am continuously made aware of the exceptional importance that horses have for mankind. In that respect, Xenophon's suggestion that the horse is a friend, not a slave, is particularly important to me. "Introduce [the horse] to the pleasure of work and voluntary obedience!" he writes. In doing so, Xenophon emphasizes that the only effective means of education are praise and punishment, whereby—and he makes this very clear—praise takes absolute priority. The aim of our riding at the top of the sport must be to bring the maximum level of difficulty together with the greatest possible effortlessness, combined with joy and expression, into the dressage ring.*

"Consult the masters of equitation." This is what should be said when the classical principles of riding are interpreted differently.

A debate about the training of horses developed in the early 2000s: a fierce argument about the direction in which the schooling of dressage horses was heading. The clashing views were not always clearly defined and mainly led by riders and trainers from Germany and the Netherlands.

The friction between camps was due to photographs taken at competition warm-up arenas—pictures that made followers of the classical principles of riding break out in a sweat. The focus was particularly on riders who forced their horses into an artificial outline—the so-called "rollkur" or "hyperflexion"—for extended periods of time. In the process, the horse's head is pulled toward his chest to its extreme, the neck curls up, and it appears as if the horse could bite his own chest at any moment. Taken further, the method—with the help of the reins—pulls the horse's head around to the side (sometimes the rider uses both hands to do this). The question of whether the hyperflexed position causes a horse pain has never been fully answered, but one thing is very clear: It is unnatural for him.

The best known, and therefore, the most criticized protagonist of this method was Isabell's long-time rival, Anky van Grunsven.

The topic is precarious, especially for a still-active rider like Isabell. A fair athlete avoids, whenever possible, criticizing fellow competitors in public. Thus, commentaries on the rides of colleagues are rarely heard, outside of exchanges perhaps in a more intimate setting. Usually, the athlete does not talk much about the competition and instead gives answers on the state of the playing field (in this case, the ring), in the form of better performances. The fact that the discussion surrounding hyperflexion became more and more fierce and emotional *outside* the traditional boundaries of professional rider comportment obscured a clear view of the issues and compromised the chances of a cognitive process and reflective discussion that might have otherwise arisen from such a subject-specific controversy. The bitter formation of sides that shaped the sport of dressage during that time influenced the internal climate so adversely that it was captured by mass media outlets, who fed the story to the "non-riding" public—adequately simplified, of course.

The term "hyperflexion," still popular today, is an inadequate label, as it leads to undifferentiated views and generalized judgements. Isabell still uses it, but not without raising an eyebrow. She is repeatedly dragged into hyperflexion discussions and confronted with criticism that is not the result of in-depth study and understanding, but instead based on superficial knowledge. Snapshots caught on camera are generalized rather than carefully considered, and key questions are always attached to particular incidents. The communication problem starts as soon as someone asks what "rollkur" actually is. Thus, fruitful discussion of a topic that is important to Isabell is often drowned in pandemonium. Her own position on the matter is actually quite clear.

*Rollkur for me is the forced "screwing in" and "rolling up" of the horse's neck in front of his chest. The horse is held in this too-tight position for a certain time. When this happens, the necessary stretching and lengthening of the neck is completely neglected. It doesn't correspond to my understanding of dressage training at all. Truly gymnasticizing a horse is something completely different. The templates are out of place in every respect. Xenophon's standard still holds true today: A horse's nose should ideally stay in front of the vertical. Yes, but the way to this ideal has to be adjusted to each horse. For example, when I am starting a young horse whose body is not yet trained or muscled, I want to form that horse into an athlete with appropriate gymnasticizing. This means that, among other things, the horse is made more supple and elastic through frequent bending of his neck and stretching of his entire body. This, however, has nothing to do with rollkur. The aim of the right kind of gymnastic training is that the horse can use his body elastically and be supple, just like a high-performance athlete, a gymnast, or a figure skater.*

How to create maximum flexibility through individual training for the horse was the central topic of many of the books by the old equestrian masters. For example, Gustav Steinbrecht's text *The Gymnasium of the Horse* forms the basis for the modern German art of riding. This classic was published in 1884, and Steinbrecht's riding theory was integrated into the army regulation 12 (*H.Dv.12*) handbook of the German cavalry, which was last revised in 1937 and yet has never lost its validity. Neither in Xenophon's nor in Steinbrecht's work, nor in the famous *H.Dv.12*, is there a passage from which a justification for hyperflexion could be inferred.

The language of cultivated riding masters, in its accuracy and its condensed wealth of experience, is a source of inspiration for many of the people who seek to train horses in the best, most correct ways. These are the riders and trainers who think about their actions, what they do around the horse, their entire life. It gives Isabell visible pleasure to paraphrase Steinbrecht: Correct dressage is natural gymnastic exercise for the horse through which his strength is steeled, and his joints are made flexible. The horse's stronger parts are encouraged to greater activity in support of his weaker parts, and the latter are strengthened through the gradual exercise. Sources of force and energy, which the horse usually holds back because of his natural tendency to just want to be comfortable, are awakened.

And finally, utter harmony and coordination of the individual joints and their forces is created, which enables the horse to, continuously and without force, perform controlled and beautiful movements from the slightest of rider aids, which, when the horse is at liberty or in a wild state, would only briefly show in moments of excitement.

Hyperflexion's effects are slavery, surrender, and absolute submission. This method stands in stark contrast to true goals of dressage training.

*Total obedience, the achievement of so-called "blind obedience," is an essential aim of rollkur. With this in mind, I have also pondered how such an exaggeration of position might relate to other exaggerations in training, such as remarkably frequent repetitions of movements. I have asked myself why a pirouette is constantly repeated, even after it has been carried out successfully several times before. Even in the time of Xenophon it was said that praise for the horse doesn't only mean patting his neck or giving him a treat. "Calling it a day" when something goes well is another reward through which the horse learns to identify when he has done something right. That is a guide post that The Doctor firmly installed in me: If it goes well, it's "home time." The only explanation that I can find for the constant repetitions we so often see in dressage schooling is that they are hoped to lead to an automatization of the horse. People must feel that mistakes can be eliminated this way.*

*I principally respect my competitors' achievements and don't want to denounce anyone. My goal is to advance myself. But the great pleasure I take from my work mainly results from the fact that I work together with animals that have their own personalities, that are confident, and that I am on par with.*

100

*A horse may and must live his own personality. Of course, I expect obedience, I wish to be in control, and I want to be the one who decides what happens when. But, my horses are also allowed to resist; they are allowed to tell me what they think. Live and let live. I have to lead my horse so skillfully over the years he is in my barn that he plays along voluntarily and has fun doing it. Don Johnson, with his quirky personality, is the best example. Only a horse that has fun can develop the kind of charisma that captivates people in the show ring. The foundation of what connects us to our horses every day is affection and respect. It helps us see through all phases of doubt.*

It was an equestrian magazine that labelled the controversial method "rollkur." The term stuck, because it was easier to remember than "hyperflexion," which FEI officials brought to the table when they entered the discussion. The new word was hoped to help take the edge off the debate. Under the third label "Low, Deep, and Round" (LDR), a framework was created that stipulated what was allowed under international federation rules. However, the Dutch dressage riders, especially Anky van Grunsven and her trainer Sjef Janssen, pushed the boundaries of the method now officially called LDR to its limits.

Some top horses—not only from the Netherlands—managed to produce a particularly expressive movement from this tense body position. At the time, the expression was particularly liked by the judges and rewarded with high scores. And the gap between the traditionalist trainers and their challengers grew wider and wider. According to the Dutch, the "antiquated dogmatists," who preferred the old regulations of the German cavalry (last modified 70 years ago), were fighting against the cool and unconventional innovators. Subsequently, trainer Sjef Janssen not only defended his questionable method, he defended it as if it was its own training philosophy. The more criticism they received from traditionalists, the more the other side hardened and carried their views to the extreme.

At shows, spectators—many still rooted in tradition—had issues with what they were observing and how it contradicted the classic principles of riding theory that had once been taught to them. Criticism intensified as considerateness diminished. Onlookers suddenly saw hyperflexion everywhere and characterized the entire sport of dressage as animal cruelty. They labeled relevant and temporary disciplinary measures as examples of the problem, as well as basic gymnastic stretching. Unregulated "hyperflexion alert" is still a popular pastime for some amateurs who constantly evaluate the work of professionals and keep the topic viral using the leverage of social media. Isabell, too, has been and still is accused of practicing rollkur by certain people.

*Of course, it hurts when people put the "rollkur-label" on you. I don't see myself there at all. Naturally, I cannot absolve myself from making mistakes sometimes, and not-so-pretty pictures happen to everyone sometimes. While I do believe that this can happen to every rider, I have to accept that I am particularly high-profile, which means I am always out there and vulnerable to criticism. I take that on board, but I don't want to be judged by people who only form an opinion about my daily work with horses through a few particular photos and video sequences, without looking at the entire situation in context.*

It was the fall of 2017 when the last of such accusations was launched. The never-tired Don Johnson put his head between his front legs and bucked somewhere on the outskirts of the

Stuttgart indoor show grounds. Somebody took a picture of the exact moment with a smartphone, and while Isabell sat in the post-competition press conference, the picture was posted online, along with negative commentary that completely distorted the facts.

Organizers of bigger events now plan ahead to protect riders from such malicious activities. At the CHIO in Aachen, Germany, the entire proceedings in all training areas are recorded on video so that, in case of accusations or doubt, the complete order of events can be analyzed. Such a system is expected to be installed at the show in Stuttgart in the future.

All told, the ideological battle between Germany and the Netherlands has lost much of its energy in recent years, especially when a new era started with British dressage riders Charlotte Dujardin and Carl Hester taking over the leading roles in the sport while espousing the classical way of riding and training. But Isabell is still suspicious of insiders who have gained popularity through their own definition of hyperflexion.

*I find those opportunists, who have all ridden themselves, who have all fought for the same goals often enough, but who want to use these discussions to their advantage, almost ridiculous. In my opinion, experts (who should really know better) make a name for themselves as critics in the rollkur debate in order to position themselves as the "good ones" in the business (even though there are compromising photos of them as well). They can count themselves lucky when they are no longer active competitors, thus no longer in the spotlight. Moreover, with many, there was no social media in their time, so they never had to deal with such consequences. They're obviously looking for a niche to market their training, their courses, and their books. To neglect critical discussion in favor of populism is not only short-sighted, it is negligent, as they have damaged the social reputation of dressage and equestrian sport.*

*Don't throw stones if you live in a glass house. Every rider will have a problem with a horse at one point. Everyone will have difficulties dealing with a certain situation at one point. None of us can claim that we do everything right, all the time. But that is not the worst part. You can't don a halo at the expense of others. You always have to return to yourself and think: "How can I do it better? How can I reach my goal differently?"*

The broad generalization of the topic even led to Dr. Schulten-Baumer being subjected to criticism related to hyperflexion. The reason for this was that, in the heat of the moment, the participants in such discussions often lumped together all aspects of the topic. Indeed, at the end of the eighties, The Doctor had succeeded in making Nicole Uphoff and her Westphalian Rembrandt the most influential pair in dressage with the help of riding the hot, anxious horse deeper in the neck. It was very clear when the two came to Schulten-Baumer that, for the most part, Rembrandt knew his movements, although in some ways incorrectly. What Nicole had to learn to manage were his nerves. Rembrandt spooked at every fall leaf flying through the air; his high-strung temperament made it difficult for him to focus on specific tasks and the guidance of his rider.

Through a lot of gymnastic work, repeating transitions from one movement to another thousands and thousands of times, The Doctor managed to focus Rembrandt more and more on the essentials, and Nicole was able to very quickly bring him back on track if he became distracted. This did not just school his mind, but also his body. It should be noted, he was not at all brought into a forced frame, but ridden deep and stretched, with his back arched. This meant that in what he might deem a "scary situation," he no longer reacted as dramatically. Over the course of his training, Rembrandt became so light-footed and elegant that his way of going developed into a new ideal. It was dressage at the highest level of difficulty with hardly any visible physical effort—as if somebody was driving a Formula One race car with only a little finger on the wheel. Rembrandt literally flew through his most difficult tests in his prime.

But there was no "system" or rule of thumb at the Schulten-Baumer stables. The Doctor was not fascinated by the horse's submission. His goal was to bring the horse into a physical and mental state where he could easily do everything that was asked of him. The technical terms for this are hardly comprehensible to the layman: "Throughness"—the ability to understand all aids of the rider (the signs the rider gives the horse through shifting weight, the back, hands, and legs) but to also realize them without fault. The horse has to be prepared for his tasks in such a way that there is no more "grit in the gears" when he has to perform the complicated movements of the dressage test, which can best be compared to gymnastics in human sports. "Gymnasticizing"—the training of muscles to the point where the horse, despite the rider's weight, can still make his own body light, can carry himself and move gracefully, and can maintain his balance in the most difficult of movements. "Elasticity"—supple movement and perfect body control.

It was important to Dr. Schulten-Baumer, and it is important to Isabell today, to work with every horse individually. For example, her horse Hannes (Warum Nicht, "Why not") was very tall—over 18 hands. But he was also extraordinarily long. To build up the horse's muscles so that he was able to meet the demands of dressage at the highest level was a challenge. As few as two centimeters made the difference between whether his topline was in a beautiful position or his neck was in too high a frame or he was too tight in front of his chest. To transform Don Johnson's body, which was technically not made for dressage at all, was yet another challenge. Likewise, to build up Gigolo's neck muscles. To turn an ugly duckling into a swan, *that* is Isabell's goal. But whatever the horse's weaknesses that need to be improved, he ought not to become stiff by permanently working in one position.

Once again, Steinbrecht addressed this in *The Gymnasium of the Horse*: "The more perfect the conformation of the horse and the more noble the pedigree, the more he will have the desired harmony in his natural movements. But such horses, of which one used to say that they already carry their father's dressage genes, are very rare and precious. And...these horses hardly end up in the hands of professional riders. Thus, this rider must spend his skills mainly on weak and less favorable horses; yes, even those with conformation faults, and for the latter, in effect elevate dressage to therapeutic gymnastics. But in the same way physical therapy has found such great recognition in our time, and plays such a great role in human medicine now that we are convinced that weakness or pathological conditions of the human body cannot be healed or lessened by machines, but only through appropriate exercises, so can the professional rider, on the basis of a proper understanding of his art, remedy many natural flaws in the horse and work wonders for those, as well as weaknesses the horse may have acquired through abuse or ignorance of previous riders. Professional riders are able to 'cure' these horses thoroughly through the appropriate training, sometimes even after veterinary aid has been applied in vain."

*Riding dressage means gymnasticizing, and additionally, "preserving" the horse. People stretch their bodies to prepare for maximum performance, and to bend, lengthen, and loosen muscle to avoid injury. I'm proud that our horses live to be very old, even though they spend many years in the competitive dressage arena. Many have lived into their late twenties. And, to be fair, we can't forget that Anky's Bonfire was also very old when he passed. It puts a lot of things into perspective.*

*Dr. Schulten-Baumer invested all his personal experience into the training of his horses. It was his opinion that a horse that was permanently worked in an ideal competition frame would get "stuck." It would become a habitual posture, and there was a risk that the horse would stop using his body to its full capability. In this, The Doctor was thinking about his own body and the experiences that he gained on a naval ship as a young man. As a cadet, he always had to stand at attention—"Attention!"— with his hands behind his back. And, that's how he actually still often stood in the following decades. He recounted that it took him a good while until it no longer felt strange to just stand without placing his hands behind his back.*

Horses are, in this respect, like people. Their conformation is rarely perfect, but you can work on opening up all the options that movement offers for them. Learning to use one's own body to its potential, to shape it so that it looks round and beautiful, to keep it so supple that no natural movement causes it pain, to train it so that the body and what it can achieve brings one nothing but joy...who would not wish for that?

# 5  SATCHMO

Satchmo has become quite a bit rounder ever since he turned twenty. In winter, his hair grows long, fuzzy, and soft. He looks like a dark-bay teddy bear with a playful half-moon on his forehead. He spends his day in the field, munching away, together with his partner-in-crime (of his later days)—the pony, Kelly, who he never lets out of his sight. In his stall, he enjoys visitors. He is always gentle, lets people scratch his ears, blissfully stretches his head forward, and purses his lips. The message is clear: He wants more.

When it is very quiet in the barn, you can almost feel the resonance of a whisper in Satchmo's stall...a quiet voice that will never rise to the point of audibility. What kind of story is it that Satchmo would so much like to tell us, but cannot, since he is lacking human words? He carries a secret with him that seems to, at times, stretch toward the daylight, yet will likely remain forever in the dark.

Satchmo stands in his stall and looks innocently with his bright, black eyes. He is enjoying wonderful years of retirement; he has achieved enough in his life; he has the right to rest now and enjoy just being a horse. He is not in any pain. At one point, he decided that he no longer wanted to be a riding horse, but just wanted to be out at grass, and so he shall now do as he pleases. Isabell has taken his saddle off for good. Still, he is not shoved out of the way or forgotten. His barn neighbors are all Isabell's current stars.

*I walk by his stall regularly, think about old times, and talk to him. "Satchi, old boy. Why can't you tell me what your thoughts were on all of it? I would find it fascinating to finally have an explanation for your mysterious behavior."*

*I trusted him in every phase of our life together. I would have lain down to sleep in his stall without hesitation. He was never mean. Feisty, yes. Sassy, too. Even wild. But never mean. But why were there horrible moments again and again? The ones where he suddenly stopped in the middle of his dance? What did he see in those situations? Why did he forget me, there on his back, all of a sudden? Why did he freeze out of nowhere—those moments where he couldn't be persuaded to go on? Why did he spin around out of sheer fear and horror because of nothing more than a wall of air, whose dangerousness only he saw? What kind of scary world did he live in? Was it really full of ghosts, demons, and flying missiles?*

Isabell does not talk about any horse in more detail or for longer than she does Satchmo—not even Gigolo, her original superstar. Satchmo, the hectic, electric, little guy with his short body, kept her busier than any other of her complicated horses.

*This horse was my true mission in life as a rider and opened new dimensions for me with the challenges he posed. And his story is not closed. It never will be. I still blame myself that I was unfair to him at times, just because I didn't manage to find a way to understand him. These thoughts hurt.*

Yet today, Satchmo has a mellow look in his eyes and whatever may have left the mysterious wounds on his soul that caused his unrest in the show ring seem to have healed completely.

*Satchmo was the horse I fell off most often. And it wasn't just me, it was everyone in the barn. When Satchmo was still young, narrow, and small—more of a "horsey" than a horse—I said to Dr. Schulten-Baumer's professional rider, a tall guy, who at the time sat in this horse's saddle: "Careful, you will fall off this one faster than you can imagine."*

*The tall dude grinned and sneered, saying, "What? This little stinker?"*

*He hadn't quite yet said it, when he was in the dirt.*

*Despite this, I always had a very special bond with Satchmo. Even during his rowdy teenager phase, I just had to hold on up there. But he was my kind of horse. We are very much alike in character. We suit each other perfectly. It was complete symbiosis, and I have always believed in him.*

Satchmo and Isabell have spent more than twenty years together, and she sometimes jokingly calls him her better half. Born in 1994, he came to Rheinberg at only two and a half years old. The Doctor had bought him on one of his trips to the auction in Verden, the home of the Hanoverian horse. He went to the stallion market and bought him for 70,000 deutsche mark—that was a lot of money for a stallion that had not been selected for breeding purposes. But the fact that the famous horse dealer Paul Schockemöhle was The Doctor's main bidding opponent in the sale shows that, even back then, Satchmo made a great impression with his extraordinary ability to move. Dr. Schulten-Baumer came home happy and proud...and the usual doubts came shortly after. "Did I buy the right horse? Did I make an expensive mistake? Will it work?"

Of course, a horse should not yet be ridden at two-and-a-half, so nobody knows what kind of difficulty the horse will cause his rider. The Doctor first gave Satchmo to Hannes Baumgart, who operated a training facility close to Verden. There, the horse was to get a proper start. As early as that, the young Satchmo already began to feel people out. He was highly sensitive and would get charged up, go "ballistic," and begin to buck. He was completely uncontrollable.

*When Hannes Baumgart was headed toward another crisis with Satchmo, he always just called out: "Turn, turn, turn!" and the horse was led in small circle after small circle. When turning, it is easier for the rider to bring a tensed horse to a point of relaxation. It takes away the horse's ability to run forward and start bucking. Through these turns, Satchmo learned to calm down a little while moving. Only when that was successful was Hannes able to ride the horse as he wanted to ride him. Eventually, it became possible to have him move forward normally under the rider.*

But still, tensions were high. One day, the phone rang in Rheinberg, and Baumgart was on the line. When Dr. Schulten-Baumer hung up, he grinned and chuckled. "They seem to have problems with Satchmo," he said.

The horse was so sensitive and explosive it was discussed as to whether he should remain a stallion. The decision did not take long: Satchmo, who was to become a dressage star and not the founder of a dynasty, was gelded. But the matter was far from solved, even after the operation that was supposed to help "get the sass out of him." He was still full of energy. After she and The Doctor picked the horse up, Isabell had a chance to marvel at his sizzling personality.

*He was so agile that he could shake off anybody. He was able to turn in mid-air, go up to the right, to the left, could run backward, buck, throw his legs. It was impressive. Judging by his flexibility and elasticity, he was an ideal dressage horse. But not by his discipline. Satchmo wanted to dominate and call the shots. I saw it all (albeit from the ground sometimes, where I had just landed, yet again), and it made my heart smile. He was a challenge on four legs.*

*I tried to get at least some control over the feisty bundle of energy. It was about the basics under the saddle. Walk. Trot. Canter. Downward transition. The first milestone was to find a way I could channel this tremendous temperament. The Doctor, who also progressed in his learning with every horse, coined the phrase: "You have to solve this one forward." I have ever since included this advice when I speak and follow it every time I have to deal with horses like Satchmo, who constantly lose their temper. Don't hold on, don't drill, don't hold your breath—let it out. If he doesn't want to walk, trot—don't hold back. Don't think whoa, or he will get charged up even more. Solve the problem thinking forward. Let him go until he has caught himself again. Satchmo was and remained a time bomb, got excited, pulled, and wanted to go—but I found control in movement.*

The Doctor provided a *modus operandi* that suited Isabell's nature. *Always forward.* Take risks and learn to manage them.

From the beginning, the tango between Isabell and Satchmo went all out.

"Satchmo at a show" was unthinkable for the longest time. If he became too hot five or six times in competition, showing his worst side in a class for young dressage horses, he would have not been able to get rid of the "rowdy" label any time soon after. That is how it is in the dressage world: Those who have been put in a certain category cannot redeem themselves quickly. Thus, Satchmo was prepared for a show very carefully; he probably hardly knew what happened. At first, Isabell only brought him with her to competitions. At the Frankfurt Festhalle show, he was allowed to get accustomed to the atmosphere in a demonstration. At seven, he was finally entered in an advanced dressage test for the first time in Hanover. And from there, he quickly reached the top category, the Grand Prix. Things went to plan. He was still very excitable, he remained a hot ride, but he did not show signs of going berserk and Isabell had fun with him...until the day at the European Championships in Hickstead in 2003, where everything changed.

*That's when it started: his stopping, standing still, freezing. The first time it happened was in the warm-up ring. It kind of blew my mind, but I initially forgot about it and considered it to just be tension that wouldn't last. It wasn't until it occurred repeatedly during the test that I knew that we had a problem. I just didn't know the reason.*

*What kind of ghosts had my horse met in England? I thought about it and came to a quick conclusion. The problem had possibly had its start in Germany. Maybe, the memory of an accident that had happened during our "training camp" had caught up with Satchmo, again and again. Back then, I had perhaps made one of the biggest mistakes that I have ever made as a rider. It seemed blatantly obvious in hindsight. Back then, I would never have guessed the drama that was in store for me and Satchmo.*

*The entire team had prepared for the European Champion-ships in Warendorf, Germany, where the German Equestrian Federation (FN) has its headquarters. I was pleased with how Satchmo had presented himself in his first engagement with the German Team. He was only nine but my great hope for the future after Gigolo's farewell. It was only one year until the Olympic Games in Athens in 2004. With Satchmo, it was looking good in terms of the continuation of my career. But then, the accident happened. My groom led Satchmo into a dark wash stall and started to hose him down. The horse's hind end slid and fell to the side. In the process, one hind leg ended up in a crack between the floor and the wall planks.*

That a crack of this kind existed is fascinating in its own way. Experienced horse owners know that their animals have a very special talent for getting stuck in gaps, getting caught in wires, and generally speaking, getting themselves into all sorts of scary predicaments, injuring themselves severely when doing so. There simply should not have been a crack in a wash stall of the German Olympic Committee for Equestrian Sports, the sports department of the German Equestrian Federation.

Although Satchmo was stuck at first and desperate to get his leg free, he did manage to do so quite quickly. It seemed as if the accident had not resulted in any serious consequences, considering he could have broken his leg. He was on his feet and had only a little cut—a mild laceration that was immediately stapled.

And now? Should they participate in the European Cham-pionships or cancel? Ambition and concern fought inside of Isabell following the accident. But the entire German Team and her support staff were in favor of her riding Satchmo at Hickstead. And Anton Fischer, the Chef d'Equipe, whose task it was to organize German success, agreed.

*We should have gone home. Given him a rest. Hand-walked him. We should have taken the staples out after ten days and started over. But no. We believed it was only a superficial injury and would quickly be forgotten.*

*I only led him and didn't ride anymore until we arrived in Hickstead. I started riding again after the vet check there. But that a nine-year-old horse was completely overwhelmed by what had happened is easy for me to see from today's perspective.*

The incidents in the warm-up in Hickstead were just the beginning. The accident in the dark wash stall had become deeply engrained in Satchmo's mind. At the showgrounds, there were "black boxes," about 3 feet high and 10 feet long, with plain, smooth walls that could be seen from the ring. They were used to display individual marks during the class for the spectators. These black boxes put the fear of God into him.

*I felt in the saddle how Satchmo froze before the first piaffe, when he suddenly saw one of those boxes—how he took a deep breath, and panic came over him. I sat on this horse, my favorite, and we were of one mind—we were both unable to cope with the situation. The test was ruined and the European Championships, for me personally, were a disaster. Of course, we won team gold, and I was happy for the others (Ulla Salzgeber with Rusty, Heike Kemmer with Bonaparte, and Klaus Husenbeth with Piccolino). But insecurity ate me up inside. I wouldn't ride the final individual test.*

What Isabell didn't know was that the mental breakdown that Satchmo had at Hickstead was harmless, compared to what was yet to come. He worked himself up more and more, each time he was ridden. He winced at the same movement in the test: the piaffe. Everyone, even the spectators at the shows, eventually just waited for a reoccurrence of the freeze. Soon his strange behavior started even earlier during the test program: at the first passage, before turning right to the apparently very scary piaffe. Just seconds before, he would be in the midst of a supple and majestic transition to his almost celebratory elevated trot. And suddenly, he fell directly into his "psycho-hole." The weird thing was that, generally, he quickly took a deep breath right after the moment of horror, and carried on with the test normally. Maybe he was relieved when the horrific creature he imagined did not appear as expected? Who knows?

*His fits came in more frequent intervals and built up to the extreme; Satchmo suffered downright panic attacks. He not only paused, seemingly terrified, but he aborted the movement we were performing and "paddled" with his front legs, turning around and trying to run away in the other direction. Sometimes, I felt signs that he was about to get hysterical and so I was able to prepare for it. Other times, it came out of nowhere, and I wasn't able to anticipate it. I fought for almost two years, again and again, in front of a large audience—and failed repeatedly. It came to the point where I was accused of harassing Satchmo too much, and allegedly that was causing his fits to become worse.*

The truth was very different. In the saddle of the horse that was beside himself, Isabell, the Olympic and World Champion in dressage, was at the end of her resources. The Olympic Games in 2004 were the first Games since 1992 that took place without her. She could no longer qualify for the team with Satchmo. She had to surrender the gold medal without a fight to her old rival Anky van Grunsven with Salinero, a horse that may have had his own strengths, but Isabell was not—and still is not—sure that this horse came even close to Satchmo's quality in any way.

*I sat in front of the television, desperate. I was convinced that I could have actually won the gold medal with Satchmo. I was sure that he was the best dressage horse at the time. And I blamed myself that I couldn't find the way to help him.*

*In the end, his episodes also happened at home. I rode across the diagonal in the outdoor arena, another horse suddenly came from behind the hedge, and Satchmo behaved as if a UFO, fully manned by hostile aliens, had just landed right in front of his feet. He suddenly could think of nothing else but leaving the practice ring to the left, and I wracked my brains about what could have frightened him now. Should I give in? What did he want to run away from? What did he see that my eyes couldn't? Was he really scared? Or was he simply a brilliant actor?*

Breeding experts claimed the problem was genetic. His father Sao Paulo should have really been given a different name, they said: "Sau" Paulo ("sau" means "pig" in German). But that was really nothing more than a stupid joke.

*I had to find out what was behind his behavior in order to react correctly. But I really had a tough time with this question: What should I do? I tried to tire him out by riding more, hoping to bring his excitability down this way. Nothing. I tried to take it easy so he would be less stressed. Nothing again. I tried to repeat the movements he was anxious about to ease his fears. Nil. I avoided repeating the movement that caused him fear. Still nothing. I turned him out more in the field, to relax with a pony. Negative. I took him for a gallop on the racetrack. Nothing. I tried a shorter warm-up before a test. No change. A longer warm-up before the test. Also not it. If somebody had told me back then that it would help to run around the churchyard three times, holding a rat, I would have done it.*

*I never felt like I had found the solution to our dilemma. There was no breakthrough. Sometimes, everything was just fine. If I made it through a test, smoothly, I received top scores immediately. And at home, it felt like he deserved a score of 80 percent on some days—90 percent according to today's judging standards. Satchmo's phenomenal talent was unquestionable. But I couldn't breathe a sigh of relief. When it went well, it only meant that we made it through the test under the highest tension and that it had not ended in disaster for some mysterious reason. Just riding along in a natural and relaxed way, even at moments of joy or pleasure, was impossible. I always knew that the next time, he would expose me again with his public show during the Grand Prix program.*

*I lay awake at night, brooding—without result. Because the panic attacked Satchmo usually without warning, I sat in his saddle with sloping shoulders, always living in fear that the sky would fall on us again. I talked to Satchmo's new owner—and my compassionate friend, Madeleine Winter-Schulze—sometimes several times a day, and we discussed the problem back and forth, made assumptions, discarded them, developed new approaches, and, ultimately, discarded our ideas. Sometimes, I had hope, just to sadly let it go again soon after. My own* phobia was soon just as big as that of my horse. Inside, I was trembling when I sat on Satchmo, sending fervent prayers, knowing that I couldn't give up—that I had to find a solution, just as I always did when a horse had difficulties. There had to be a key. But which one? I had tried so many and none had fit.

I remembered my experience with Antony, whom I once had to give "a good talking-to." Maybe I had to show Satchmo once, too, who was in charge. Maybe I had to tell him to stop walking all over me and that he had to learn to submit to my wishes, to accept that he had to keep going, that he wasn't allowed to stop, no matter what ghost he imagined seeing. Maybe he made up those ghosts to give himself a reason for his disobedience. He had always had a very dominant personality. Could it be that he just became more and more rude and that all of this was his extremely hysterical form of refusing to work?

My correction had worked for Antony right away. Sanctioning him consequently in the right moment—and thereafter he had always obeyed. I thought about the story of this horse that had had a strong career as the reserve for Gigolo.

Antony was a capable Hanoverian. And he was very smart. He had proven himself willing and able to learn and work until he was eight years old. He finished the career path for young horses without any unpleasant incident. He was very well behaved as he learned piaffe and passage, and he didn't resist the flying changes. I could request anything. It seemed to be running along smoothly. Only my father said, every once in a while, "Be careful. That horse has two faces." This sentence had dual meaning: He had a blaze that ran askew so that, from one side, he looked like an unmarked dark bay. From the other side, the blaze framed his eye. From one side, he looked as if he was very well-behaved and innocent; from the other side, he appeared clever and a little mischievous.

*It happened, out of the blue, at his first start at Grand Prix at the indoor show at Bremen. I entered the arena with Antony…and he suddenly flipped out and started to buck, almost jumping on the table in front of head judge Heinz Schütte. The Doctor and I were so surprised that we believed he was sick and asked the vet to check him over. Could it be a colic, maybe, which caused him so much discomfort that he was unfit for any controlled effort? Or did his back hurt? But no, Antony was perfectly healthy.*

*Three months later, at the May-Market show in Mannheim, Antony's attitude had increased and his refusal was more extreme. He now only moved forward in little steps. He stopped every 16 feet, and during the test, kept me at arm's length up there in the saddle. I worked hard to influence him, using all the options available to me, which at that point in my career were not few. I succeeded in making him move forward briefly, immediately patted his neck as a praise, but a dozen or so feet later, he stopped again as if he were a tree that had taken root.*

*That's how I crawled through the test. A little bit here, a little bit there. After, Dr. Schulten-Baumer said that if Antony kept getting away with his behavior, I could give him away for free. He said that the next morning we would ride the test again, just as if we were in competition. And if he stopped again in the same spot, I would really punish him once. He said I had to get my point across once. And so that is what I did. He stopped in the same spot as the day before: We came around the corner, trotted, and again: BAM, he stopped dead in his tracks. And so I followed The Doctor's instructions and used the whip.*

*Even though I felt bad about doing it, it was an important and correct sanction of his bad behavior at that point.*

*A journalist saw me do it and I got bad press. But it was an educational experience for the horse. Antony said: "Okay." He never stopped again.*

*Antony had understood that lesson, but there was another problem still to be solved. When we arrived with him at a show in the Belgian town of Schoten one day, we found that the arena had almost flooded…and Antony hated water. He had always refused to walk through puddles. He would rather take a long detour if it meant he could bypass on one side. The warm-up ring at Schoten was under so much water that training and warm-up rides had to be moved into the parking lot. However, one look at the competition arena and I completely broke out in a sweat. Puddles everywhere. How was I supposed to manage even one test with Antony? I said to The Doctor, "I don't even know how I am supposed to get across this arena." We finally agreed that the most important thing was to convince Antony to set foot in the arena. Then we would just see. He would either learn to swim, or he would stop in the middle of the water, and we would go down together. But at least I would have tried.*

*And that is how I did it. I entered the ring at full speed, and before he even knew what had hit him, he was in the middle of a puddle of water. And, lo and behold, he learned to swim in this moment of surprise. He fulfilled his duty that day as if he had never had a water phobia. And he never refused to go through water again.*

With Antony, the behavior had only been a mood. The horse did not put up another fight with Isabell after their confrontation; he seemed to have decided to cooperate. He subsequently developed into a confident serial winner, who even won a World-Cup qualification in Neumünster at nineteen years old. Every once in a while, when Antony felt that Isabell had relaxed and thought herself safe, he treated himself to some naughty action—much to the joy of the audience. But he never again stopped during a test. Antony may only have been the Number Two in her barn (his great colleague Gigolo shone at all the major championships), but at the more modest shows, Antony collected impressive lifetime earnings of 531,246 Euros. And, he achieved his greatest successes when he was already at an older age for a competitive horse.

Antony's famous role was to be the clown. His Freestyle played to the German folk song: *"Im Wagen vor mir fährt ein junges Mädchen, ratta-ratta-radadadada."* (Translated loosely, the title means, "In the car in front of me is a beautiful girl.") There was one point in the Freestyle where the two of them pretended to turn left, before an offstage voice sang, "Oooooh," whereupon they corrected their course to the right. Antony, the comical party-animal. It matched his rascal personality, which he had previously used to test Isabell.

*As a rider whose goal it is to win the absolute trust of my horses, it was very hard for me to take such measures with Antony. However, I felt Dr. Schulten-Baumer encouraged me to make the right decision. Like parents who have to tame a child at a defiant age, I learned that it is important to sometimes set firm limits in the training of horses, if necessary.*

*I thought about this and looked at Satchmo, my favorite, the horse that I didn't understand, and I pondered. He had tested the authority of his rider fiercely as a very young horse. I asked myself again and again if we had to try more pressure on him as well. And I finally did it, as I did not have any other better ideas.*

*I had always ridden him without a whip. But now, I used the whip to force him to move forward. It was an act of desperation, but the entire idea of disciplining was just as ineffective as all my previous attempts to get through to him. Satchmo's behavior didn't change; his fits still came over him regularly. If anything, he became even more scared and erratic. In his case, it wasn't a struggle for power. Both of us remained baffled and helpless.*

*Later, when I finally received the first clues as to a possible explanation of his behavior, it made me feel even worse. I could have kicked myself because I had completely misunderstood this horse, and I had done him wrong when I assumed that perhaps he was looking for a showdown. He hadn't put on an act at all; his panic was real. I tried to comfort myself, reminding myself that I had used calmness and patience at least 90 percent of the time, but it still stung. But I also said: "From now on, for as long as I breathe, I will believe in this horse."*

June 2005: A familiar picture was playing out at the show on the castle grounds in Balve, Germany. Isabell had not given up on Satchmo; she continued to start in competitions, even though, by now, every one of her tests looked like a suicide mission to the entire circuit. Satchmo made an excellent first impression in the warm-up—he was supple and seemed to move forward full of confidence, working through the practice movements without any noticeable difficulties. Then, Isabell entered the ring, came around the turn...and it started all over again. Satchmo hit an invisible wall without warning, tensed up, stopped breathing, and stopped for two seconds. Isabell rode on again, and continued as if nothing had happened.

*I quickly had a feeling that the bucket seats in the stadium had reflected sunlight and blinded him. Or was this just one of the many theories that would turn out to be a fallacy?*

124

*I went to the barn after the Grand Prix, where Satchmo, already hosed down, was being cared for from head to toe by Hacki, our excellent groom. As Hacki reached up to clean his head with a sponge, I suddenly noticed that Satchmo made a suspicious movement when the sponge startled him. I had an epiphany: On my way home, I called a friend who worked at the animal hospital in Hochmoor, described what I had seen and said, "I think we have to get his eyes checked."*

*I didn't even take Satchmo home, but drove him directly from Balve to the vet clinic. And indeed, the check-up came back with a result: He had small striations in his eyes—kind of like little fish that swam through his vision. They were very bad on one side and fairly considerable on the other side. The vet warned me to not get my hopes up too high with regard to the test results and what they could mean. Technically, it wasn't anything unusual, but a degenerative process, as could happen in humans and horses alike—in horses as early as six years of age. Essentially, every horse has the striations to varying degrees, and most of them live with it easily. Corrective surgery was relatively simple: The fluid in the eye was sucked out and refilled. However, the vet preferred not to perform the procedure, unless he was very sure that it was the reason for Satchmo's problems.*

*I tried not to get my hopes up. Too often, I had jumped at alleged solutions and had only been disappointed. But I couldn't help but wonder: Were the ghosts that haunted Satchmo in his eyes?*

*I took Satchmo home. We tried for a week to figure out if he had an actual eye problem. We gave him a patch on the right eye, then a patch on the left eye, then blinders to the left and right. Did Satchmo relax? I couldn't tell. I drove to our riding club, where they were going to hold a show on the weekend,* and faked a test situation. I even wore my tailcoat! Satchmo was braided, was warmed-up as if it was regular show procedure, and everything was the same as our usual competition. Satchmo needed to feel the usual tension we would experience at shows. I had the club farrier make official-sounding announcements over the loudspeaker. And then I rode into the ring with the blinders, looking a little bit anxiously toward the first piaffe, which had become the normal location of the first episode by now. And Satchmo? He rattled off the entire Grand Prix as if nothing of the sort had ever happened. I took the blinders off and rode the same program again. Satchmo stopped before the first piaffe and turned around. The old phenomenon was back.

The decision was made: The eye surgery would take place. But I didn't make a big fuss about it. I informed as few people as possible. I had become so thin-skinned that I was afraid of the pressure to succeed, which became stronger with every attempt at a solution with this horse. I withdrew Satchmo from the German Championships and took him to the vet clinic.

Ten days later, I was allowed to ride again. We took it slow, giving him lots of time to recover.

I was full of anxious anticipation as I planned to take him to the indoor show in Stuttgart in November. Pretty much everyone had given up on Satchmo: Madeleine sympathized but doubted; national coach Holger Schmezer remained sceptical; the journalists deemed his "psychological problem" beyond repair, despite my persistence.

And then...the Grand Prix in Stuttgart. Everyone in the arena felt a tingling sensation, and when Satchmo got underway—supple, honest, without even a trace of anxiety—everybody was astonished. Where had the strange fits gone? Satchmo went brilliantly in all gaits, glamorously in every *movement. He was light and elastic, stretching in the lateral movements and the half-pass, which were his highlights anyway. He was focused in his flying changes, and he performed the piaffe without hesitation. I sat in the saddle and couldn't believe it. It was truly a real breakthrough. I had found the way to Satchmo. My heart rejoiced. Finally! Finally.*

The entire arena in Stuttgart shook on a very wintery Saturday morning in November. Everyone felt it: It was as if a door had burst open after all the months of uncertainty and demoralization. The judges were smitten and showered the pair with points—they received a world record score. Joy and relief brought tears to her eyes in the arena at one of her most familiar showgrounds, where she had already cried so much… at Gigolo's good-bye five years before. She had been certain then that she had found a more-than-worthy replacement for her superstar in Satchmo—but then, the big setback. Instead of proving to The Doctor that she was good enough to win gold medals without him, she instead had been painfully reminded of the limits of her abilities, and on top of it all, she had to endure ridicule from the press and her competition. All the tears that she had swallowed during her most challenging time yet spilled freely in this moment when Satchmo seemed to have finally shaken his demons.

And yet, one day later, they came third in the Grand Prix Special. Their test was nowhere near as focused as it had been in the Grand Prix. A brief hesitation before the first piaffe cost her points, among other factors. It was a tiny trace of a reminder of what once was, and it seemed perhaps a suggestion: "Don't let down your guard." But this time, the nightmare was over before it had even started, and it was a happy Isabell who left a load in Stuttgart that had weighed her down for months. She knew that the following year, the World Equestrian Games were to take place at another familiar venue for her, in Aachen. She had missed the Olympic Games in Athens, but Aachen had become a goal within reach.

The officials of the German Equestrian Federation did not fully trust Satchmo's sudden transformation. Somehow, it looked a little too much like a "miracle cure" to them. They considered it unlikely that his issues were "fixed"—all of them were experienced horse people who had a tough time with any phenomena that remained mysterious somewhere along the line. Of course, they saw the talent that Satchmo had, and the potential when he made it through a test without trouble. But what if he did not?

Eventually, it became apparent that the competition at the World Equestrian Games on the German's home soil would be filled with very strong Dutch riders. The team victory that the Germans expected was no longer guaranteed. This challenge did not leave room for experiments, in their opinion, and the officials were not prepared to say definitively that they felt the bomb that had been ticking inside of Satchmo since 2003 had finally been disarmed.

And so, it was hardly surprising when Warum Nicht (Hannes) scored higher than Satchmo at the German Championships in the early summer of 2006. It was more than just a matter-of-fact ranking. When in doubt, the results of national title fights, which are used to select potential pairs for upcoming major events, are an easy way to read the preferences of the German Olympic Committee for Equestrian Sports. The judges at the German Championships tend to nuance their judging in the way the Federation expects of them. Thus, it was quickly very clear to Isabell how the officials would decide. Their favorite for WEG was Hannes.

Hannes was a tall, long chestnut with an imposing appearance, but not necessarily the best horse for individual success at major championships. He was a gentle giant that Isabell could rely on. Hannes did a decent test in Münster, but Isabell believed that Satchmo had shown the better performance. While she had to accept that she was nominated for WEG with Hannes, she insisted that Satchmo went with them as the traveling reserve.

*As much as I was disappointed, because Satchmo was my favorite, I still complied with the judges' choice without complaint. After all, there was no way I wanted to risk being held responsible for potential problems later. What happened then seemed to me like a twist of fate—although at the expense of poor Hannes, who, fortunately, didn't have to suffer long. Later, some haters with a notorious inclination to gossip accused me of having manipulated everything to impose my wishes, but I swear to high heaven that this was not the case, and I can refer to the assessment of two independent vets.*

*But one thing at a time: Shortly before the World Equestrian Games, the German team trained together close to Aachen at Nadine Capellmann's facility. Holger Schmezer, the national coach, had mainly argued in favor of Hannes: our trainings with him were satisfactory, and the rational decision seemed to be justified from the Federation's view. But, suddenly, team vet Björn Nolting discovered an inconsistency in his gait. When he came through the corner, Björn questioned if he was really sound. We decided to take Hannes back to the barn and wait until he had recovered from the training session and was relaxed to then examine him. Wolfram Wittig, my trainer at the time, and I were schooling Satchmo in the meantime, while the rest of the team went inside for lunch.*

*For everybody else, the decision had already been made. I enjoyed my ride on my lifetime horse that I had just reclaimed from the world of threatening shadows, and I realized: He was in top shape.*

*When Hannes had cooled down, Nolting went to the barn, looked at the horse's hind legs, and winced. It did not look good. He shook his head, saying, "I don't think this will work." The vet had diagnosed a swelling in the aponeurosis (connective tissue) in the fetlock groove, a rare injury in a dressage horse. Since he wanted a second opinion on his serious diagnosis, he suggested we consult the Swiss horse specialist Hans Stihl, who I think is the best diagnostician in the world. Stihl initially said that he couldn't imagine such an injury, since he had checked on Hannes only a week before. But he came out the same day, went to the barn, felt the hind legs, and came to the same conclusion as Nolting. He couldn't compete. Satchmo had to take his place.*

*You have to imagine the situation. The emotional progression. It was not fake. This was not a laughing matter. I would have ridden Hannes, even though I would have three thousand times over rather have ridden Satchmo. I would never fake an injury. I am utterly superstitious when it comes to that.*

The unsound Hannes was sent home; Satchmo was taken to Aachen. Holger Schmezer broke out in a sweat when he heard what had happened. On the inside, he had already braced himself for the thought of having Satchmo in the ring. He had hoped to save himself the stress that was connected to this horse. The riders from the Netherlands, however, rubbed their hands together. Needless to say, Isabell's difficulties were not news to them. They no doubt hoped that Satchmo would once again make a fool of his rider at the World Equestrian Games.

*Team vet Björn Nolting told me: "You are not the red-hot favorite. But maybe you can be the joker."*

The scales began to tip. The long nightmare had come to an end, and an enchanted time began.

For many, Aachen is one of the most beautiful locations of equestrian sport. It has style. It has history. It has tradition. And, it has a unique arena, which was renovated specifically for the World Equestrian Games. A giant grass area, surrounded by impressive bleachers on four sides, with a view of softly rolling hills in the distance. This lawn is as holy to riders as Wimbledon is to tennis players. Some horses take a deep breath when they enter the stadium; others, when they first enter, try to beat a hasty retreat backward, it would seem out of sheer respect. At the annual CHIO show, the jumping competitions are usually held in the main arena, with the Grand Prix of Aachen as the highlight. The dressage has its own pretty, but smaller arena off to the side. At the World Equestrian Games, where World Championships were held in seven disciplines, the dressage ring was moved to the center and filled with the usual sand footing. It can be assumed that never had a dressage competition been held before such an impressive backdrop. It was a bit risky, considering the sensitivity of most dressage horses. But it was unmatched in its glamour.

*I was looking forward to the WEG in Aachen, my beloved Aachen, with Satchmo. First, I walked across the extensive showgrounds on foot and looked around as if I had all the time in the world. Wow! It was like being in a movie. I so enjoyed walking across the lawns to the entrance of the arena. For me, it was a magical moment.*

131

*My view wandered to the giant scoreboard that technicians were working on. They tested it with a fictitious class. Then I suddenly saw the writing flash up on the screen: Grand Prix Special—Gold Medal: Anky van Grunsven. And the World Championships hadn't even started yet! I still get a lump in my throat today when I think about this moment. I said to myself, "Well, well. So it's Anky." I also thought, "I am here with my favorite horse. That I am allowed to ride him here feels like destiny, providence, fate. And here, on the screen, there is this writing, inviting a challenge." It was a sign, a moment of clairvoyance, which had never occurred to me, either before or after. And so I said: "Okay. We will see about that."*

*It was unbelievable to ride there. Just the thought of it still inspires me, even though it is more than a decade ago. During that moment, I felt so safe on Satchmo's back, as I never had before. And never before or after have I experienced such an atmospheric event as those World Championships in Aachen.*

The team title went to the German Team, despite all concerns; the Dutch attack was once again warded off. Heike Kemmer with her Hanoverian chestnut Bonaparte experienced a magical moment right at the beginning of the competition, laying the foundation for a title win. Isabell and Satchmo contributed the third-best result of the class to win the World Championship title. Also on the team: Nadine Capellmann with the chestnut gelding Elvis and Hubertus Schmidt with the mare Wansuela Suerte. Once again, Isabell stood at the top of the podium. She said in the press conference that it was the most important gold medal of her career. She had proven wrong all those who had doubted Satchmo. And now, after this golden comeback, she was free of all obligations and expectations and could enjoy the rest of the World Equestrian Games.

The Grand Prix Special, the classic test requiring a set catalog of movements, in which the first of two individual medals at World Equestrian Games is awarded, followed two days later. Compared to the Freestyle to music, the Special does not leave room to play down a horse's weakness or to score with the help of artistic vision. The Special is the more reputable, honest comparison of ability and schooling—basically, the moment of truth. The Freestyle, on the other hand, is more entertaining, and so, more popular with the audience. In Aachen, however, where the bleachers are filled with an expert audience, people are definitely familiar with the importance of the Grand Prix Special. The audience wants to see how pair after pair fare.

*I could hardly wait to enter and start my test. But first, Dieter Earl Landsberg-Velen, then the President of the German Equestrian Federation, gave a lengthy speech. I was thinking to myself, "Gosh, Landsberg, don't talk forever. That's enough! Let me ride." Everything felt so right and I wanted to get going.*

*I rode into the "inferno" with my Satchmo, the ring where 45,000 spectators were waiting for me, and all of a sudden, I felt something very big in the air. Something was up, something very special, something electrifying.*

*While I was riding the test, I noticed that the audience had started to murmur. I continued, heard the noises, yes, but I moved as if in a cocoon in which I was alone with Satchmo. He stayed true to himself. He soaked up the atmosphere that was transferred from the appreciative audience to him, and he radiated his energy back onto the audience—and I let myself be carried on these waves. Everything went very smoothly, naturally, and Satchmo didn't hold his breath, not even for a second, when he began his piaffe…unlike the audience! I didn't doubt him for a second. Everything was completely seamless.*

133

*I felt like I was sleepwalking from movement to movement, in a dream. The last centerline, to the center of the ring in a passage, then a piaffe, then continue in passage—it was magnificent. You felt that everything was just right. And then the halt. I will never forget that.*

And then: The clenched fist with the upward arm-swing. The "Werth-fist." The gesture hadn't been seen for years, eight years to be exact, when she had won the World Championship title with Gigolo in Rome in 1998. The way to this final halt and salute and the World Champion title had been long and painful for Isabel. She and Satchmo had worked their way back to the top of their sport. She was now 37 years old. Satchmo was only 12, and the door to their future was open again.

*Tears? Of course. They were falling again. I stood there and bawled my eyes out. This is where I cried my most beautiful tears. It was the emotional highlight of my career. That's why you do it all. To experience a moment like that.*

The last day added a bonbon in bronze to the two gold medals she was awarded. Isabell came third with Satchmo in the Freestyle. A happy ending? Those who may think that still underestimate Satchmo. His mission as Isabell's "horse of a lifetime" was not yet over.

However, Isabell was now sure that the spook was over. For her, the reasons for his behavior all those years had been a mix of the trauma of the slip in the wash stall in Warendorf and the eye defect. The surgery seemed to have been the solution. Satchmo finally learned to relax.

The year after may have seen the end of the Germans' historical winning streak. In La Mandria, close to Turin, Italy, the Dutch finally managed to pass the Germans and win the title. But the individual European Champions in the Grand Prix Special were about Isabell and Satchmo. It was now as if nothing had ever happened. He felt fantastic, she confidently told journalists in La Mandria. She knew now that she was no longer chasing the other competitors. Once again, she was the one being chased.

It was obvious that she was a joint favorite, flying to Hong Kong, where the equestrian competitions of the 2008 Beijing Olympics were held. Finally, she was going to the Olympics again, after she had to miss out on going to Athens. And with Satchmo, she was ready for her second individual Olympic gold after the one she won in Atlanta in 2006 with Gigolo.

Despite seemingly irreconcilable difficulties, she had once again made a potential Olympic Champion, very much in the manner of Dr. Schulten-Baumer, but this time under her own management. And it went well in Hong Kong. Her contribution to the team gold competition was optimal. They had the highest score of the day. Satchmo was 100-percent focused and in top form. Isabell had a clear lead over Anky, even before the Grand Prix and the Freestyle, which, back then, was added to the result from day one to determine the Olympic Champion. Everything was ready: It looked as if the individual gold medal lay on a tray for Isabell; she just had to take it. And indeed, in the second step, the Special, the intermediary scores for Isabell were fantastic—she was on the way to a dream result, to the next, even more spectacular highlight of her grand career.

And then: the piaffe.

It was like a clip from a bad movie. Disaster. Satchmo froze. He spun around. And tried to get away, full of panic. It looked as if he would have rather run from Hong Kong back to Rheinberg than cross the invisible line that frightened him so. Isabell

135

sat on him, a helpless co-pilot, as she had in the past. Except this time, it was possibly even worse. A haunting reminder of a past they believed they had overcome. There was horror in the stands.

The entire nightmare only lasted a few seconds. Then everything went on as if nothing had happened. It was the same old story. That Isabell managed to continue intently, and at the highest level, shows her unmitigated world class as a competition rider.

*It was a complete shock. It felt totally unreal. You don't think that something like that is really happening. A nightmare. But you can't really register it either. I experienced it as if I were in trance. Your automatism kicks in; you continue riding, but partly because you just don't believe what you have just experienced.*

*My head began working frantically. What could have been the cause for this devastating déjà-vu experience? I questioned every step. Had I judged anything incorrectly, missed anything, ridden through the problem, not felt it? Jumper rider Karsten Huck even came to me and showed me videos had been taken of my warm-up to confirm that there had been no incidents that would have foreshadowed such a situation.*

*Today, however, I am at peace with myself and what happened. There is nothing on my conscience when I think about Hong Kong. Everything was relaxed, nothing was pointing toward the possibility that something was going the wrong way for my horse.*

*The Satchmo we saw in Hong Kong was certainly still the new Satchmo, no doubt, the entire time in the Grand Prix and in the Grand Prix Special…until the piaffe.*

One possible explanation for Satchmo's flashback was that when they were allowed to ride in the Olympic arena for the first time to familiarize the horses with the space, a huge video screen was showing pictures from the last Olympic Games in Athens. Riders and horses were magnified larger than life, threatening like dinosaurs, and some of the sensitive dressage horses reacted with panic. When Isabell rode toward the screen with Satchmo, the horse Weltall with Martin Schaudt in the saddle was just appearing on the screen. They seemed to run directly toward Isabell and Satchmo. In shock, Satchmo stood on two legs, turned around while rearing, and almost fell over backward. Did this experience potentially revive his buried trauma? It seems in many ways a clue. But this theory has one catch: Such a memory should be particularly strong when it was still fresh—so during Satchmo's first test. But he had been completely relaxed then; no Weltall-shock was felt.

Something else had happened in this arena in Hong Kong. Something that only Satchmo had perceived and nobody else.

*I wondered a lot about this. I looked at the videos, thinking that somebody might have pointed a laser at him. They were just becoming trendy back then. I considered everything you can think of. High-pitched sounds? This might sound nuts, but this is what I thought about: Did somebody maybe use a dog whistle? Was there an intentional attempt to spook him? I couldn't find anything.*

And those who cannot find anything to turn off or turn down cannot turn off or turn down anything. After the incident in the Special, Isabell's lead over Anky was only a fraction. The Freestyle remained. The great show. A potpourri of movements of the highest difficulty to festive music by the Greek

137

musician Vangelis, newly put together for the event. Satchmo shone...until he was supposed to show a particularly difficult movement. The piaffe-pirouette, the elevated trot on the spot, and all while turning. Clearly, Satchmo had mastered this task before this moment. But, once again, the ghost jumped up at him from the ground. Without warning.

He saw no chance to open himself up and go forward.

The gold medal was gone.

Isabell patted his neck and smiled.

With a spectacular Freestyle, whose level of difficulty was not even close to Isabell's program, Anky on Salinero secured her third subsequent Olympic title. The team title and the individual silver medal that were left for Isabell were a rich consolation, but all that went wrong in Hong Kong still haunts her thoughts today.

Isabell rode her lifetime horse competitively for three more years. Satchmo's panic attacks never came back. He was retired in 2011.

*I regret that he was unsuccessful in perfecting his career in Hong Kong, after the initial times of doubt were over. The unaccountable, the liveliness, that something special about him still fascinates me to this day.*

Satchmo was a mysterious teacher. He did not give Isabell the desired individual Olympic gold, but instead, the opportunity to leave the Olympic stadium with a smile on her face, despite a dramatic loss.

# 6  MADELEINE

When Madeleine Winter-Schulze sits on her deck, she notices everything that is happening at her barn. To the right, she looks at the large outdoor arena, where her two riders train the competition horses that she owns for pleasure. A little bit to the left is the stable, where horses nibble hay contentedly or relax under the equine solarium. Farther to the left is the entrance to the tack room with the giant trophy case full of ribbons from almost 60 years of showing, as well as the door to the indoor arena with a style that has the distinct feel of the seventies, but still fulfills its purpose perfectly.

Madeleine sees constant bustle; horses are led here and there. She hears people call to each other, horses neigh, hooves clip-clopping on the intricately patterned stone pavement. On her property in Mellendorf in the Wedemark region of Germany, it is not just about owning horses. It is about life amidst horses with all its noises, smells, and rituals. The arduousness that comes with horse keeping is her way of life.

Madeleine has been able to let her gaze wander across her property and its work of art since 1978. She was still a long way from 40 when she moved to her farm. On June 28, 2016, she celebrated her seventy-fifth birthday on her deck. She has enjoyed the atmosphere over all the years and is certain it was one of the best decisions of her life to buy her property. The facility was once owned by the German show jumper Hartwig Steenken, who was killed in 1978 following an automobile accident.

When Madeleine turns around, she sees the pool, which she had built for her husband, Dietrich, who was simply called Dieter by anyone who was close to him until his death in 2008. It is gurgling behind her. Dieter's doctor had prescribed exercise. The pool is still in use, even now—her bathing suit is hanging over the rail to dry—but it is empty at the moment. Deserted. No matter how often it is used, it is, in a way, abandoned forever. Like all the other rooms, the bench in the tack room, the chair on the deck, the couch in the living room—all of them seem to say one name: Dieter.

When she's at home, Madeleine prepares breakfast for the entire barn staff at half past six every morning. Then she sits happily at a full table. But she cannot sit still for long. She needs to move. Nowadays, she travels so much that she does not even want to have her own dog anymore. She feels he would only get attached to the girls at the barn and not to her. She stands up, runs outside to get cream for the coffee. Then the phone rings, and she chats for a while, smiling. Her housekeeper prepares her lunch in the kitchen, but that won't be ready for a little while. Madeleine jumps up to get a piece of paper with notes pertaining to her phone conversation. "Why don't you sit down?" That is what Dieter always said to her. Sometimes, Isabell says it to her now. "Stop running from A to Z all the time." Of course, Isabell is the same way, all day.

Dieter is still omnipresent, not just in the countless photographs around the facility that are, of course, visible to everyone, especially in the living room, where Madeleine and Dieter's life together is framed and documented. There is hardly a picture where one of them is portrayed alone, and hardly a picture without a horse. There are even horses in their wedding photo. The two of them look into the camera next to a horse and rider with a ribbon at festive events and prize-givings in the many arenas in which they have celebrated overwhelming successes. Often shown are show jumper Ludger Beerbaum and Isabell—their two star riders.

There are several pictures of Goldfever, the chestnut stallion that Dietrich Schulze had discovered for show jumping. He bought the Hanoverian from a breeder "two villages down" from his farm in 1995, furtively—he did not even tell his wife. Ludger got up in Goldfever's saddle, supposedly to try him, and Dieter only confessed his solo purchase decision when Goldfever turned out to be a talented jumper.

Thinking about this story still makes Madeleine smile.

Goldfever was a difficult horse. More than once, Ludger came out of the show ring and angrily made a "snip-snip" gesture, which to many in the industry is a symbol for castration. Goldfever was sassy, rebellious, aggressive toward male horses, and constantly chasing mares. He was a red-gold testosterone bomb. And, he hated grays, especially Cento, the horse ridden by Otto Becker, who would later become the German national coach. He did not miss one chance to pin his ears at Cento. Goldfever's stall wall had to be secured with electric wire so that he would not jump it furiously to attack his next-door neighbor. He was a devil in a horse's body.

Dietrich Schulze talked about this gleefully, for Goldfever could produce ingenious rounds on a show-jumping course.

He was especially brilliant in the wide arena at Aachen. Of course, at the Olympic Games in Sydney, he ruthlessly let his rider down, bringing him the worst individual result possible: accepting a team gold medal as the producer of the "drop" score. But in total, Ludger won almost 3 million Euros in prize money with him. Dieter was right.

Goldfever is still Madeleine's favorite jumping horse. He was, after all, the last horse that she ever rode herself. She was already around 70 then, and, at first, she was not even really up for sitting in the fiend's saddle. But Goldfever was no longer as wild as before and retired from competition. He was only active as a stud. It was a gorgeous ride, Madeleine said. While she was cantering along on her four-legged star, she had the idea that this would be the crowning glory for her. After all, she could count herself lucky to have survived a decades-long career in the saddle in one piece. Despite her lifetime passion for riding, she had woken up every morning without injury, pain, or regret. She patted Goldfever's neck—and that was it. Her very last ride.

The cell phone rings again. It is Isabell, who, along with Ludger and their respective families, makes up Madeleine's family today. They call each other almost daily. She calls them her "jockeys," although this is usually the term reserved for riders at the racetrack. The tall Ludger and athletically built Isabell do not have much in common with the petite racehorse riders, but Madeleine likes to use such expressions. She does not want to be the "grand sponsor" who is above all; she prefers to be right in the middle of it, by any means. She sometimes refers to her money as "bucks," and even calls it "dough" flippantly, on occasion, in a rough Berlin twang. The colloquial language slightly contradicts her voice, which always sounds soft, almost like a whisper. She is a categorically friendly person, with a tendency to a conciliatory approach. She is smiling in virtually every photo on display in her living room.

This may be the reason why her two "jockeys" have really let her into their lives. That, along with the fact that both of them are steady, grounded characters with a stable family background. The equestrian industry, especially the jumpers, is rife with rich people who have become infected with the horse bug, and are then, in extreme cases, taken advantage of by professionals who use every trick in the book to fund their own lives with the money of others. It is the fervent desire of many to be part of the inner circle that opens the pockets of the wealthy. As a rider, you must make sure that *you* are the beneficiary of those with funds and the desire to invest in talent, and not one of your spurred competitors. But real friendship with sponsors is not usually a possibility. Even horse dealers have a certain sense of honor: Their respect, no matter how it is measured, cannot be bought. Normally, sponsors remain outside the lives of their riders—they do not get any closer than the wood-paneled fireplaces of the old farms where guests are received. Riders may drink with them, offer them company when it is requested, and share a homey country ambiance, which may give their lives special importance. But confide in them? Never ever. After all, sponsors are there to be milked.

Madeleine, however, is of such disarming generosity, of such unwavering loyalty, and so nice to her riders that they cannot help but open their hearts to her. They rave about her reliable fondness and call it friendship. There is always a bed available to her at Ludger's facility in Riesenbeck, and she has a close relationship with his wife Arandell and their daughters. Madeleine also has her own room in Isabell's house in Rheinberg and gets along perfectly with the entire family. Whenever

Madeleine feels like it, she boards a train and is quickly on her way to drop in on one or the other of her jockeys. If she wants, and if her property in Mellendorf becomes a burden for her one day, she can move in with either one of them permanently. That is a done deal. Or she might commute, she says, and laughs, and you can feel her happiness that she is so well cared for by those she sponsors. She says she trusts both riders one hundred percent. And she is overjoyed when she can buy them new horses.

Madeleine asks why she shouldn't live in the here and now. This is the time when her two riders *want* to ride, although Ludger has taken a step back since the Olympic Games in Rio in 2016, which Madeleine has accepted with a faint regret. It is foreseeable that soon he will withdraw even further from the sport.

Madeleine enjoys accompanying her riders to shows, partly, of course, because she loves the success. Her jockeys are two defining figures of equestrian sport, both as riders and entrepreneurs, and so ambitious at competitions that Madeleine thinks it unnecessary to put additional pressure on them. They do that themselves. Madeleine greets them when they exit the arena and gives them a hug, even when their rides have not gone satisfactorily. And they explain the reasons for it to her, unasked. But if it has gone well, Madeleine enjoys the triumph to the fullest.

So why save money until it is too late? The memory of Dieter's passing resonates in this belief. How suddenly it can be too late! One day, he went to see a doctor for his backache. He thought he would get an injection and that would be it—problem solved. But everything went completely differently from how he imagined it would...instead, he received a devastating diagnosis: bone cancer. And all of a sudden, they realized that their days together were numbered. Of course,

Madeleine said, as was her habit: "We can do this." But she also knew that his fate had been decided. She had to look on as he dwindled, as he deteriorated; she wanted to hold on to him, but it was impossible. He died in December 2008, one week before Christmas, at sixty-eight years old. Ever since, the activity in Mellendorf turns around a deserted space that nobody will be able to fill in this lifetime.

Isabell hadn't lived at Mellendorf for some time when Dieter died, but she still visited regularly.

*In that dark December, when Dieter was getting worse and worse, I was on the way from Rheinberg to Frankfurt, to the Festhallen show. El Santo, whose barn name was Ernie, then my future prospect, had qualified for the finals of the Nürnberger Burg-Pokal. This series offers potential championship horses their first dance on a big stage. I had planned to visit Madeleine and Dieter soon anyhow, maybe after the show, but then I thought, "Should I go before?" I don't have a tangible reason why I spontaneously decided to take the detour and steered my car toward Hanover and Mellendorf. Dieter lay there, in the same apartment that I had lived in for two years. It's on the ground floor; he had moved there because he had a hard time getting around. Basically, I just wanted to say hello to him. And yet, it was the evening when Dieter's condition became dramatically worse and when he eventually died. Madeleine and I were with him.*

*It was like a stroke of fate. And it is also a little bit symbolic of our relationship: Each of us is there for the other one when it gets important. It was a dramatic experience and has bound Madeleine and me even closer together.*

*It was hard to immediately go back to a daily routine afterward, but Madeleine said that I should get in my car and go to the show the next day since it was what Dieter would have wanted. I reluctantly pulled myself together and competed in Frankfurt—and won the Burg-Pokal with Ernie. I didn't feel able to participate in the performance later, but Ernie's win made me smile under my tears. The reason being that Dieter had always affectionately mocked Ernie a little and referred to him as the "little riding pig" because he is a slightly dispro-portioned creature with a fat belly and doesn't look as elegant as you would want in a championship horse. "See," Madeleine said, "Ernie wanted to prove to Dieter that he is the little horse that actually could do something!"*

Isabell and Madeleine had known and liked each other during the days of Dr. Schulten-Baumer. As early as then, when she was still an active rider herself, Madeleine committed herself to German teams as the Chef d'Equipe—for example at Isabell's first European Championships. She was an authority, always at the center, and a point of contact for all those who, from time to time, needed a refuge from the coldness of high performance sports to warm up again. Despite the age difference between her and Isabell, she never took on a maternal role, rather that of a good friend and a kindred spirit. Isabell, constantly under pressure to perform from The Doctor, and in addition, hardened by her own ambition at times, enjoyed Madeleine's friendly manner and her habit to not only ask for results, but to also ask the riders from time to time if they were doing okay.

On one hand, the way The Doctor treated Isabell discon-certed Madeleine—like when he had a real go at her just as she dismounted her horse, still beaming with joy, only to face his criticism. That cannot have been easy to swallow, Madeleine thought. But when asked, she also quickly makes excuses for Dr. Schulten-Baumer: "Maybe that was how it had to be in the course of training Isabell," she says. "You have to be tough every now and then. Kindness doesn't always get the job done."

The chemistry was instantly there between the young woman and the one twenty-eight years her senior, although their relationship started with a "bad buy." Madeleine tried out the Hanoverian Aurelius at Dr. Schulten-Baumer's; Isabell had ridden him at shows thus far. Madeleine bought him, but did not really get along with him, and so she and Isabell exchanged ideas and tried to improve the partnership, without pressure or stress—although on this occasion, also without any success. Madeleine eventually gave up and made the ride on Aurelius available to professional rider Karin Rehbein. The calmness with which Madeleine accepted the failed mission impressed Isabell, who was accustomed to being at odds with every little mistake.

The Doctor was no exception with regard to the interaction between professionals and rich patrons. This is why his attempt to solve his own problems meant arriving at the solution that led to his breakup with Isabell. Madeleine was to buy horses from him, Isabell was supposed to train the horses in Rheinberg and compete them as usual, and so only one thing would change for The Doctor: Madeleine's money would change hands and secure the future for his barn, which also had to pay for his stepdaughter's dressage career. Apart from a little fame as the owner of the horses, there was not much in the deal for Madeleine.

When Madeleine tells the story with her soft focus, it sounds a bit different: "He said, 'Oh, well, I have so many horses, don't you want to buy two? Then I am no longer burdened with so many of them.' So I bought two from him."

Those were the two prospects: Satchmo, who Isabell rode to the World Championship title in 2006, and Richard Kimble, whose career ended too early due to an injury. The discomfort that this deal caused Isabell, as we know, was the beginning of the end of her cooperation with The Doctor. He let her go, at least a little bit. Nobody would have guessed back then that Isabell would eventually completely align herself with Madeleine and Mellendorf. Least of all, Dr. Schulten-Baumer.

*I met the right person at the right time twice in my life. First The Doctor. Then Madeleine. Two lucky breaks.*

After the split with The Doctor, a fresh start had to be arranged. Isabell considered boarding her horses at the German Equestrian Federation in Warendorf. Even a move to Ann Kathrin Linsenhoff's facility, based at the Kronberg Schafhof, was discussed. Finally, she decided to transfer her training location to Madeleine's. At first, the German national coach Holger Schmezer supported her in her training. Then she hired coach and former competition rider Wolfram Wittig. He frequently came to Mellendorf, where Isabell slowly found a way back to her old self again. Of course, he did not have to practice flying changes with her; what she needed was a calming influence who filled the vacant position in the background. She would never again find as congenial a partner as Dr. Schulten-Baumer had been, that much was certain.

Dieter probably did not foresee what Isabell moving to Mellendorf meant. Her presence rattled their tranquil life and former rhythm. Sometimes, she came home in the middle of the night—often exhausted and a lot later than expected. The always generous Madeleine did not mind. Dieter complained occasionally. But somehow, they still grew together. It was as if Isabell suddenly had two families. She was the daughter of the house, not only in Rheinberg, but now also in Mellendorf. This was a new feeling for Madeleine and Dieter, since they did not have children of their own. They did not want children for a long time. And then, it was too late.

Madeleine and Dieter first met at a horse show in Berlin. Both were competitive riders at the time: She rode dressage; he was a jumper. But, apart from this, the worlds they belonged to could not have been any more different. Madeleine was the sheltered daughter of a well-off business family. Dietrich had fled the German Democratic Republic with his family in 1953; he was twelve at the time. He lived in Spandau, and at first, made some money driving a taxi before he became a professional rider. When the two of them first set eyes on each other, Madeleine was eighteen years old, and he was twenty. They met again and again at shows: the young, blonde, tall Madeleine, and the smaller, sturdier Dieter, with that jumper rider mystique that automatically captures the hearts of girls for mysterious reasons. One day, he suffered from a bad fall and had to go to the hospital. Madeleine visited him there...and they fell in love with each other, despite all social differences.

Time proved their love to be true, but of course, the people talked back then: The taxi-driving jumper rider snatched the rich girl. Madeleine accompanied her mother regularly to the annual Bayreuth Festival, at which performances of operas by the German composer Richard Wagner are presented. Dieter had no interest in this whatsoever. He also rode differently. Not as finely and elegantly, but as some said, professionally and effectively. But neither of these differences played a decisive role in their relationship. Both had the "horse bug," and it brought them together and connected them their entire lives. They were engaged, but not married, for seventeen years, only because Dieter did not want to have it said that he was only after Madeleine's money. "My late fiancé," she sometimes said, self-mockingly, and just putting up with it during a time where many people were significantly more narrow-minded than today. Dieter, now a member of the "ensnared jumper rider club," remained persistently at her side, before their wedding in 1987, and after their wedding. At shows, you always saw the two of them together. And also at the crowded hotel bars, where relevant connections were made and cultivated.

"We could have gotten married earlier," Madeleine says. "We belonged together."

Madeleine was the younger daughter of Eduard Winter, a major figure of post-war Berlin. He sold cars in the 1920s, then became an economic miracle in person, so to speak, making a considerable fortune with two German cult-products of the era, Volkswagen and Coca-Cola. He sold VW, Audi, and Porsche vehicles in his dealerships, which were spread all over Berlin, with an elegant headquarters on the Kurfürstendamm—one of the main avenues in the city. Germany motorized itself en masse with the beetle from Eduard Winter. If people were able to afford a fancier ride, they would get that from him, as well. Moreover, Winter purchased the Berlin brand license for Coca-Cola, which was a bubbly source of money. A businessman of his time could not have lined himself up any more lucratively, yet still within legal limits. And he was popular. On Eduard Winter's seventieth birthday, the Kurfürstendamm was blocked, a Volkswagen stood at every corner, and he paraded through with his driver as everybody honked and waved.

Eduard Winter obviously did everything right. His marketing genius could already be seen when he named the first promising show horse he bought for his daughter Madeleine Coca-Cola. At eighteen years of age, she became the German Dressage Champion in September 1959 with this mare, dark bay and fizzy, just like the caffeinated soda. It was a class with prominent competition: Liselott Linsenhoff, Rosemarie Springer, and Ilsebill Becher. And, at the very top of the result list, the newbie, Madeleine Winter, appeared. The first to congratulate her was publisher Axel Springer, also someone of the entrepreneurial generation and well acquainted with Madeleine's father, who unfortunately, did not live to see his daughter's magnificent success. He had died in July of that year at seventy-four years old. His picture is up in Madeleine's office—a serious man with heavy glasses.

"He was an unbelievable person," says Madeleine. Even today, she imagines hearing his voice when faced with difficult decisions. "I always think, 'How would Papa have solved this problem?'"

He could only watch from up above when she became the German champion for the first time. It would have been so nice for him to have been there...after all, it had been he who had kindled her enthusiasm for horses.

Originally, Winter had only wanted to hack out for a little while in the Grunewald, a forested region within the Berlin city perimeter. Then, he had the idea to bring along his daughters Marion and Madeleine, ten and eight years old at the time. They got horses from the riding school around the corner and went with their father. As different as the two sisters might have been—the older one introverted and quiet, the younger one bubbly and social—the relaxed rides with their father became a passion for both. Marion Jauß, née Winter, later won harness races, still runs a breeding farm close to Hamburg today, and supports jumper rider Christian Ahlmann as an owner. Madeleine's ambition drove her into the equestrian arenas early. She competed in her first show at twelve years old. After the German championship title in dressage at eighteen, she became a German jumping champion in both 1969 and 1975. Clearly, she was a fearless woman.

Eduard Winter, who became a father late in life, provided for his family after his death with his usual acumen. A five-person advisory board still manages and multiplies the assets that he acquired for his daughters. Madeleine assists in this work. The car dealerships have been sold, but the real estate is still owned by the family and yields rent.

Thus, when Madeleine has coffee on her deck and looks around, it is not only her husband who comes to mind, but also her father. "Without him, I wouldn't be sitting here," she says to herself. That is why she often radiates a slightly perplexed gratitude, as if she had to ask herself over and over again: "Why was it me, out of all people, who was so lucky and was so well taken care of?"

Madeleine does not want to say how rich she really is.

"I can live well," she states. "I really don't live badly here."

Not lavishly and not crazily—but she can do what she likes to do. And that, she says, is to make sure, first and foremost, that her jockeys have rides, and to make horses and riders happy.

"And I like to do so in a way," she asserts (and yes, she really says this), "that really shows they deserve it."

Madeleine tries to pass on some of her luck. Hence, she expanded her reach into other equestrian disciplines in 2008. She brought two-time Olympic Champion Ingrid Klimke into the circle of her protégées. Ingrid had won team gold with Abraxxas in Hong Kong, and now the horse's owner, who saw Abraxxas as a lucrative investment, wanted to cash out. When Madeleine heard, she reached for the phone, called Ingrid, and offered her help. She waited a few more months until the asking price had become slightly more normal, and then Madeleine conquered eventing and expanded her fitness program to include cross-country course walks. Later, she also secured the mare Escada, whose biggest strength was dressage, for Ingrid. Ingrid won the World and European Championship title and won the event in Luhmühlen, Germany, one of the most difficult competitions in the world. Ingrid also feels very close to Madeleine, who she calls "a gentlewoman."

Often, people who think they can talk Madeleine into doing some other "good deed" call her. For example, she hears: "My daughter's pony is too small. Could you not give her a bigger one?" Or: "Doesn't Isabell have enough horses? She could probably easily give one to my talented daughter." Madeleine has a hard time saying no in these situations, but her good sense commands her to control her contributions. She founded a charity in 2015 that helps sick children in Berlin, and she funded a "chill out room" in a home for mentally ill children, where they can let out their aggression and calm down. Of course, her efforts were named after her father: Eduard Winter Children's Charity.

*The charity is an affair of the heart for her, since she has created something for the future in memory of her father. He would have been very proud of her. She is a person who takes real joy in helping others. If she feels she is being addressed nicely or if she feels badly for someone, she has to give that person something. Her father must have been the same. You can't learn such generosity, and it is not a question of wisdom. You have it or you don't. It is a fundamental philosophy that is yours in the first place. It is, of course, easier to live by this philosophy if you are financially independent. Yet there are thousands of people who are well off and a different kind of being, completely out of touch with the real world, arrogant, not compassionate at all, and only asking, "Why should I be bothered?"*

Madeleine often goes to her hometown of Berlin where she visits her parents' graves, participates in board meetings, and attends to asset management and new investments. Madeleine says she monitors everything closely, managing her part alone, without a secretary: keeping appointments for the children's charity, looking at new projects. Sometimes she is accompanied by Isabell. She always has a suitcase in Berlin, and most of the time, she stays in a hotel on Kurfürstendamm. Shopping, however, is very limited. Her clothing is practical and unpretentious. She often wears light-colored jeans and a freshly ironed blouse, a piece of pretty jewelry, hardly any makeup, and her hair styled in a simple fashion. Allegedly, she buys a jacket at a discount store every now and then, which is, after all, good enough for whirling around at the barn. Style is secondary to her. She is happy to be with the horses. They have absolute priority in her life.

Madeleine not only provides a home for competition horses in Mellendorf, but also for some of her riders' retirees. When Gigolo followed Isabell from Rheinberg to enjoy his retirement, Madeleine even rode him a little bit. The most successful competition horse in history! She just loves being around horses, with their many different character traits, and their quirks, which are never the same. And, she loves the professionalism with which her jockeys judge horses. Whenever Ludger might have discovered a potential superstar, the fever infects her, too—even though a show-jumping horse can get very expensive these days. The market is keyed up, some bidders, for example, come from oil money. Or their name is Springsteen. Or Onassis.

"Ludger," Madeleine says, "will need a horse every once in a while that costs a little bit of dough. After all, he is a little bit older and can no longer wait for a horse to develop."

It does not cause her sleepless nights to spend money on a jumping prospect. On the contrary, it pleases her. And if it does not work out as expected, she will comfort Ludger and they will move on. It is still like it was when they first started working together, when their new relationship began with a fall. Dieter had stopped riding and was looking for someone to ride the horses he still had in the barn. They tried several acclaimed people: Hauke Luther. Gerd Wiltfang. When they hired Ludger in 1994, they knew right away he was the right man for the job...even though he fell off the horse at their first show together in Nörten-Hardenberg.

To Ludger's surprise, Madeleine apologized to *him*...for having given him such a stubborn animal to ride. It made them both laugh.

Isabell is very close to Madeleine; Ludger was closer to Dieter—as is often the case among men. The two of them traveled a lot together and talked about riding incessantly. Dieter arranged the horse deals for Ludger. Madeleine financed them, but gave her husband free rein on making the purchase decisions.

Today, Madeleine sees to those deals and also takes in the more "rugged" atmosphere of the jumper scene. If it does not go well for Ludger on course, he sometimes becomes slightly unpleasant...even grumpy, says the always conciliatory Madeleine. "But that's just how he is." And, of course, it is a little annoying for anyone that the poles fall down so quickly in jumping, sometimes only by lightly brushing them, and then in an instant, everything is ruined. Especially since high monetary sums are involved.

Madeleine does not like to judge and does not want to change anyone. She would rather brush the peculiarities of her fellow human beings away with a smile.

*It could happen that Dieter sat in the living room with Madeleine's cell phone ringing next to him, and he simply wouldn't answer it because he wanted to have his peace and quiet just then. He would call out, "Mado, your phone is ringing!" When she came running downstairs, out of breath, and having missed the call, all she said was: "Really, Dieter. Why didn't you just answer it?"*

Isabell's concept to buy dressage horses for a reasonable price and train them to excel is more cost-effective than to buy a show-jumping stunner for millions of dollars. Isabell still sticks to what she learned from The Doctor. Reason takes priority. But Madeleine notices, of course, what is up when Isabell's voice starts to vibrate on the phone as she describes a prospect, when she sounds electrified. She says then, "Let's do it," and both are ecstatic. Then they just have to play it cool to not get taken advantage of by the seller.

*The Doctor set an example for me in the way that the relationship between financial input and return has to add up. And that you make something out of the horse that you have bought...that you never say, "Okay, this one is no good— next, please." This standard has followed me to Madeleine's. I don't act according to a price tag. Some people are quick to add another zero to the price as soon as they hear the name Madeleine, because they think she is made of money. But I still follow my principle today: If a figure is over the top, then it is just not our horse. Never mind all the risks that you take when buying a horse. They can become sick, for example, and could, in an instant, no longer be a contender in the sport.*

The highs and lows of the training stages with each horse and contemplating solutions to challenges give Madeleine a lot of food for thought. She is all in with great enthusiasm, although she does not like to interfere with her advice. When she does offer it, she will begin with a complicated introduction: "Just so you don't get me wrong..." For example, she shared many thoughts and worries about Bella Rose's injury with Isabell for years. She, too, worried whether the mare would fully recover. The glorious beginnings of Belantis, the radiant gray stallion from Brandenburg, did not just please Isabell, but Madeleine as well. And when people catch their breath with amazement when they see him, she is proud to be his owner. She bought him from the state stud in Brandenburg, and her heart is full when she sees Isabell on the horse.

"I would be an idiot if I didn't feel that way," she says.

When she accompanies her jockeys to shows, Madeleine is in her element. At the CHIO in Aachen, one of the international highlights of the equestrian world, she always has several horses on the start list. That means she is always on the move. Equipped with all the necessary access authorizations, bracelets for the stabling as well as for the VIP area, she hurries across the extensive grounds, waving different start lists around, and tries to pry herself loose from the many acquaintances wanting to chat with her, so she can always get to the right place in time to see her horses go. "Oh, I have to be at the jumping arena—Ludger is up next." Or: "Oh, I have to hurry—Isabell is about to enter the dressage stadium. Wasn't she great yesterday?" Madeleine covers a lot of miles during a week at Aachen. But it does not matter, she is physically fit and always wears proper shoes! Often, she also has to attend ceremonies and parties at night. Very often, she is one of those being honored. The industry has awarded her pretty much anything in their repertoire. Everyone knows what she does for the sport. The continuous success of German equestrian teams would not be possible without Madeleine's horses.

Without Madeleine, Isabell might have had to decide on a completely different life. Madeleine has played a crucial part in the fact that Isabell was able to keep her high level of success, because horses come and go, and riders only remain at the top if they can continuously bring good youngsters into training. But Madeleine also gave Isabell a monetary jump-start for the reconstruction of her parents' farm in Rheinberg, despite the fact that Isabell's decision to take over that farm meant that she would leave Madeleine's facility after only two years. Isabell is proud that she has repaid that loan in full. Next to everything else, there is a monthly fixed rate for the board and training of Madeleine's horses, which is the economic basis for Isabell's show barn. Stability is everything in such a fluctuating business, and to be able to look calmly into the future is good for one's nerves. Isabell and Madeleine split prize money fifty-fifty.

Dieter once had doubts that "the little girl," as he thought of Isabell, would manage. He believed more in the economic success of show jumping—higher prize money can be won. But he did not count on Isabell's perseverance and ability to learn. Nor on her determination to interpret Madeleine's contribution as a foundation upon which she would build a functioning system of training and competing.

When she left The Doctor, Isabell still had different ideas. She had finished her law degree and had taken her first steps in the legal profession. Yet, it had always been clear that riding would remain her priority. This was the simple, but irreversible, plan ever since she had gone to high school. Eventually, when she was "old" (at thirty or thirty-five), she would take care of her "bread-and-butter job." School was a side stage; she rode before the bell rang for the first lesson of the day and she rode after school was out. Schoolwork was not very important to her, and she certainly did not meet the expectations of her teachers, who said that, if Isabell was still able to advance a grade the next year, despite her manner of learning, think of how good she could be if she took learning seriously. Her parents were upset about the first notification from school, but she kept her promise to do enough to get by and just made it from year to year and graduated. Heinrich and Brigitte Werth got used to Isabell's strategy and no longer gave way to panic. They never said that she was not allowed to ride anymore if she was not better at school. They believed in their daughter's potential.

Thus, cramming at the expense of riding was never an issue. And, later, the same applied for her university program, which she started right after graduating: Don't lose any time; it will take more time than is the norm due to riding anyway.

Isabell registered at the University of Bochum, since she could be close to her horses that way. She met the compulsory attendance during the first semester, but other than that, appeared only sporadically and took her first final exam after twelve semesters. She actually liked going to university as she could occupy her mind with other things and was able to mentally relax a little away from the "performance machinery" of The Doctor's facility. It was already about Olympic victories and World Championship titles back then, but she really wanted to finish university. Even Dr. Schulten-Baumer urged her to establish a second source of income for her professional future. After all, the fear of becoming impoverished through equestrian sport had haunted him his entire life.

After an exhausting day in the saddle, Isabell took her boots off and pulled many a nightshift studying—for example, when she had to hand in a paper. Since everything always had to happen at the last minute, she soon learned the exact time the mailboxes in her neighborhood were emptied. This way, she could send her paper off at the very last minute. At some point, her computer crashed on her last sentence, and she thought, "Now you've really screwed up." But somehow she managed. Her famous strong nerves helped her through it. And nobody asked about the grade later.

Then, a time of transformation announced itself. Suddenly, the public saw a completely new Isabell, with glamorous makeup, her hair down in waves, and chic clothes—and all of it larger than life, on posters hung up at relevant horse shows. The department store Karstadt had hired her as the model for their new clothing line aimed at businesswomen. Show spectators stood before the giant pictures, stunned. "That is Isabell, our 'natural' girl from the Lower Rhine region?" Her confident look under slightly lowered eyes made an impression. The transformation was stunning.

*I enjoyed being cleaned up professionally just once. "Well, well," I said to myself, "this is how you could look." But the styling didn't catch on. On a day-to-day basis, I prefer not to wear makeup and I tightly tie up my hair. The reason is simple: Every day, the moment comes when I have to get on a horse. And I find mussed styling worse than no styling at all. And I don't have the time or patience to constantly fix it.*

The professional boxer Henry Maske was the male model for the clothing line, called "Sir Henry," as well as the chairman of the soccer club FC Bayern, the former national soccer player Karl-Heinz Rummenigge. Isabell's world was becoming larger and larger.

She met Wolfgang Urban at the opening of a Karstadt sports branch in Hamburg. He was introduced to her as the designated chairperson. He gave her a tour and explained how a department store worked.

After the second part of her final law exam, Isabell began working part-time at the firm Oexmann in Hamm, Germany, where she was able to work flexible hours. She focused on equine and medical law. Sometimes, she stayed at the office until ten at night because she had ridden so long and had started her work late in the afternoon. A life like that was not feasible in the long-term, as the highway became her second home, and after two years she decided that it was enough. She had been invited by Wolfgang Urban to a meeting where he offered her a part-time job in the marketing department at Karstadt, which was on track to set up a program for sport sponsorships, and she accepted the offer. Isabell was in charge of promotions, events, and the design of sales space. The sponsorship of the Ruhr Marathon was a project, for example, that she was part of.

*There was a spark between us from the beginning. We got along very well and it turned into more. Today, Wolfgang is my common law partner and the father of Frederik, our son, who changed my priorities once again in 2009.*

Her new job was in Essen. Finally, shorter distances to travel between work and the barn. But the initial happiness was not to last very long. It was shortly after the job change that she decided to leave The Doctor and take her horses to Madeleine's. Once again, she raced across the highway from Essen to Hanover twice a week, or got stuck in traffic. Sometimes, the estimated two-and-a-half hours turned into five.

Isabell was everywhere and nowhere at the same time during these two intensive years. At the office. In Rheinberg. At a show. At training. It was a time of movement for Isabell. Of change. Of searching and finding.

In the years at the beginning of the new millennium, all tracks changed for her. Like a chain of logical consequences, it became apparent how she had to position herself for the next phase of her life after the breaking off with The Doctor. The cocoon of Mellendorf kept her warm for two more years. She drank a large portion of the ideal world, sat comfortably at the table with with Madeleine and Dieter, and was so much at home that nobody noticed when the three of them sat in front of the television together, in silence. Or when everybody was dwelling on their own thoughts over dinner, before one of them started talking again. It was almost like a last remnant of childhood, after which Isabell, once again, set out to conquer the world for a second time, now at thirty-four years of age, and this time at her own expense. She was done with having a second job, which was only an insurance policy to minimize the risks of riding. She had overcome the need for a boss and mentor. Her new dream came true.

The renovations at her facility in Rheinberg were finished in 2003, and she moved into her own house with a view over the fields, and her horses moved into her own barn.

*Sometimes I thought, "Phew, hopefully I didn't overdo it, and I can get everything done the way I had imagined it." The profitability had to be established with time; it wouldn't come overnight, and the pressure was especially high in the beginning, even though I always knew that Madeleine would help me—and my parents, whether with physical work or financially. But at the end of the day, you want to get it done yourself.*

After Dieter's death, the apartment where Isabell had lived at Mellendorf was restored to what it had looked like before. Now, when she comes for a visit, she sleeps there in a familiar bed, and enjoys never having really left. But her life takes place in Rheinberg now, and revolves around Frederik and her partner. Wolfgang is twenty-four years older than Isabell; hours spent together seem even more valuable and the passing of time is ever more noticeable with such an age difference.

*I needed someone next to me with authority, someone I can look up to, where I don't have to think, "He lies at my feet." That's not me. I can't do that, and I don't need that. I need someone with whom I can have a controversial debate, not someone where I have the feeling he is weaker than me.*

Both Wolfgang and Madeleine fought at Isabell's side when she was confronted with a case of doping and, later, with a medication case that threatened her reputation and her existence as a rider. They gave Isabell the support she needed, since she was determined to hold her ground. The investigation cost a lot of money, and once again, Madeleine supported her. In the second case, which was related to a stomach toner that was found in Ernie, Isabell swore not to rest until she was exonerated, and Madeleine pulled herself together and bravely agreed to stand by her jockey. She tried to conceal how much the dispute with the German Federation affected her. Not only because, by that time, she was a board member herself, but because the situation contradicted her need for harmony. Madeleine has to feel at one with herself and the world. As much as the way Isabell rides in her competitions may inspire her—a fight to the finish!—her feeling is please, not outside of the arena. "Children, play nice!"

One day, Ludger approached Isabell and said, "Let it go. Accept the suspension. Madeleine is suffering." Hearing that, Isabell did not have the heart to continue. Reluctantly, she finally agreed for the proceedings to be closed. But only for the sake of Madeleine, who sat on the couch at home, crying.

The man who asked Ludger to intervene at that time, was "a kind of stepson," as Madeleine refers to him today. He was part of her life for a while. It was a strange period in her life that caused many to worry, not only her riders. During this time, Madeleine sat at her sponsor's table at big competitions, with a young man at her side, and people all around her turned toward them and pinched themselves in disbelief. Was it Dieter sitting there? But he had died recently. And now a man suddenly appeared at Madeleine's side who looked just like Dieter in younger years. It was Dieter's son from a previous relationship, about whose existence Madeleine knew, but whom she had never met before her husband's death. The man got in touch with her after he learned of his father's passing, and Madeleine quickly welcomed him and his family into her heart and her home. She envisioned it to be wonderful to have a family in Mellendorf, particularly now that it had become so quiet and lonely. She even added another apartment to her house for the new addition. Isabell still blames herself for not having slowed Madeleine's euphoria, because her hope proved deceptive. It was impossible, of course, that life would give Madeleine another Dieter. The alleged idyll was not to be and "the kind of stepson" eventually moved away again. It was the only time that Madeleine, the notorious giver, really felt she had been taken advantage of by someone.

Madeleine has not been able to let go of the incident, even today. But the disappointment has not lessened her generous perspective on people. And she still has her jockeys.

Of course, professional riders and competition barn managers never have enough time. That's why she uses her standing invitation to Riesenbeck or Rheinberg rather frequently. But every once in a while, it does happen that a swarm of "family" invades Mellendorf and livens things up. A while ago, during a show in Isernhagen, very close to Madeleine's home, *both* her jockeys and their families were her guests. Isabell's son Frederik and Ludger's daughters got into a golf cart and raced along the paths on the property, hooting and hollering loudly. Nobody felt like going to a restaurant, and instead, the entire company dined together, chatting cheerfully on the deck.

And Madeleine was happy.

1  At a fox hunt on Funny. *Photo courtesy of Isabell Werth*

2  My sister Claudia on Fairy (left) and me on Funny (right).
*Photo courtesy of Isabell Werth*

3  With Monica Theodorescu, who would later become
the German dressage coach. *Photo by Werner Ernst*

4 My proud parents accompanied me to shows whenever possible.
*Photo by Werner Ernst*

5 Up in the air... *Photo courtesy of Isabell Werth*

6  Victorious with Gigolo at the European Championships in Donaueschingen, 1991.
*Photo by Hugo M. Czerny.*

7  The Werth family at a show. *Photo courtesy of Isabell Werth*

8  Taking a break with Gigolo. *Photo by hz/Foto, Heribert Herbertz*

9  On Gigolo at the
Barcelona Olympics
in 1992.

*Photo by Werner Ernst*

10  With Dr. Schulten-Baumer and the Honda DAX. *Photo by Jacques Toffi*

11  Training with The Doctor. *Photo courtesy of Isabell Werth*

12 The Doctor sees everything. *Photo by Jacques Toffi*

13 Winning gold at the
1996 Olympics in Atlanta
with Gigolo.

*Photo by Jacques Toffi*

14 The award ceremony in Atlanta.

*Photo by Lutz Bongarts/ Bongarts/Getty Images*

15 At the European Championships in Verden, Germany, in 1997, with the then chef d'equipe Madeleine Winter-Schulze. *Photo courtesy of Isabell Werth*

16  With a proud Dr. Schulten-Baumer at the party in honor of my Olympic gold medal at the local riding club in Rheinberg, 1996. *Photo courtesy of Isabell Werth*

17  The Doctor giving Gigolo his usual bit of sugar. *Photo courtesy of Isabell Werth*

18 My stint in the fashion world.
*Photo courtesy of Isabell Werth*

19 Satchmo feeling cocky. *Photo by Jacques Toffi*

20 With my archrival Anky van Grunsven in Turin, Italy, 2007.

*Photo by Jacques Toffi*

21 Emotional on Satchmo in Stuttgart, Germany, 2008.

*Photo by Jacques Toffi*

22  Edward Gal on Totilas in Aachen, Germany, 2010. *Photo by Jacques Toffi*

23  In the stable with (*left to right*) Satchmo, Hannes (Warum Nicht) and Ernie (El Santo). *Photo by Jacques Toffi*

24  It is what it is.... With Ernie (El Santo) in Stuttgart, Germany, 2010.

*Photo by Jacques Toffi*

25 With German dressage coach Monica Theodorescu and my groom Steffi.
*Photo by Jacques Toffi*

26 With Madeleine Winter-Schulze. *Photo by Jacques Toffi*

27  With my Bella Rose. *Photo by Jacques Toffi*

28  With my partner Wolfgang Urban and our son Frederik. *Photo courtesy of Isabell Werth*

29  My Olympic ride on Weihegold in Rio de Janeiro, 2016.
*Photo by Rob Carr/Getty Images*

# 7 TOTILAS

There is no question: Gigolo was a celebrity on four legs. As were Satchmo, Rembrandt, Bonfire, Salinero, Valegro, Weihegold—all names with a powerful ring to them in the world of dressage. But the story that evolved around each of these horses is only a mild breeze compared to what happened with Totilas, the shining black stallion with the expressive face, heaving muscles, and stunning movement. Totilas managed to propel the sport of dressage out beyond its prestigious but small pond for the first time. He is one of the very few horses who have made it into the collective memory of the Occident—a Black Beauty, in the flesh.

It helped that his first rider, with whom he became famous, was just as good-looking. Edward Gal, a perfectly styled Dutchman, sometimes even came to the barn with pink fur boots on his feet. He is an excellent and experienced horseman. Once, at Aachen, when Gal passed a shining, highly polished blue bus with Totilas, he could not resist pausing to quickly admire his mirror image: His immaculate hairstyle, perfect facial expression, and Totilas, his black steed. A sight for the dressage gods! That weekend, so many people piled into the dressage stadium, which was by no means small, to see them compete that the show management in Aachen had to eventually close it off and turn people away.

Totilas first managed to capture the attention of the international audience at the European Championships in Windsor, England, in 2009. What spectators saw there seemed to be the realization of a dream. Totilas had the enormous strength that it takes to perform the key movements—piaffe and passage—to perfection. The mobility of his shoulders caused people to rub their eyes in disbelief. In extended trot, he fired his forehand into the air like a can-can dancer. In addition, he radiated a magic beyond comparison. Power, masculinity, confidence. He was far superior to the crazy chickens, his competition, who spooked at every flowerpot. When he left the ring on a long rein, he seemed to look around gleefully, bathing in the admiration that the audience showed him and proud serenity in his eyes.

The small but determined dressage society in Holland rejoiced. Two years after their coup in international competition, a reversal of power was finally accomplished through Totilas, and the Germans were deprived of their power. At long last, Oranje—the national sports team of the Netherlands—stood at the very top of the *team* rankings at international Championships, which went beyond Anky van Grunsven's individual successes. Totilas received two World Record scores in Windsor. The judges were spellbound, pulling out one top score after another. Gal became the European Champion with the team and in the Freestyle. Totilas would keep the Dutch Team at the top for a very long time, the Dutch were sure of that.

What they did not realize was that in those areas where the industry's movers and shakers sat and ate, the pulse of one of Europe's leading horse dealers and stud owners had quickened. Former German show jumper Paul Schockemöhle followed Totilas' performances with a desirous look on his face. His passion for horses and his business sense were dancing a duet. What a dressage horse! Even he, who had studied thousands of horses and had never once forgotten one, had never seen such movement. And the horse was only nine! Many more successful performances should be possible—and why not for Germany instead of Holland? The controversial Paul, who in his life as a horseman had taken a lot of criticism, could all of a sudden become the savior of German dressage. He just had to find the right rider.

And Totilas was a stallion! "Rattatttattt" went the sound of Schockemöhle's inner calculator, whose precise work had supposedly led to him making his first million at seventeen. Now, it churned out attractive profit projections. Totilas would be sought-after as a sire, and one could ask a high price for the cover fee—per year that would bring in...the possibilities were immense. Schockemöhle decided to tap his network and look at the options to purchase the horse a little more closely.

Yes, but...there were critics of this spectacle that at first could not quite make their voices heard. What they said was dismissed as "German propaganda," especially when it was connected to criticism of Dutch training methods. Party poopers. To the Dutch, everything was just perfect. And yet, strictly speaking, Totilas was a little bit short-legged: essentially tall enough at 16.3 hands, but he appeared smaller. It was his charm and mind-blowing expression that made one forget his tendency toward stockiness.

*Those who saw Totilas at the World Championships for five-year-old horses remember him not as a beauty, rather a little*

*cutie, compact, with lots of impulsion. You could imagine that*
*you could do something with this horse. And he let you ride*
*and work him.*

But the physical price that the stallion's exalted, unnatural
movements would claim threatened to be high. Experience
had shown that the risk of injuries increased the more exaggerated a horse's movement. The aim of the classical way of
riding is the preservation of the horse, not a harmful extreme.
In his extended trot, he kicked up his front legs, but his hindquarters did not develop the needed thrust that would have
given the entire drama its purpose. An old cavalryman would
have said, the music was playing in the front with all its "bad-
umbumbum," but no troops followed.

But those were details that hardly anyone was interested
in. The waves of emotion this horse conjured up washed away
all concerns. One year later, at the World Equestrian Games in
Kentucky in 2010, Totilas' fans went into a frenzy when he cir-
cled around in a perfect pirouette to the sound of the Big Ben
bells. Edward Gal and Totilas took home all three gold medals.
The Dutch rider still raved about the stallion the same way
he had on the day he had got him, age six, when he had first
felt the amazing energy that emanated from him. But many
did not know that the joy was mixed with melancholy in Kentucky, and a mood of farewell secretly dominated the party.

The insiders knew it: Totilas was for sale. And that was
only wise from the owner's perspective. He was ten years old,
at the zenith of his abilities, and nobody was able to tell how
long his body would withstand the extreme strain of his performances. "Sell your horse before it's too late"—that is an old
rule. He could already be sick or lame tomorrow. The owners,
Tosca and Kees Visser, who were also the breeders and who

had made their money in real estate, were negotiating with Paul Schockemöhle. Technically, the deal was done before Gal was tacking him up for Kentucky.

Isabell also competed in Kentucky, with Hannes, with whom she did not stand a chance for a medal in the individual competition. German dressage was at a low, third place after the Netherlands and Britain, but nothing more. None of them could challenge Gal and Totilas; they had been carried away to impossible scoring spheres. So it was true: The German Team was in dire need of points at that time to win back the old prestige.

*I felt bad for Edward when Madeleine and I strolled across the venue and he came toward us. Of course, I knew the rumors that Totilas would likely be sold and that Paul Schockemöhle already had the right of first refusal. I said to Madeleine, "This must be a really shitty feeling, to know that this is your last championship with a horse with which you have created such a stir and with which you have grown together so much." To my surprise, Madeleine didn't only agree with me, she turned around and said, "Oh, I am so glad that you are saying this."*

*I said, "Huh? Why?" And then Madeleine came out with the truth. Paul Schockemöhle had been to see her before the WEG and had asked her if they could work together. If she bought Totilas for a price in the millions, I could ride him competitively, and Schockemöhle would take over the breeding rights. Madeleine did not want to tell me before Kentucky, but now, here it was. She had told Paul that she did not want to make a decision just yet. She would talk to me about it at some point; when he insisted she do it in Kentucky, she told him, "Talk to her yourself."*

*A long discussion followed in the lobby of our hotel. Paul does know me and my position, a little—at least he began our* conversation with the sentence, "Don't say no right away... listen first."

At the time, any high-caliber rider would have probably found it appealing to try Totilas; to compare the feeling that this horse gives you to the feeling on your own horses. Also, to feel how Gal schooled his horses and to benefit from it, learning something to apply to your own work. I, too, would have found it exciting, simply out of curiosity, out of interest as a rider and trainer...but behind a hedge or at home, where nobody could see.

Paul said: "You can do it so much better than Edward. You can really bring the horse together, but you can also release." But the compliment didn't have the desired effect. I felt that he shouldn't underestimate Edward.

I asked him what I should be happy about, when I was aboard Totilas. "Edward is going to become a three-time World Champion here in Kentucky with the stallion," I said. "What, in your opinion, should I do better than him? They are an established team. A symbiosis. Even if we became Olympic Champions, what about it should make me happy? I already have a few medals. This isn't for me. I wouldn't even know how to look Edward in the eye afterward. Losing Totilas will take away a piece of his heart. Some things can't be compensated for with money."

It would have been the first time after my very first apprenticeship with The Doctor that I would have sat on a finished horse and ridden him in an international competition. I would have felt as if on a pre-packaged holiday, where everything is planned for you. The entire fascination, the joy of teaching the horse, would have been missing, whereas the risk to place behind Gal in my performances with the stallion would have been huge. Plus: How would it look, spending millions for a *gold medal? My expertise would have been unused, and show-ring success would have been the only intent and purpose of the operation. This is not my philosophy. It would have been a betrayal of my own horses. It was no to the proposal in the beginning, and it was no to the proposal at the end.*

At least, our discussion led to the idea that Totilas should not be bought directly by a rider or that rider's sponsor. Schockemöhle purchased the stallion and then sold the right to use him in competitions. Naturally, he wanted to collect the income from his breeding potential himself.

When it became public that Schockemöhle had bought Totilas, there was enormous outcry in Holland. It was almost as if one of their soccer players had taken up German citizenship. The upset was despite the fact that two parties in the land of merchants had conducted excellent business: the sellers, Mr. and Mrs. Visser, and Edward Gal, the rider, who received his customary share of the sales price. That said, all that money did not seem to console Edward with regard to the loss of Totilas. He kept his stall at his barn empty for months. He could not bring himself to give it to a new horse.

Reportedly, Schockemöhle spent ten million on the stallion, but he never confirmed that amount. It would be the highest sum ever paid for a dressage horse. And this *despite* the fact that the deal dragged on for a long time due to significant doubt with regard to Totilas' health. How much money the genius businessman Schockemöhle contributed himself will remain in the dark. He found a rich and solvent sponsor: Ann Kathrin Linsenhoff, previously Isabell's closest friend. She wanted Totilas for her husband's second son, Matthias Rath. Her goal: to continue the family tradition. Her mother Liselott had won a gold medal in Munich in 1972, and Ann Kathrin had won in Seoul in 1988. Matthias was to continue the series in London in 2012. Certainly, there was still room for it in the glass cabinet she had at home. A few million did not seem too much to fill this space. Once again, the question whether one can and should "buy" gold medals was present. Naturally, criticism was particularly loud in the Netherlands, where emotions were boiling over. But not only there. And what was ultimately the source of all this criticism? Was it class envy or a sense of justice? Needless to say, the two sides evaluated the situation differently. Isabell looked at it simply from the perspective of an Olympic athlete.

*The manner in which success would have been achieved doesn't conform to my idea of competitive sport.*

When Totilas arrived at the Linsenhoff farm in Kronberg, Germany, it became apparent for the first time how great the interest in him had become. Television crews and journalists awaited his appearance at his new home. They called him the "wonder stallion." His management set up his own personal website. He had his own press secretary. Later, even bodyguards. A merchandising program was introduced. Now, one could drink from a Totilas cup and wear Totilas jackets. The German paper *Bild* assigned two journalists to him who found it particularly inspiring that he was busy at stud when not pursuing his competitive duties. From then on, his sex life, which took place in a sober setting in a laboratory by means of a "phantom" breeding mount covered with leather, provided reporters material for stories: "Sex Ban for Totilas," which was indeed once the case. And when he hurt himself while jumping on the phantom? "Sex Mishap."

The small dressage community marveled, accepted the unusual drama around the black stallion for the sake of the media attention that every event where Totilas was competing suddenly received. People hung in trees like fruit at the Wiesbaden castle grounds to snatch a look at the horse. At the German Championships in Balve, a hidden corner in the German Sauerland region, the masses arrived only to find their cars bogged down in the mud.

The gold could come any time now, they thought...but it didn't. The most serious problem was the result of the different ways of riding in the Netherlands and Germany. Edward Gal might not see himself as an imitator of Anky van Grunsven and her trainer Sjef Janssen; however, he did not only follow the classical principles in his training. Totilas moved so eccentrically not least because of the tension that Gal put him under.

*Totilas endured it all and cooperated. And Edward rode him really well during their peak together. I wouldn't say that he tortured him or oppressed him, something many people accuse him of. I have asked myself, for example, sometimes, "Do you really have to ride that many pirouettes?" You can argue about the intensity in many people's training. But they were a close-knit team. That the expectations grew and, of course, with that, the pressure—that's a different story.*

Matthias Rath and his father and trainer, Klaus-Martin Rath, probably knew all of that. But they wanted to approach the task immaculately, and initially, keep solely to the methods of the classical principles of riding, with the end result being becoming Olympic Champions as the role models of perfect riding. At first, Totilas was confused. Indeed, he moved with more relaxation under his new rider, but also, it was less spectacular. When he did figure out that he was no longer under the familiar force, he did not really show his gratitude with good behavior. Obedience through trust has to develop over years. Instead, Totilas became naughty and picked a fight with his rider—a nice, peace-loving, young student—and claimed supremacy in the arena. He wanted to be the one leading the dance. Basically, he wanted to be "the man." Rath, a competitive rider with comparatively little experience, risked losing the fight. Ultimately, the family threw out their model program and engaged a new trainer: Sjef Janssen.

Now classical equestrian Germany was appalled.

Even the then ninety-five-year-old, retired major Paul Stecken, the head of the Westphalian Riding and Driving School for decades, raised his hand from his townhouse in Münster, and insisted on the German Cavalry *H.Dv.12*, in whose revision he had played a part in 1937. He denounced rollkur as "misconduct" and criticized Matthias Rath as bringing little experience as a horse trainer to the task of riding the stallion, and explained that, post hoc, one would not be able to change a horse of Totilas' age. He assumed that the stallion had already suffered physical damages.

*It was not a secret that the horse had health problems. And he had to work a lot harder under a younger rider, so that they could grow together. When it was finally working out between the two of them, his health no longer cooperated.*

Pretty much everyone who saw this struggle wondered where Isabell would have been with Totilas at this point. She, however, was busy with Ernie's piaffe problem at the time. The good boy tried really hard, but he just could not manage to trot in one spot as was asked of him. Over and over, Isabell and Ernie dealt with the same embarrassment, while Totilas basically still performed his piaffe like clockwork. Isabell continued to fight on.

Don Johnson, who, at the time, could have taken over the lead role in her barn, was also not fit. He had injured himself and could not start at the qualifications for the 2012 London Olympics. What was needed was a Totilas for Germany with Isabell in the saddle! But, she saw the scenario differently. "There is," she said, when it became clear that she would not be going to the Olympics again, "also a life after London."

It can be assumed that she might have found Totilas' "buttons" in much less time than young Rath, due to her experience with many different horses. But even Isabell could not have delayed his physical vulnerability. Totilas regularly had to sit out important championships due to injury. It can be assumed that the vet bills alone were enough to buy several other talented young horses with which a rider could have worked very differently to form a competitive partnership.

Totilas did not give his new owners the desired Olympic gold. They also did not win gold at the World Championships. At the European Championships at home, in Aachen in 2015, his athletic career came to a sad end. It became obvious during the Grand Prix that he was suffering from an injury. The vets must have shown the black stallion leniency during the vet-check, but it was very visible during the test: Totilas showed obvious irregularities. It felt as if the last little bit of his genius was supposed to have served for this team title. The entire Totilas entourage, and the experts from the German Federation, who later even expressed their regret that they had put the desired success of the Team above the well-being of the horse, made for a rather bad example. It also could not be forgotten that the rider claimed that he had not noticed the injury in the saddle. The judges also cut a bad figure. They could have called off the test…if they had had the courage. The smart co-owner Paul Schockemöhle preferred to stay home during the European Championships, because he must have guessed the fiasco that was about to unfold.

The dressage horse that had moved the equestrian world—and beyond—like no other, became living proof for a succinct piece of wisdom: The higher you climb, the farther you fall. The team, of which Isabell was a part with Don Johnson, only came third without the expected top score from Totilas.

*He was an exceptional horse and would have deserved a nice goodbye, worthy of him.*

Totilas' homepage was taken down, his press secretary was no longer needed, nobody wanted the mugs anymore. The "wonder stallion" had not worked wonders. The book of Totilas was closed, garnished with two headlines: When it became known that he was no longer competing but only used at stud, the papers read: "Totilas in Sex Retirement." And when, in the light of certain events, Paul Schockemöhle lowered the stud fee from €8,000 to €2,500, it read: "Totilas Semen for a Bargain."

# 8 BELLA ROSE

Bella Rose is a born diva. When she performs, the crowd goes quiet and everyone watches her. If the chestnut mare with three white stockings and a long curved blaze was running across a field somewhere with ten other horses, all eyes would be on her. Even in a group of horses, everyone automatically looks at Bella. She radiates the same magic as some people do—those who pursue a career on the big screen, on the catwalk, or in politics. They have this mesmerizing effect, this charisma that you cannot learn and that can unleash a magnetic power of attraction for everything with eyes and ears. We do not want to exaggerate—Bella Rose is still an animal and not a Hollywood actress. But that is exactly it. Her gaze is not only captivating and confident—at the same time, it is defined by infinite gentleness, and thus, free of any vanity or arrogance. It is a loving greeting from nature, although she does not lack in personality or power.

*Bella Rose is my dream horse. A dream that has materialized in reality. I was allowed to enjoy it for a short time without restrictions. There were perfect moments where nothing was missing. No questions remained unanswered. There was nothing to criticize, to correct, to mold, to change. Just delight, and the feeling of what it is to finally learn what perfection feels like. She has given me pure happiness on four legs—moments that I would have loved to continue, but that were hard to hold on to, as is so often the case with happiness.*

At first, Isabell did not even get to enjoy an entire international season with her "ultimate" horse. They only had eight performances on the grand stage before, in the late summer of 2014, a painful ordeal started for the then ten-year-old Bella Rose. The dream-like rides were over, almost as soon as they had begun. Searching for the problem, finding it, treating it, and rehabilitation took three and a half years—but then the chestnut mare gave Isabell a World Championship that transported her to Cloud Nine. At the 2018 World Equestrian Games in Tryon, North Carolina, the two of them won the Grand Prix team competition and the Grand Prix Special. And, if the Freestyle had not been cancelled—the FEI did not manage to organize to have the final test moved after heavy rainfalls during Hurricane Florence wreaked havoc on the venue—it was possible they would have danced through to their third gold medal. Isabell laughed with happiness during her rides, and tears of joy streamed down her face afterward. It was yet another high point in a lifetime of career highlights—and felt all the more indulgent on the wonder-horse, Bella Rose.

*I saw Bella Rose for the first time when she was three years old. Finding the horse had a somewhat complicated background: My employee Anna was friends with Matthias Bouten, the individual who took care of the young horses at the facility of a family of breeders named Strunk from Bochum, Germany. Anna had seen Bella Rose there and tipped me off, and so I went to Bochum one day to look at the mare myself. I still remember what it was like when I stepped onto the Strunks' property. I went through the gate and down the barn aisle. To the right, a little entrance opened up into the indoor. That's where I stood, chatting with the breeders, while watching with one eye through the door of the arena, where Matthias was longeing the young Bella Rose. The mare started to trot, and I was breathless.*

*It was like electricity in my body. I felt like I had been zapped—it was incredible. It was a kick, an ignition, and I immediately told myself: "This is your horse."*

*While I enjoyed the view of Bella Rose trotting past me, I was thinking, "Let's hope this is not an illusion, directly followed by a fall from grace—some problem in the canter, some deal-breaker that will ruin my excitement." But the horse went in walk, trot, and canter, and I tried to keep my facial features in check. This narrow, long-legged horse, the equine equivalent of a fashion model, had completely enchanted me. I knew that I had never met a horse like her and that I would also never find one again. And her name was Bella—the same name I was and still am called by some very close friends: Monica Theodorescu, former Olympic Champion and German National Coach, calls me Bella, as does Heike Kemmer, with whom I have ridden together on the same team at numerous championships.*

*I made an effort to contain my euphoria. We left the barn as Matthias kept working the mare, and I was only capable of one thought: "How do I get this amazing horse?" All I said aloud was, "Interesting," but Anna could read the truth in my eyes.*

*The breeders suggested a fair price for a horse of her class that had just been started under saddle, and I called*

Madeleine, who could already tell from my voice what was up. She didn't even ask much about the mare, but only said, "Okay, go ahead."

Of course, the Strunks knew that Bella Rose was a fantastic horse, but they might have not been aware of her entire potential. They did, however, ask to be allowed to present her at the annual Westphalian mare performance test. The German breeding associations award their permission for targeted reproduction at these events. In this case, however, their scores were slightly off. Bella Rose only received 6.5 points out of 10 for her trot. "Whaaat?" Madeleine asked. "What kind of animal did you buy there?" I just said, "Relax, Mado. This horse can never move in a way that she would only get a 6.5 for the trot. It would be like Kate Moss getting a D for modeling on the catwalk, or Michael Jackson a D for dancing."

I didn't care about the performance test scores. All I cared about was Bella Rose coming home to Rheinberg with me and spreading her charm in the dressage rings of the world. It was 2007, one year after Satchmo and I won the World Championships and time to build up the next "golden horse." Bella Rose was one of those, I was sure of it—certainly, the best horse I had ever had. Not a day went by when I didn't feel the fascination I first felt watching her all over again.

Bella Rose was my horse, the culmination of everything I had experienced before...she was the perfect image, formed from the best puzzle pieces of all my top horses. She had Gigolo's athleticism, and his commitment, willingness to move, and sportsmanship. She had Satchmo's charm, flexibility, and his genius, but lacked his madness. And, just like Weihegold, she was not complicated at all and highly talented for passage and piaffe.

The best of everything.

*When I first sat on Bella Rose, I felt almost apprehensive. I still don't have words to describe the feeling. It was incredible. The freedom of movement she had in her shoulders and hind legs—the elasticity. It was a completely new feeling. It is ineffable how this horse could use her body. And then the canter: I could see her front legs flying. Bella didn't only captivate you from the ground, she did so from the saddle.*

*A God-given ability to move: Satchmo's half-pass, for example...those kinds of lateral movements that require the highest degree of elasticity have always seemed perfect to me. Bella Rose added another nuance on top of that. And her passage and piaffe—the most elevated, celebratory movements, which, simultaneously, require physical effort, balance, body control, and feeling for rhythm—well, I had never felt before how intensively these movements could go through the horse's entire body. With this mare, the transition from passage to piaffe was hardly perceivable; it was as if her body continued to produce the rhythm like a metronome. I could bring the piaffe into her body in one spot, almost by simply wishing it to be there. In and out, it was always swinging through her entire body. After all my years riding, it was an eye-opener for me, even though I had not done anything else in my life other than trace the movements of a horse's body and swing my own body in time with it. The mixture of asking and receiving is what constitutes equestrian sport; we need to grasp the idea that limits are perceivable and revocable at the same time. Riding is an experience of great intensity because of this.*

*Bella Rose was extremely sensitive and delicate. Once, when I was riding her in a rain shower as a five-year-old, the drops drummed lightly on her croup, and she immediately started to prance in a little bit of a piaffe. At the same time, she was so excited to move, had such an urge to move, that she was hard to control. When I rode Bella on our racetrack, it was a major effort. She wanted to go, and she wanted to do so with such motivation and enthusiasm that I could hardly hold her.*

*As it had been with all the other horses with which I had followed a path to great success, my most important task with Bella was to channel her temperament in the right direction.*

*Bella tended to overdo her forwardness and to go out of her way when it came to keenness. I had difficulty achieving mental relaxation with her. That was the only challenge with this mare, and it has remained the only one until today.*

*Bella Rose had such reserves of energy that she didn't tire easily. Working her for an hour to "let out the steam"—that was pretty much a waste of time with her. She also never got distracted by her surroundings or succumbed to hysteria. She could cope on her own and was not interested in flowerpots or umbrellas. She fed on excitement from her own self. When she got going, it was because she was excited by her own activity and movement, especially in the canter. She was like an engine that runs and runs and becomes hot in the process. She learned all the movements easily. The question really was, how was I to get her to perform them in the arena without incident?*

When Bella Rose turned six years old, Isabell presented her to the world of dressage experts for the first time at a show in Munich. The news spread like wildfire. Everyone wanted to see Bella Rose. The Dutch star Edward Gal, still riding Totilas then, and his partner, Hans-Peter Minderhoud, who was also riding on the international circuit, asked, surprised: "Who's the chestnut mare you have there?" Bella competed in a dressage test, not yet at the Advanced Level, and the insiders stood along the side of the ring, mouths wide open, taking in the horse's aura. Already, Bella Rose showed a trot "tour" that silenced onlookers. During the walk phase, between the two required turns-on-the-haunches and out of sheer *joie de vivre*, she started to piaffe, which was not even asked for at her level. The spectators grinned. The mare's urge to move was overwhelming. And besides all her other qualities, she was also a model student. Sadly, she was just starting to learn the sport when she injured herself. Isabell did not get to keep going with Bella and her training; she didn't get to develop the "fireworks" and to fire them when she wanted them. The mare's training and development would only continue—eventually—after years of delay.

*I don't even want to imagine what could have happened, had I had been able to focus totally on Bella Rose's progress. Naturally, we would have grown even closer. The mare had learned quickly what was important—that, for example, sometimes, she had to calm down mentally to do her "job." She had quickly grown accustomed to the daily show routines, had gained more and more experience, and had become quite comfortable with the competition business. I can imagine that we would have rocked the scene. Even British star Carl Hester, rider and of course trainer of the then dominating pair that was Charlotte Dujardin with Valegro, believed that there was only one horse out there that would have made their life difficult: Bella Rose.*

Charlotte Dujardin on Valegro became World Champion, European Champion, and Olympic Champion. But Hester was deeply impressed by Bella Rose. Their first remarkable performance: the qualifier for the World Equestrian Games 2014 in Normandy, which was located in the remote Province of the Saarland in Germany, at the luxurious facility of a pharmaceutical company owner in Perl-Borg. All of Brazil, as well as public viewing areas in Germany, were in the grip of the FIFA World Cup soccer playoffs at the time. But, on the neatly raked showgrounds where the potential team horses and riders for the World Games were to be evaluated, Bella Rose performed as if she had to score the deciding goal. She easily cracked the 80 percent mark with her score in the Grand Prix—the invisible borderline where "good" becomes "world class." It was a particularly important result, since this was the test that decided the team ranking at a World Championship, and *that* was what the German Equestrian Federation was most interested in. Individual medals were a bonus.

It was as if audience members were guests on a launch pad as Bella Rose rocketed to victory with almost provocative coolness and nonchalance. She knew everything already, it was just patience that was not her thing. She had to learn to *wait*. She sometimes shot ahead, before her rider's signal from the saddle had even reached her. Because of this, Isabell had continuously halted when riding the test during training, letting the mare catch her breath, and giving her a sugar cube. When it finally counted, however, this method proved to be a source of errors: Bella Rose hesitated in all those places where Isabell had made her work sweeter before, awaiting her reward. Instead, she now received a leg aid telling her to keep going, which she now felt was a little bit too strong. Rather than continuing her elegant walk, then, Bella Rose started to jog. The knowledgeable bystanders noted down in their programs: *mistake*. Of course, it was also proof that this mare reacted to every little signal in a highly sensitive way. Her finely-tuned reactions cost points for the time being, but Isabell took it in stride.

"She doesn't make the mistakes," Isabell said about Bella in Perl-Borg. "*I* make the mistakes."

It was a time when Isabell's seasoned fighting spirit had a break. The "old Isabell," who took pleasure in climbing into the ring with each of her unruly horses, was not needed in Bella Rose's saddle. The new Isabell did not have to fight for control or for answers for the first time; she could just enjoy.

In the meantime, it had also gotten around amongst the stallions present that a very attractive equine model was out and about. First, they became nervous; then, they tried to put the moves on her. Totilas, the forever injured, neighed, although he was not known as a particular go-getter. Matthias Rath played it safe, preferring to isolate his horse and move his training sessions from the outdoor warm-up to an adjacent indoor arena. It is rare that a single mare has a measurable effect on her male surroundings. You have to consider that studs are not generally known to have a particularly differentiated taste in the mares in their lives. They usually even function pretty well at the sight of a leather-covered, wooden rack upon which they are perfectly happy to jump. But Bella Rose awoke unexpected amorous desires. Desperados, Christina Sprehe's beautiful, well-behaved, black stallion could not resist the chestnut either. Usually, his rider had control over him, even when pretty mares coyly waltzed past. But at the sight of Bella Rose, Desperados lost all composure. The risk that, this time, he would rather follow the call of nature than his obligations as a mannerly dressage horse was high. He made it very apparent he wanted to be free to follow his desires, and Isabell on Bella Rose's back was in serious danger. They had to separate the two horses.

"In any case, the gentlemen," remarked Isabell later when she was safely on the ground, "have good taste."

By now, the Dutch national coach had already called out to Isabell: "Have fun in Rio! They will be your Games."

It was still two years until the Olympics.

First came Aachen. This was the first CHIO with Bella Rose in a setting that seemed made more for her than any other horse. Totilas also competed—the glossy black who attracted so much attention because he seemed to perhaps be finally ready for his first big Championships, the World Games, without the usual health problems. Bella Rose played the second main role at the show, confirming everything that she had promised Isabell. A world-class horse, on her way to an international career. When Totilas was withdrawn before the final day, because, again, he was not fit to compete, Bella Rose's star finally rose.

The Freestyle to the sounds of "Ode to Joy" was the best and most beautiful thing that Isabell had yet achieved with her dream horse. It really seemed to be surreal for all involved. Nobody was looking for faults anymore, as dressage spectators usually like to do. Instead, everyone enjoyed the mare's talent, her impulsion, her grace, and her power. Isabell, already prone to crying when things become emotional, did not wait until the prize-giving ceremony this time. The tears started streaming down her cheeks during the Freestyle performance.

Oh, Bella Rose!

On this day, in front of a full dressage stadium in Aachen, Isabell cried, as if she already knew that what she was experiencing would be the emotional highlight of her own Hollywood movie with this superstar main actress, and that she would have to fight tenaciously for a repeat of the event. This international judges' panel at Aachen was one of those that is extremely slow to catch on and tends to follow the mainstream rather than scoring what's actually happening in front of them. They put Isabell and Bella Rose in third place. But, in this case, Isabell couldn't care less. The audience rose from their seats and gave her a roaring ovation, and she just kept crying. Forget the other star of the show, thought many people who stood there, clapping. That stallion in a black suit. Here comes a supermodel in a ginger fur coat.

*Totilas and Bella Rose—we have two completely different horses there. The mare naturally had extraordinary freedom of movement and talent. Of course, Totilas also had talent, but he was also very much "produced." I never had to go there with Bella, since she already offered so much herself. I think that was the big difference between the two. Both horses had lots of charisma and expression, but with the mare, the movement was part of a naturally supple flow of her body. To ride trot half-pass as expressively on Totilas, you had to really grip him between your aids. You had to hold him, keep him in the air. It all came naturally to Bella.*

Bella Rose always made Isabell look good. For the moment there were no more compromises necessary, no need to transform ungainly body proportions, no constant psychoanalysis for disturbed equine souls. Bella Rose demonstrates progress in breeding. She was a horse that had everything that clients ask for, as well as, technically, robust health. She did not suffer from intense training but always seemed to draw new strength from somewhere. Her performance was modern, chic, effortless. This mare no longer mirrored the "old times," where horses where still used as work or draft animals, or even weapons of war. Bella is a pure leisure horse, a fun, highly functional toy. Fine-tuned, like a Ferrari. She is the future of dressage sport and equestrianism in general.

Bella Rose won her first big title, the Team World Championship, at the showgrounds of the World Equestrian Games in Caen, Normandy. She contracted a cold on the trip, which developed into laryngitis, and she was only allowed to walk on the first two days there.

*And then, during training, on the day that still feels like flying to me today when I think of it, she suddenly went like a dream. I sat in the saddle and thought: "There. Nobody can reach me now. I have everything that I have ever dreamed of as a rider. You just go to the Games, stir up the scene with your horse, and take everything you can get." It was still two days until the first World Equestrian Games test, and I saw before my eyes how one door after another would soon open for me.*

*But on the morning of the Grand Prix, I was brought back to reality with a jolt. I was the first rider in the ring at eight in the morning. Bella Rose had been really hot the day before, had felt good, and had signaled with every fiber of her body that it was high time to start the competition. But it was impossible to prepare her as I would have liked that morning. I couldn't ride her again before the test—I would have had to ride at four in the morning to give the mare a sufficient breather before all the stress in the ring started.*

*It was raining that morning—August in Normandy—and was cold, dark, and uncomfortable when we left the barn. The morning made for a bad mood. And then, the arena: When I was already on my horse, because the schedule was tight, tractors were still roaring across the ring, preparing the footing. This was a disaster. My already sensitive horse, who had not had the chance to get rid of her excess energy, had to go into the ring at once following these tractors.*

*I started off carefully, and at first, I thought, it wasn't even going that badly. Bella Rose went forward, if not as freely and enthusiastically as two days before. Something was different— annoying to both her and to me. The footing was very hard.*

*While I kept on riding, I thought to myself, "Maybe she doesn't like it much." She wasn't completely through…Bella Rose, of all things! The boisterous one, the disciple of readily available obedience! Despite everything, she delivered an outstanding performance, cantering with impulsion very beautifully, and if I hadn't counted my strides wrong in one of the half-passes, it would have been very good. It gave me hope that maybe I was only imagining her stiffness…but that is usually not how it works. Even if you only have the thought as a rider, "Oh, is there something there?" you have to take it seriously. Pushing it to the back of your mind doesn't usually make it go away, but, of course, everyone still tries.*

*During Bella's last extended trot, which should have been an impulsion-filled, blissful, floating dream, I knew it no longer felt as it should. The test went well, yes—but not as well as expected.*

Isabell still received the highest score on the German team, and the World Championship title was safe. But in the afternoon, Bella Rose was taken out of the barn for a walk, and doubt quickly turned into certainty. There was a problem. At first, the mare moved stiffly, like an older person who has just gotten out of bed. When the team looked at her more closely, it was obvious: She was lame in one of her front legs. It was a shock, and an emotional crash for all involved. Isabell's grooms, Steffi and Anna, who weep even more easily than their boss, cried. They did not want to abandon their dream of watching Bella Rose enchant Normandy.

*Anna asked, "Why don't we at least wait a day? Maybe it is just a temporary problem." I knew immediately that I didn't want to take the risk. Experience has taught me that these things don't vanish into thin air within a day.*

*We removed the shoe on the leg in question, and Bella seemed to immediately feel better. We had put a new set of shoes on the mare during the training camp, shortly before our departure for the WEG. The new shoes and the hard footing at the showgrounds obviously didn't agree with her. My worry for my horse raced in circles in my head, while I had to answer the journalists' questions during the press conference. Up on the podium, I forced myself to cheerfully rave about Bella's qualities, while she was being examined by the veterinarian a thousand yards away. Somehow I managed to get the press conference over with, still with the desperate hope at the back of my mind that we might get off lightly after all. In the end, the vet's diagnosis didn't sound all that dramatic: An inflammation in the laminar corium, meaning the mare's sole.*

*Even though Bella Rose was already feeling a lot better, we went home. It was tough, but acceptable. After all, I believed I knew exactly what the problem was and that it was harmless. Just bad luck, and those kinds of consequences we would quickly leave behind. The world was still open to Bella Rose! She was only ten, and it was still two years to the next Olympic Games in 2016 in Rio. There was plenty of time for great deeds, still, so why fret? Instead, I must get back to work. First, I had taught Bella Rose how to wait for me. And now, Bella Rose was teaching me how to wait for her.*

After a few days' rest, Bella Rose trotted soundly again. After a thorough examination under anesthesia, the doctor gave her the all-clear. Nothing stood in the way of a start at the show in Stuttgart in November, where Bella Rose moved as effortlessly as before her injury and turned on her charm to captivate the southwest of Germany.

*I was perfectly pleased that I was able to experience a happy ending with her in Stuttgart at the end of show season. But then one day, during winter, Bella did not feel as good as before again. It was not a dramatic lameness, but she was not one hundred percent. A painful process began: She was checked, but we didn't find clear answers. There was nothing tangible. I worked her less over the winter, and there were no changes in the leg. Spring 2015 came around; the mare was brought back into work, now eleven years old. The world should have been on hand for her. This was the time where things should have gotten underway. But nothing got going. Bella Rose was lame.*

A long time of uncertainty followed for Bella Rose, Isabell, and her entire team. Again and again, they experienced hope that they finally had a handle on the problem. Many treatments were undertaken, without anyone getting to the root of the problem. Many examinations yielded different interpretations. Another transport to a different clinic; another anesthesia for the horse. The X-rays still did not show anything serious. But the pain undeniably always came back. Forever alternating between hope and desperation, Isabell was asked about Bella Rose time and again by fans, journalists, officials. She repeatedly expressed optimism, because she believed herself that, finally, the horse was on the way to recovery. But time kept on passing.

*By this point, I had started to scour medical literature for answers. These repeated setbacks! There were many times when I thought we had finally pulled through. But then ...*

It took a long time until it was eventually certain what was actually wrong with Bella Rose. Evidently, she had been troubled by a problem that had existed for a while, and it had only happened to come out in Normandy. More than two years after the World Equestrian Games, the truth was revealed through the comparison of three pictures taken with magnetic resonance imaging (MRI) at greater intervals. They confirmed a dramatic diagnosis.

The problem was in the bone. The mare had a bone edema, caused by a lack of nourishment. In the spring of 2016, it was clear: Bella would not be sound in time to compete in the Olympic Games in Rio. They should have been her Games. As Johnny was also injured, a new solution had to be worked out. The hour of Weihegold struck. While Isabell prepared the black mare for her fifth Games, Bella Rose's bone was elaborately stabilized. And when Isabell returned from Brazil, having attained the title of the most successful rider in history, Bella Rose stood in her stall, a convalescent. Her muscles were gone; her state of training was zero. And the following spring, while Weihegold was on point to also dominate the World Cup Finals in Omaha, Nebraska, Bella Rose stepped into a pool and began to tread water. Very slowly. The prognosis was favorable, as the newest check-ups showed that the treatment was working, and the bone in her foot was again filled. But nobody in Rheinberg dared to be joyful. Isabell announced that she expected to return Bella Rose to competition in the fall of 2017...but, then she also had to let this date go by.

At first, the mare was only allowed to walk. Meanwhile, time was racing on at a gallop. It galloped right past Bella Rose—that beauty, all that talent, the ideal dressage horse. For her, now, there was no bold forward impulse, full of relish; no playful learning progress; no magic; no moments of elevation. She was twelve years old when Rio came and went. It could have been the highlight of her career.

*Bella Rose seemed to know that she had to rest. She stopped herself, put herself into a new mode where she stoically endured anything happening around and to her. In the wild, a horse, which is born an animal of flight, would not survive a leg injury like hers for very long. As a domesticated animal, she turned into a tolerant patient. She crept around, at the walk only, for twelve months. And yet, all the while, she remained the queen.*

*She began every morning with dignity and her wonderful expression of interest. She kept her friendly nature. When I opened the stall door, Bella Rose, who had gone through so much with vets and therapists, still came cheerfully toward me. It was as if she knew that all the uncomfortable and scary procedures were needed to restore her health. She has just always hated one thing· When other horses were walked up and down in front of her stall. She used to observe this very closely, pinning her ears back, and becoming even a little mean toward the passers-by. It was as if she also knew something else: That, if there wasn't whatever this was going on here, all the attention would be on her, as it should be, and not the others.*

*Her old impatience started to pipe up again when she was back in work. It felt as if she knew she had been given the go-ahead. She wanted to get going. To move forward, to move thoroughly, to open her heart, fill her lungs, feel her body, and enjoy who she was. She wanted to jump around, buck, turn, and twist in mid-air. I have never been squeamish, but our entire team cringed when Bella Rose moved too fast. Please, please, please, not another setback! There was the fear that her eagerness to move would turn into a risk to her well-being.*

*I couldn't say, "Bella, let's just putter around a little." She was so hot that she wanted to overdo it right away. I was constantly scared that she would sustain more damage. Rehab is the same for horses as for people, but with a person, you can say, "You are only allowed to put 20 percent weight on it, and you have to build it up, step by step," and the person might listen. But try telling Bella that.*

Isabell is a dressage rider by profession. One could also say: she is a problem solver. Whatever difficulties her horses may have, she will work on them. Every minute. During the golden fall of 2017, her barn was overflowing with four-legged stars and great hopes for the future. The FEI had awarded her Rider of the Year. The number of her annual wins was close to forty, her prize-money was past half a million Euros. She led the world rankings with Weihegold and was in the top ten with Johnny and Emilio, who had matured into another leading horse. She had started to show the dressage world her young gray stallion Belantis, and the people reacted with true storms of enthusiasm. An exemplary year of success lay behind Isabell. The signs seemed to indicate that her hard work over the years were finally paying off and the time of harvest had come.

With these great gifts in her heart, Isabell has always turned back to Bella Rose, the unfinished one. She still talks fondly of the way the mare carries herself and her look and gracefulness, which the horse never lost during her long time of suffering. Everything had gone to plan for Isabell in this year that was now slowly coming to an end.

Oh, beautiful Bella Rose.

Isabell always knew this story would continue. The year 2018 came around. Bella Rose was back. And Isabell danced with her into the skies, crying with happiness.

# 9  THE PIAFFE

What exactly is a piaffe? When a layperson dares to step foot in the dressage scene and ask such a simple question, she is likely to be waved aside with a generic answer along the lines of, "It is the trot on the spot." When a person has watched a Grand Prix test or two, then she will have observed for herself that piaffe is often the movement that most horses seem to not like to perform or seem not able to perform well. Sometimes, the piaffe looks like tense fidgeting. Sometimes, it is more like an unwilling thrashing about. Sometimes, the rider appears to simultaneously step on the gas and the brake pedal, the horse tries to get away by going up, and is more or less rearing with his front legs. But when the piaffe is *successfully* performed in the dressage ring, even the amateur's expression is transfigured. This is when you see a horse dance.

This animal that was born to move forward, to transform power into ground covering strides, is able to express his noble brilliance, his personality, in the smallest of spaces without forward momentum. This movement is by no means just a "trot on the spot." It is a special, rhythmic, very powerful, elevated athletic endeavor, which expresses pride and confidence. It is magnetic; a drum roll should truly accompany it. And the rider who has the privilege to enjoy such a movement from the saddle? This rider appears sublimely happy—as if she is floating on clouds as she indulges in a particularly special swing of the horse's body, a rhythmic swaying.

In the piaffe, the rider experiences "a piece of perfection." That is what Isabell calls it. Riders like her, Anky van Grunsven, and Edward Gal could celebrate being part of an outright piaffe cult, having had the right horses. And then there is the passage, which is usually shown in connection with piaffe—the majestically slow, suspended trot with short moments where the horse gives up all contact with the ground and seems to hover in the air.

Isabell's piaffes with Bella Rose are for her, evidently, the ultimate feeling. She feels likewise with Weihegold. She performed piaffe and passage so gorgeously and seemingly effortlessly at the European Championships in Gothenburg in 2017 that the audience started to clap rhythmically along with her. Under normal circumstances, such enthusiasm from the crowd would have been considered a cardinal sin in the sport of dressage, where some horses are on the verge of jumping out of the ring at any moment, much less when faced with such disruption. But Weihegold seemed to soak up the people's excitement and transferred it into even more radiance. As her experience grows, she performs in an ever more confident and positive manner.

*I have discovered the piaffe anew with my horses, especially with my mares. It is critical to never develop the rhythm of a piaffe from tension, but always from a calm focus. Suddenly, I have experienced the movement in a way that is a very special luxury. After having worked with dressage horses for twenty-five years, a new world has suddenly opened for me.*

Isabell's most important teacher in the process of piaffe was El Santo, the somewhat bulky bay Rhinelander with lots of impulsion. He has two question marks on his face, mirroring each other for good reason (one on his forehead and one on his nose). The challenge he presented Isabell was tricky, yes, and almost unsolvable. No small number of people were surprised that she did not give up on him at some point. But Isabell remained tenacious and from her experience with El Santo grew tremendously as a rider and trainer.

As a reminder, El Santo, known as Ernie, was the horse that, in the beginning, Dieter Schulze affectionately mocked as a "riding pig" because of his round belly. In the ring, however, his persona gained from his enormous amount of expression—and his long, elegant eyelashes were legendary! His greatest physical challenge was his hind legs, which deviated considerably from the ideal. Seen from behind, they were not straight, like those of supermodel Bella Rose, but instead curved outward. They were proper bow legs. Isabell used to be very unhappy about Ernie's "soccer player legs." It is different today, however, as the bay's legs have managed to provide a kind of mental release for Isabell.

Ernie was not able to perform a piaffe in one spot with his hind legs. He had to move forward in order to withstand the strain of the movement. This was a grave flaw for a dressage horse. It was clear from the beginning that Ernie was not a super-talent for performing piaffe. His strong suit was movement with impulsion. His ground-covering canter was impressive, and his extended trot—in which the horse surges forward as if powered by a rear engine as they stretch their front legs to the max—was full of vigor.

*"The rest," I thought to myself, "he will learn." The training steps leading to the piaffe did not give him any serious trouble, but when it came time for him to have to perform the steps really on the spot, it was no longer working.*

*Asking for the movement he couldn't do squashed his courage. He simply couldn't carry himself through the piaffe. And then I never really got out of that hole. His conformation just wasn't suitable.*

In order to understand how important a role Ernie's hind legs play in this story, you have to understand how a piaffe, which was developed from the horse's natural movement, is supposed to be performed. The purpose of this exercise is apparent in the ideal silhouette of the horse in piaffe: the croup, and so the hind end, is lowered. One can see that the horse carries a lot of his own body weight and that of his rider with his hind legs. This shifting of weight is important—after all, a horse is not naturally built to carry a rider. He has to be trained to do so, in order not to suffer physical harm in the long run. A Warmblood, commonly used for dressage, weighs at least 1,300 pounds in his own right. He is certainly not small. But a rider on his back still becomes a burden over longer periods of time. Essentially, the horse is being asked to carry a living backpack: a human, who, in the best case, aligns her own motions with the horse's, but who, in the worst case, interferes so much that the horse's balance is seriously compromised.

In nature, where a horse only has to carry his own weight, more of his body weight rests on his front end than on his hind end. When a rider sits on the horse's back, this unequal ratio intensifies. The forehand then carries 60 percent and the hind-quarters 40 percent of the horse's total weight. Thus, the horse's balance has to be improved through appropriate training.

Dressage schooling progressively enables the horse to step under his body with his hind legs and take up more weight. Experts call this process *collection*. Through this shift in weight, the front legs become lighter; in a way, they gain freedom through collection. The highest degree of collection is achieved in the piaffe. As a result, the horse can lift his front leg until the upper leg is almost horizontal. The hind leg shows the so-called "flexion in the haunches," which is a lowering of the major joints—the hips, the stifles, and the hocks. This lowering action is extremely strenuous for the horse and requires a lot of muscle strength. It is most comparable to squats in human exercise, but be sure to imagine the squats performed by weightlifters, as horses are dealing with the addition of the rider's weight. The movement of the piaffe is similar to the trot, meaning the horse's front and hind feet lift off the ground in diagonal pairs. This should occur in a clear rhythm, whose quality plays a main role in judging a piaffe. Twelve to fifteen steps are required in a dressage test. And only the slightest forward movement is permitted—a maximum of one hoof's-width per step.

*And Ernie? He wanted to move forward in the piaffe as his hind legs were too weak to endure the strain of the movement. He would start to wobble slightly, even during normal training exercises. I would try to shorten him more, to detain his urge to move forward, and to teach him the art of maximum movement at maximum stasis. After all, he had answered all my questions brilliantly, so far! He had won the Nürnberger Burg-Pokal competition for young horses in Frankfurt, Germany, in 2010, shortly after Dieter's death. He had learned all the movements quickly and reliably. Most importantly, he had a fantastic character: One could hardly imagine a horse that was any less complicated or more willing to please. He was easy to handle in the barn, eager during training, determined to perform during competition. But, the question of the piaffe rapidly developed into a problem. His conformation predestined him to sit too low on his hindquarters, and that made it difficult for him to "swing" elastically through his body on the spot.*

The work of art that is the piaffe is not part of the Burg-Pokal, which is a competition series for young dressage prospects in Germany. Because of his performance there, Ernie "moved up" in the barn the following year. At only ten years old, he advanced to become "Horse Number One" for the major events. Der Stern, the potential championship horse following Satchmo, had injured himself as a young horse and he then never reached the necessary resilience for an international mount. Ernie had the chance to step up to the plate, and he was ready and willing to give it his all. But what he could not do, he could not do.

Isabell was lucky that, during the 2011 European Championships in Rotterdam, the Netherlands, all eyes were directed at Totilas, with whom Matthias Rath rode for Germany at a major championship for the first time. Thus, her problem with Ernie and his piaffe became a mere footnote in the press and with the spectators. But, in fact, a major drama was taking place between rider and horse.

*Ernie's progress with the piaffe not only came to a halt, it started to regress. He was so frustrated that he could hardly be motivated to even try to attempt a reasonable start to a*

202

*piaffe. He didn't even go into it properly. He lifted his legs very little, and the entire thing hardly displayed any dynamic action. Eventually, the movement died completely, just like a four-cylinder engine that skips and then stops. In the silence I could hear people in the audience clicking their tongues, trying to coax at least a few steps of the movement from him.*

*No other movement will reveal a horse's weakness like the piaffe does. A pirouette that is performed larger than ideal still leaves you with the feeling of a wonderful movement. A flying change that is late in the hind legs—that is just nuance, and if another change follows immediately after, someone from outside the dressage scene won't even notice. But to flat out refuse to dance? A horse that just hangs about awkwardly in the middle of the arena? That is a major disgrace.*

*I sat in the saddle, desperate, and didn't know what to do. All my expertise didn't help me. And both of us, Ernie and I, developed an outright complex about it all. Ernie's entire personality froze: He changed from being the sunshine of the entire barn to a frustrated brooder, who no longer could get out of the mental trap related to the piaffe. He suffered in light of his own shortcomings. It was as if he wanted to tell me that he was scared, so he became rigid in anticipation of what was ahead of him. He already knew he wouldn't be able to complete the movement, because he was unable to carry his own weight in the way that I demanded of him. The truth was, he simply couldn't perform a piaffe on the spot the way I wanted him to do it. But I was incapable of listening to him.*

Isabell did not recognize at first that she had disregarded one of her most important principles: namely that the art of schooling a horse consists of adapting to the horse and developing individual solutions that make the task at hand easy for the animal. And this happened to her in the piaffe, of all things—the movement that is so decisive for the modern dressage horse. Those who cannot score in the piaffe do not have a chance to win a medal at the international level. This was quite different back at the end of the twentieth century, but since then the horses, as well as the training, have improved. Piaffe, passage, an elevated trot, and the transitions from passage into piaffe and back, now make up one quarter of the total score in the Grand Prix, one of the most difficult tests in dressage competition. Piaffes, of which three are required in the test, have a coefficient of two. (Every test has an associated score sheet where the judge assigns a score along with a comment for the movement performed. There are also five marks given at the end of each test called the Collective Marks. Some of the test movements and Collective Marks have "coefficients" associated with them, which means they are worth two times the points assigned.) The end of Ernie's career as a Grand-Prix horse seemed imminent.

> *We were approaching the turn before the piaffe, and both of our hearts were quickly beating. Neither of us was breathing. When it was actually time for the piaffe, it was like we had arrived at a dead end. It felt like a balloon that had all the air drain out, and I did not have time during the test to pump it up again. Neither Ernie nor I had an idea about how to continue. Our desperation joined us together as helpless companions in fate.*

Isabell did not manage better than seventh place in Rotterdam; at least she came second in the team competition, but there was no individual medal. And it was certainly no consolation that Rath and Totilas had also come away empty-handed. Isabell knew she had reached an impasse.

*Whatever I tried to do, whether I rode with less or more pressure, it was irrelevant. I always had to encourage him to do more…and he did less and less. It was a turning point in my life. It led to me to taking a step in another direction and approaching the topic of the piaffe from a completely different angle.*

The piaffe is not a "trick" developed for the horse by humans, as are, for example, somersaults for people. Rather, it is a movement taken from nature—horses use the piaffe to express emotion. Born animals of flight, horses convert their feelings into actions. This may be one of the reasons why we perceive their body language to be so very expressive, as well as why it triggers an emotional reaction in us. Excitement can be one of the reasons why a horse starts to "prance" in one place with his feet. It is, in a way, a form of impatient stomping, and shifting weight from one leg to the other. Some horses start to show piaffe when their barnmates are led to the field and they have to stay inside. Others trot on the spot in their stalls when they hear the feed buckets being filled. A stallion displays piaffe when he is about to be led to a mare but is being held back. Horses both release and contain their urge to move in this way. One could say that, in the piaffe, they are behaving like fidgety children.

It has been said of Otto Lörke, personal guard and horse trainer for Emperor Wilhelm II and defining dressage master, that whenever he entered the barn at his facility in Berlin, his horses started to piaffe—out of sheer respect, maybe. Or because they knew: *It is time to work.* As mentioned earlier in this book, Gigolo, forever the athlete, still showed off his piaffe in the barn aisle at twenty years old, whenever the farrier came and he expected some action.

The most impressive piaffes are the ones shown by stallions when they want to appeal to a mare. It is then pure display behavior, driven by testosterone. The horse starts to almost "glow," making himself appear bigger in the front, rounding his neck, and flexing his muscles. But mares also like to show off every once in a while. Sometimes, when Isabell watches the broodmares let out into the fields, she pauses to enjoy the sight: how they play amongst themselves, parading up and down the field in a floating trot, tail raised. She then thinks: "Yes. *That* is the feeling I want to enable my horse to have when he floats across the centerline in a test." The passage should be an elevated, celebratory form of the trot, which then turns into a piaffe with the same rhythm. Both should say, "Look at me! I am a star!"

It is wonderful to witness this inherent pride, and the pristine emotional world of these elegant animals. And Isabell asked herself, "Should this be denied to Ernie?"

*I had coincidentally seen a movie about the natural movements that horses show when they are with a herd in the field: Flying changes as perfectly normal strides as a horse moves in a new direction; pirouettes, where a horse turns around an imaginary center with his hind legs when he plays with others (they gallop toward each other, and then turn on the spot at the last moment); and, of course, passage and piaffe when the horse wants to show off.*

*Only when I had completely exhausted everything I knew about dressage did it become obvious to me how much potential for the training of horses lies in their inherited, natural movement spectrum. Of course, the following applies: The better the natural disposition, the easier it is for the trainer to teach a horse those movements and to later celebrate them with the horse in the competition arena. Ernie taught me to lay the teacher's "pointer stick" aside and, instead, to observe horses more carefully. Why couldn't it be possible to give Ernie's inherent natural inclination to piaffe a voice?*

*With the help of Danish trainer Morten Thomsen, I loosened up the mentally deadlocked Ernie by teaching him fun little tricks and groundwork games. Then Morten encouraged him, from the ground, to move forward, but only two or three times, and then our session would be over and he was brought back to his stall. This mini-lesson was repeated five or six times a day, every time ending on a good note so that Ernie regained the feeling that he was able to correctly carry out what was expected of him. He would do something well, and we would put the horse away. He was sometimes even asked to perform a few elevated steps in his stall, and he tried without tension. Or we brought him into the indoor arena, I'd ride him briefly into the far corner, get off, pat him, and bring him back to his stall. This is how we slowly broke up the tension in his mind and body and how Ernie's self-esteem was rebuilt. While he was not one of those horses that overreacted to distractions in the environment, we incorporated interesting props, like banners, flags, and umbrellas—anything that would normally cause a horse to hold his breath. We took all manner of measures to overcome fear.*

*I learned from Morten that groundwork can play a large role in the training of a dressage horse. For me, it was a completely new way to spend time with my horses. I felt how much good it did with Ernie when I just sat still in the saddle, when I didn't constantly put pressure on him, when I let him "do his thing" and just tried to help him. The knot inside Ernie slowly began to loosen.*

It was a Spaniard who truly opened Isabell's eyes once and for all: José Antonio Garcia Mena, a dressage rider at the international level, with a twenty-first place at the 2014 World Equestrian Games as his best result and a popular crowd favorite. Born in Cádiz, José is from a region where a traditional riding art, controlled by the requirements of the *Rejoneo* (the education of the mounted bullfight) is maintained. The conformation of the horses used for the mounted bullfight differs significantly from that of Hanoverians bred for dressage. They are small and stocky, and neither develop the powerful gaits nor the engine-like impulsion of a European Warmblood. But they are exotically beautiful, and due to their ample muscles and compact bodies, perfectly suitable for the movements that require a high level of collection from the horse. They can shorten themselves like an accordion, they can sit down almost on their hind end, becoming light and elevated in front, as is required to the extreme in piaffe and pirouette—and especially for bullfighting, where a horse not only has to prove he has courage, but also mobility in a very tight space.

José did his apprenticeship at the stud farm Alvaro Domecq in Jerez de la Frontera, Spain, where both bulls and horses are bred. Subsequently, he started his own business with his father, concentrating on training horses for the sport of dressage.

Iberian horses have experienced bursts of popularity, over time marching across the entire European continent. They have served royalty in choreographed equine displays of splendor and prestige, and masters of the classical art of riding them are sought-after, even today. Horses of the breed Pura Raza Espanola (PRE) frequently mingle with other competitors in international dressage rings—vigorous, white beauties with storybook piaffes and fiery freestyles to the sounds of guitar and castanet, which have the audience clapping and cheering with enthusiasm. Only the judges hold back in their scores, because the movement pattern of these horses does not seem to entirely fit the ideal described by the FEI.

Isabell first met José at the World Equestrian Games in Kentucky in 2010, when he wowed spectators by not only acting out the role of "the passionate Spaniard" but also by throwing his hat into the crowd. Hannes and Isabell were starting directly after him, and Hannes was clearly agitated. Thus, Ground Jury President Linda Zang asked if Isabell wanted to contest his actions and her results, as José's "hat trick" might have potentially been the reason for her horse's lack of focus. But Isabell declined, rationalizing that she really could not use the event as an explanation for Hannes' spookiness. It was only later when Isabell realized that, on this occasion, it was not José who had thrown his hat into the crowd but actually his Spanish compatriot Juan Manuel Munoz Diaz with his magnificent stallion Fuego. Then, during the time of Ernie's piaffe problems, Isabell's employee Guillem, a friend of José's, put the two in touch.

*It was like another readjustment. A new inspiration. I recognized that my previous ways of teaching a horse the piaffe might have been only partially successful, and there were other approaches. Usually, for me, the path to the piaffe started with the creation of positive tension. From this state of positive tension, I made the horse "quicker" in the trot—not simply faster, but, in a sense, I put the horse into a "time lapse" with the aim to retain the movement, but without the forwardness. The Doctor had also always recommended to use any agitation of the horse as an opportunity to practice piaffe. If, for example, a horse became hot and excited during the bustle of a victory ceremony, I should use the situation, he said, and just let the*

209

*horse go into the piaffe for as long as he remained unsettled. This was also a way to use and civilize the natural, mood-driven movements of the horse. Of course, according to The Doctor's view, horses should still develop enjoyment in performing the movement. But tension remained its origin.*

*With José, it was the opposite. Not one step was to be performed in tension. He advised to take a walk break whenever a horse managed to completely work himself into a frenetic state of nervousness or overeagerness. I was to ride in the walk without any tension, and only then set up for the piaffe again.*

*This approach gave me completely new insight. It was absolutely crucial to my evolution as a trainer. All of my horses—even Emilio, who has extreme talent for the piaffe and whose piaffes go through his entire body—have benefited from this approach. I will never again make the mistake of developing a piaffe from tension, but always from relaxation. And that is why my horses today begin their piaffes with such naturalness. Essentially, you only have to nurture the rhythm.*

It was the decisive lesson. Now, José has been coming to Isabell's barn for years and is there for two days almost every month. How hugely important this development was to Isabell can be seen in how often she speaks about her paradigm shifts in conversation, and how José and, of course, Ernie made this shift possible for her. It was like a door that she was only able to open at age forty-two, a door that changed everything. Ten years after she ended her relationship with Dr. Schulten-Baumer, she accomplished another big step toward freedom. His principles had always been her guideline. Now, she had independently developed them further *and* in a direction of more naturalness. For her, this was like the discovery of a new continent.

*The Doctor had followed my development with pleasure, albeit from a distance, and I do think that he was proud of me.*

It must have been clear to Dr. Schulten-Baumer at that point that he had truly lost the most important inspiration, and creation, of his life. As a passionate autodidact, he undoubtedly would have liked to concur with Isabell's progress in his own right. It seems he would have loved to contemplate, together with her, how the potential in her most successful horse could have been unlocked with the knowledge of today.

*"Jeez," I tell myself sometimes, when I think about Gigolo, "If I had just known back then!" Gigolo's piaffe was already pretty good; he had the talent to let his body swing in a supple way. Later, a twitch of one foot sometimes disrupted the picture, but, back then, I was convinced we had reached the optimum. Today I think that he stayed below his best, due to my lack of knowledge. There was one more lock I could have opened. Rather than a good piaffe, he could have had a superb piaffe. Ultimately, I think he could have been competitive at today's level, even though dressage horses have continuously gotten better. But, you can't turn back time.*

The duel with the Dutch high-performance piaffe machines could have been rendered more unambiguous, given a horse like Gigolo, who would have danced through the exercise as nonchalantly as if it was a mambo. Anky van Grunsven scored with expressive piaffes and passages that were developed from tension—the extreme results of an idea that Isabell has now completely moved away from, with the help of Ernie and José.

With this in mind, the situation in the Gigolo-era presents itself a little bit differently: At the time, Bonfire and Salinero were the all-time favorites due to their enormous talent for the key movements. The judges were inclined to disregard deficits in the basic gaits in favor of better scores in the impressive piaffe and passage. Bonfire's weaknesses in the walk and Salinero's high croup in the canter, which repeatedly led to mistakes, were no longer discussed when distracted by the acrobatic highlights, which did not just have a strong effect on the judges, but also on an audience that dressage had not yet reached: the general public.

One should have argued in those days that, technically, a horse has three basic gaits. If one is not working, it cannot be compensated for with an extremely strong piaffe. Yet, Gigolo received the most criticism for his lack of beauty. He was able to do everything, but he was no beau. But with one point more for the piaffe? As living proof that perfection is possible without tension? The history of dressage would have been different. And, possibly, Dutch breeding history, too. Isabell is convinced that horse breeding in the Netherlands has moved too far away from the grass roots of the sport and horses are paying the price for the overemphasis on spectacular movement.

*Dutch breeding has produced many exalted, long-legged, spectacular-moving horses. But all this spectacle has cost substance. In some cases, the horses almost seemed overbred. But they have since recognized the problem and tried to react.*

Conversely, the emphasis on the piaffe also had an educational effect on German breeding. The goal today is to breed a horse with equally strong gaits, as well as talent for the most difficult movements. The number of international dressage horses that masterfully perform passage and piaffe has noticeably increased. This is another step in the emancipation from long outdated definitions of what a horse can be to us as we move toward acknowledging him as a modern partner with chic and class, who brings joy, inspiration, and a sense of achievement to those who work with him.

Isabell follows the different developments in horsemanship and training with great interest. She is intrigued, for example, by the liberty work of Lorenzo, a French horse "magician" from the Camargue region, who frequently performs in the supporting program at horse shows. Usually, his horses wear neither bridle nor saddle and obey his voice alone, his gestures, and an instinctively driven connection, which takes place at a level beyond any common communication. His shows enchant people, because they feel that, here, a person has developed the skill to engage himself in the natural social structures of the horse and to gain the unconditional trust of the animals. It is a fascinating method of working with horses.

*I was told that Lorenzo walks into the field, lifts his arms, and the horses come galloping to him. The horses also learn a lot by watching him. Don Johnson, for example, is a horse who would have done well with this kind of work, because he is so playful.*

*I like the thought that Lorenzo and his family apparently live with their horses. Not just next door, like what I, myself, already find to be a great privilege, but really close, like nomads in the old times, who lived in a symbiosis together with their animals and where different living beings grew closer through daily routines. I am still amazed today how much some animals like to follow humans. I call it anthropomorphization in a positive sense.*

*These thoughts are also cause for reflection for another reason. Many of the problems that a rider runs into with her horse have to do with the fact that the rider spends too little time trying to identify the causes of those problems. I have realized that the biggest mistakes that I make today are due to a lack of time.*

*I have to focus sufficiently on the animal and the cause. Through my many years of riding and all the experience I have gained, I have a pretty good grasp on everything that is happening when I am on the horse. I continue to make mistakes, but a lot fewer than I used to make. The daily routines are what eat me up. You have to serve many masters and work through your program, and some things are sacrificed in the process. But if you do it right, many horses have so much more potential.*

With his desperation, Ernie made Isabell stop and think, and she derived massive benefits from it. Isabell's staff members have adopted her new training approach with regard to the piaffe, and with an ease that leaves Isabell baffled—she wonders that they do not seem to realize that a privilege is bestowed on them, to learn such a thing so soon, and to apply it in their future life with horses. That it is a special thing to be able to add an overwhelming "dimension of Ernie" to your life.

*To stick to the truth: Ernie never became a piaffe-wonder. How could he with his unalterable conformation? It took two years before I managed to go back to zero, to win back the potential in Ernie, and to optimize his ability from a new starting point. I restarted him in the piaffe, this time with forward movement—more than is allowed in the rules; however, not so forward that it would have been seen as a complete failure.*

*The most important thing was, Ernie returned to being himself again. And I felt how he sighed with relief, from the bottom of his heart.*

*I am incredibly grateful to him. To this day, I am amazed how much patience horses muster, if you consider how strong they are. And yet, they want to submit themselves to people so much…though, to be honest, I don't really want to use this word "submit," since it sounds so humiliating. Adapt is probably the better word. Cooperate. They want to please us. And, they want to do everything right.*

With Ernie, Isabell never reached their previous level again; he just wasn't born to be a championship horse, and by that point, she had Bella Rose and Weihegold. But she treated herself to a number of special moments with Ernie. In 2016 they went on a post-Olympic vacation to Mallorca, Spain, and won the Freestyle at a show there. In September of both 2014 and 2015, Ernie and Isabell flew to New York to an invitation-only show in Central Park. There, in 2014, the well-behaved horse gave it his all, as always. Neither the high-rise buildings in the background nor the usual police sirens in the streets could keep Ernie from finishing his job with full concentration. Admittedly, he was a little too forward in the piaffe—but who cared? They won twice, back to back, amid resounding applause.

For the second show, huge crowds flocked to Central Park; however, it was not just to see the Freestyle of a horse with the name El Santo (in English, "The Holy One"). An even holier one was supposed to come by the neighborhood, namely Pope Francis. He passed by shortly after Ernie's Freestyle, heavily protected by security. Isabell and Madeleine had secured a convenient lookout on top of a stable container. (Ernie's interest in the Pope from Rome was rather nonexistent.)

The music to which Ernie performed his Freestyles was particularly groovy: a potpourri of hits from David Bowie. In general, Freestyle music is an important part of the performance, especially if it is providing the musical backdrop for dance-like piaffes. Ernie was allowed to present himself to the sound of howling guitars. And, of course, Isabell could not resist highlighting his piaffe with one of Bowie's megahits: "Let's Dance." It was a bit of a joke for insiders. When Bowie died in January 2016, the editors of an American video portal for horse enthusiasts included Ernie's performance in their mourning. They uploaded video of the Freestyle as an example of a very special interpretation of a grand work from a remarkable artist.

It was a lucky coincidence that Isabell was even allowed to use Bowie's music in her performance. Michael Erdmann, one of the very few professional producers of equestrian Freestyle music, had very good connections to one of Bowie's former record label managers, and he was acquainted with the publishers and copyright holders. They allowed Isabell to let Ernie dance to David Bowie hits, and didn't insist she pay a lot of money for it.

Copyright questions have turned into a delicate topic in dressage, ever since Freestyles have become so popular. This is one of the reasons why Isabell increasingly prefers themes from classical music—you can freely use them. But, the festive and ecstatic sounds of Beethoven's Ninth Symphony were, of course, also an expression of her overwhelming happiness to have found a horse like Bella Rose.

Antony's freestyle to the German song *"Im Wagen vor mir sitzt ein schönes Mädchen"* (in the car in front of me is a beautiful girl) was owed more to the slyness of this highly intelligent horse. And, the Freestyle that she performed with Satchmo at

Aachen in 2010 concealed a special irony: She had met singer and actor Roberto Blanco, and together with him, designed music for the horse that had sent her into the deepest valleys of her career, had brought her feelings of happiness at his rebirth at Aachen, and then who had let her down yet again later. Satchmo's new music would be based on another German song...this one about the need to have some fun: *"Ein bisschen Spaß muss sein"* (a little bit of fun is always good).

*It was a homage to Satchmo in memory of the entire situation we'd been through together. So much had been bottled up, and ultimately, this provided an outlet. This type of music is, of course, not suitable for the Olympic Games.*

One iconic Freestyle, possibly also the most impressive one that has ever been used in the sport with regard to the choice of music and corresponding choreography, is that of Anky van Grunsven and Salinero. At the Olympic Games in Athens, where Isabell did not compete due to Satchmo's resistance, Anky sparkled to the sounds of French chansons. Salinero flew down the diagonal in extended trot to the bar piano from "Milord." And the piaffe, which Salinero seemed to master effortlessly, was accompanied by *"Je ne regrette rien"* (I regret nothing), by Edith Piaf (of course, seeing as her name is very appropriate for this particular exercise).

In the moment, many get carried away by the show-biz feeling of the Freestyle and do not think about the effort involved in its development. There is no music that can simply be played straight through, matched to the horse's movements, without any modifications. In the early beginnings of inclusion of the Freestyle in competition, riders just "made it work" themselves by playing cassette tapes a little faster or a little slower, depending on the gaits and the movement mechanics of their horses. And the result, obviously, turned into a pragmatic cacophony, which brought few who were watching and listening joy.

Isabell remembers how she and Stefan Krawczyk, a dentist who designed Freestyle music on the side, sat in a music studio and collaged tape snippets by hand. Today, a freestyle music is first composed, than an exact musical score is written, and finally, the entire piece is completely re-recorded, tailor-made to the horse. This cannot be done on a computer alone. Electronically, a piece of music can only be made slower or faster, louder or quieter, but it cannot be adapted to a movement pattern.

One of Satchmo's Freestyles, for example, was first recorded by a symphony orchestra in a Berlin church. The musicians were giving a concert there anyhow, and Isabell was able to convince them to add a private performance for her...but not for free, of course. The fees that are the result of music copyrights are not even the most important item on the invoice. A dressage rider can expect to pay at least $20,000 for a presentable Freestyle. It can also come in a lot more expensive than that. A choir might sing in addition, or an aria, matching the soundtrack, is performed. Dressage riders with the means have also had their music composed specifically for them, and subsequently premiered it in competition.

These prices call for budgeting. After all, Isabell has a barn full of horses, and each will need his or her own program sooner or later. Thus, Don Johnson has inherited the Freestyle music for his performances from his older barn colleagues, just as children often have to wear their older sibling's clothes. This music had once been recorded for Amaretto, who never made it to the hoped-for championship outings due to illness. The same composition was eventually passed on to Johnny. Now he gallops to the outcry: "Mama!" from "Bohemian Rhapsody" by Queen, and he performs his piaffe to the theme from the first march in Edward Elgars' "Pomp and Circumstance"—true magnificence. The songs are simply two real "evergreens"; nobody ever grows tired of such festive music, especially in the traditionally minded dressage scene. Other types of music—those that are too theatrical, too pompous, or too populist—eventually go out of style. But "Ode to Joy"? The piece is a classic, just like noble horses are. Thus, it is no wonder that audiences sometimes stand in rows in the pouring rain, under the floodlights, and literally get high on a Freestyle, despite the adverse circumstances.

To ride a Freestyle is, after all, more than skill...it is art. And El Santo, despite his struggles, almost made it to the Olympic Games with this art.

In January 2016 José would try to qualify for the Olympic Games in Rio de Janeiro with the same horse that he had helped find mental relief. Since he had lost his two horses—one had been sold, the other one was injured—Madeleine gave him the ride on Ernie. It would have been a magical step, from a hopeless case at the European Championships in Rotterdam in 2011 to an Olympic mount five years later. But, it was not meant to be. Ernie sustained a swollen leg before the deciding qualifier and was temporarily out of commission.

And that is how Ernie's international career as a dressage horse came to its end. Cheerfully, he began a new career as a schoolmaster for a young professional rider at Isabell's barn, while his colleague Weihegold showed her prowess to the world in Rio having profited from what Isabell had learned from Ernie. She and Weihegold celebrated every piaffe and passage as if there was nothing more exciting in a horse's life.

*Weihegold is naturally blessed with strong hind legs so passage and piaffe come easily to her. She is the opposite of Ernie. Extreme collection doesn't cause her any problems. She trots effortlessly on the spot—even fifteen times, if she has to— manages the transition without interrupting her rhythm, and continues into passage as if the movement she was just performing was not a test of strength but a walk in the park. A large part of her abilities is due to her natural talent. But, the pleasure she gets out of it, and that I do, too—what everyone can feel who watches Weihegold—results from me rethinking the horses' training. Weihegold appears proud and confident in her work, as if she is fully aware of her own beauty.*

Sometimes, when Isabell does not have to fight to the finish, when no competitor forces her to frown defensively, when she has already won the hearts of the audience, she radiates the same pleasure as her horse...it is as if she felt the same freedom during the piaffe as Weihegold. Her mare and she displayed an irresistible presence in Omaha in the spring of 2017, when the Olympic year had passed and, for once, nothing had to be proven, at least for the moment. The moment came, far away from home, in an indoor arena in Nebraska, where she could celebrate the work she had perfected. In extended trot, she and Weihegold headed toward a corner of the ring, and Isabell was all smiles, even while Weihegold was still swiftly moving forward. Why? It was obvious to anyone who knew her program: She was looking forward to what was to come. Pure delight.

Turn right, and for the grand finale, let the horse carry her rider elastically and elate her rider in passage and piaffe on centerline. All 8,000 spectators in the arena could see how perfectly the horse had mastered the elegant movements and how

220

well they suited her. Weihegold seemed to bathe in the admiring gaze of the audience, and Isabell let herself be carried and moved by the rhythm of her mare's body. Everyone could see how comfortably she followed in the saddle, how she gave herself to the elasticity and swinging movements, and all this as the final note of a World Cup finale rang out, where, traditionally, riders fight for every point. Weihegold turned 360 degrees in the piaffe and there were virtually only two things missing: a bell jar and a strong lamp. It was as if a gorgeous gem was presented for all to see, a polished diamond that sparkled in every direction.

# 10  DOPING

There is never a convenient time for a doping charge. However, in Isabell's case, the following holds true: It came at the most inconvenient time one can imagine. She had competed at show grounds across the world for twenty years, without ever having a positive sample from one of her horses. But then, ironically, the storm unleashed at a time where the German Equestrian Federation was already in the midst of heavy turmoil and on the defensive.

It was 2009, and the events that had taken place at the Olympics in Hong Kong the year before had not yet been sufficiently reviewed. It soon became apparent that Satchmo's strike in the ring was only a minor disaster for the German riders during those Games. Even worse: Jumper rider Christian Ahlmann, protégé of Madeleine's sister Marion Jauß, had his horse Cöster test positively for capsaicin residue in his urine. Capsaicin is a hot substance found in chili peppers and is used as a "heating element" in liniments for humans, and horses, too. It is impossible to judge how severe this particular case really was, as the substance may have been used in two very different ways. Some riders use capsaicin to prevent tension in a horse's back, similar to people using Deep Heat®. But it is also possible that Ahlmann treated his horse's legs with the ointment, aiming to increase their sensitivity. Capsaicin causes hypersensitivity, so a horse that has it applied to his legs might avoid touching the rails even more than a good jumping horse will do anyway. The former would be considered an illegal medical treatment—not completely insignificant, but a misdemeanor. After all, a horse does not suffer from it, but is meant to experience relief. The latter is a doping case of the particularly reprehensible kind.

Ahlmann's story and its two possible interpretations enables one to demonstrate how equestrian federations differentiate between "doping" and "prohibited substances." This difference only exists in equestrian sports. Doping includes everything that serves the purpose of enhancing the performance of the four-legged athlete. The most prominent examples are anabolic steroids, which lead to muscle development in people, and sedatives, which can calm a skittish horse, enabling him to perform at a higher level. Different from human sports, horses also cannot compete if a loss of performance due to an illness is compensated for with medication. While two-legged athletes compete while using painkillers, equestrian sports follow the rule that, generally, only healthy horses are permitted to participate. This rule, also called Zero Tolerance, was subsequently amended at the international level in the fall of 2009, and since then, the administration of certain substances is permitted. Yet, at the Olympic Games in 2008, the rule was still in place.

The question in Ahlmann's case was, who believed what? Was the medical treatment version true? Or was it the more egregious scenario, where the horse's legs were intentionally made sensitive, which justified the doping label? Only the rider and his team know the truth, but the public made up its mind based on the bad reputation that generations of horse dealers had built over centuries. Numerous riders over the years had reinforced this reputation with their proclivity to gambling with the rules when trying to cover up problems. In any case, a general shit storm, damning all equestrians, exploded online.

The German Equestrian Federation dreaded possible damage to their image, and officials presented a united front, promptly distancing themselves from the case. Ahlmann had to fly home immediately, already stigmatized. Once double European Champion, he suddenly became a scapegoat for German equestrian sport. His punishment was contradictory. The FEI suspended him—as it did four other riders with positive capsaicin results—for four months on the grounds of prohibited medication. The German Equestrian Federation, however, was not satisfied. They appealed the decision, arguing that they did not believe their own rider and his explanation that he had solely treated his horse's back. For them, it was indeed a case of doping. His sentence was then doubled to eight months—a gross injustice compared to the other four riders, caught in the same place with the same substance. In addition, the FN excluded Ahlmann from the national team for two years. He felt betrayed and sold out by his Federation, which is not only responsible for protecting the horses, but also the riders.

Further details from Hong Kong shook the German equestrian scene: Another jumper was the center of attention—the impressive stallion Cornet Obolensky from Ludger Beerbaum's stables, whose rider, Marco Kutscher, had ridden him at the Games. The gray had shown an unusually poor performance in the first round of the Nations Cup competition, so he was given a "performance supplement" shot in his stall. The shot included arnica and lactanase, neither of which are severe or problematic substances. Administering such a shot could have been completely legal...*if* the German team vet Björn Nolting had put in a request to do so with the event's official veterinarian. But this had not been done. Matters were complicated further when it was found that Cornet Obolensky had suffered a short dizzy spell due to the injection, which had been given by Beerbaum's stable manager Marie; yet, he was brought out for the second round of the Nations Cup the next day.

It was another potential scandal that shook the German Federation. And despite the fact that several high-ranking officials, president Breido Earl zu Rantzau among them, were in the stable area during the proceedings, the FN remained indignant about the incident.

Ludger Beerbaum, Marco Kutscher's boss, was upset about the entire development for a different reason. He wanted to stand up in principle for the idea that horses with minor health conditions could be treated with medication before a competition. After all, he had personal experience: His barn manager, Marie, had treated a persistent skin infection on his horse Goldfever's foot with an ointment containing cortisone in Athens in 2004. At the time, the resulting positive doping test cost the entire team the Olympic gold medal.

Now that Beerbaum's rider was being publicly punished due to a comparatively minor offense, Beerbaum decided to take the bull by the horns. He made a statement on the topic of prohibited medication, albeit not without careful preliminary remarks: He claimed that by no means did professional riders think that the regulations that prohibited medical treatment for horses in international competition were simply in place for "cosmetic reasons" and did not apply to them, *but* he also explained: "Over the years, I have learned to exhaust the system as much as possible," and, "In the past, I had the attitude that *all is permitted that can't be found.*"

Beerbaum's statement was published in the *Frankfurter Allgemeinen Sonntagszeitung*, an influential German newspaper, the next day. The day after, it was everywhere. He had set off his own firestorm.

One could interpret his statements as a drastic appeal to the officials to give riders urgently needed leeway. But in Germany, this could conflict with the German Animal Welfare Act, Article 3, Section 1a, where it says in formal German legalese: "It shall be prohibited to require an animal, which has been subject to operations or treatments covering a performance-reducing physical condition, to produce performances its physical condition does not allow."

The FN, one of the most reliable medal suppliers of German sports, was in a predicament, and it was made worse, since negotiations for a new deal with two television stations were due. Both channels were already grappling with the doping scandals in cycling and boxing and could not afford to provide another target. What to do? The German Equestrian Federation decided to "clean house."

To begin, all top rankings, from which the national team was recruited, were dissolved. Every single athlete was supposed to do some soul-searching with regard to his or her own doping and medication procedures, and was then to profess to the compliance of the rules to a committee under the management of the former German Federal Constitutional Court judge Udo Steiner. Fifty-three riders from the Olympic disciplines and thirteen officials were invited to the commitment convocation. Of course, Isabell was among them...even though she had never had a positive doping result to date.

*I criticized the Federation for their approach. I said, "You can't place all of us under general suspicion and refer all riders, without exception, to the Steiner committee! Why would you do that, unless in your eyes, we are all doping our horses?" Any way you looked at it, it was a horrible time of mistrust. Hanfried Haring, the FN's former General Secretary, claimed it was a wildfire.*

*I thought it was outrageous and felt as if I was dragged into a story that wasn't mine. I have never been someone who pushed things to the extreme. I have never said, "We have to make this horse fit for a competition." Our sick horses stay home and don't go to shows. I still believe the Federation dealt with Christian Ahlmann's case in an opportunist and unfair manner. Unfortunately, we did not succeed in explaining the complex problems inherent in equestrian sports to the public. I am of the opinion that the FN didn't initiate their commission to make dealing with doping and medication fairer; no, I feel it was to demonstrate to the outside world, "We are taking action!" As a matter of fact, they did nothing...or the wrong thing.*

In this year of supposed soul-searching, Isabell did not hold back her personal feelings on the matter during interviews. She ranted during a press conference on the sidelines of the German Championships in Balve: "I am against universal allegations. The fact is that this has turned into a kind of aimless activism. What kind of legal institution is this commission? A confessional?"

This was Isabell animated, her underlying tone hinting at her well-cultivated irony. The press gleefully took notes. Isabell refused to be tainted by the crimes that others wanted to impute to her—maybe in order to distinguish themselves?

Not even two weeks later, on June 23, 2009, she discovered a message on her phone. Soenke Lauterbach, the General Secretary of the German Equestrian Federation, wanted her to call him back. When Isabell had him on the line, Lauterbach informed her that the prohibited substance fluphenazine had been found in the doping sample taken of her ten-year-old horse Whisper at the Pentecost Wiesbaden horse show the previous month. It was a devastating message. Her first positive doping test—and it had happened now, after she had dared to come out against the committee. The world around her began to falter.

Fluphenazine is not unheard of in equestrian sports; it was commonly used as a sedative for a long time. According to Wikipedia, it is sometimes given to horses "by injection as an anxiety-relieving medication." It was part of an equestrianism of the past, when serious doping tests were not yet in existence. And it had an inglorious history: It was the substance that was part of the reason why Irish rider Cian O'Connor had to give up his Olympic gold medal in Athens in 2004. His horse Waterford Crystal tested positively at those Games. Fluphenazine is a medicinal product which, officially, is only approved for humans, and is used mainly in psychiatry to treat schizophrenia.

*Overnight, I was seen completely differently by the world. It was absolutely absurd. Of course I didn't administer a prohibited substance to my horse! My horse didn't deliberately receive such medication just for a competition! I want to neither cheat nor manipulate. I love a fair fight.*

Isabell's wasn't the only world shattered by the news. So were those of her fans, the equestrian teenagers who idolized her—Isabell, the prototype of a "grown-up horse girl." And there was another complication: only a small group from her innermost circle knew, but at the time she was five months pregnant. She had not yet announced it, and now she certainly would not do so. She didn't want anyone to accuse her of playing the sympathy card.

Since the FN suspended Isabell immediately, she hardly had time to compose herself and think about her situation before the press fell on her like an avalanche. And from the Federation, she heard nothing. Nobody asked for her response to the accusations or about how she was handling the disastrous news. Isabell was convinced that she not only had to answer for the positive drug test, but that she also had to atone for her critical comments regarding FN politics and the Steiner commission.

*The knife's blade was face up and I ran right into it. I offered them a welcome opportunity to silence me.*

Madeleine Winter-Schulze, who, even then, was literally the reason for the continued success of German equestrianism, suddenly saw her two "jockeys," Ludger Beerbaum and Isabell Werth, caught in the crossfire of the FN's criticism. With the words, "I stand by my riders," she withdrew from the various boards on which she served for the German Equestrian Federation and its performance-focused arm, the German Olympic Committee for Equestrian Sports.

Shortly after news of her positive test became public, Isabell released a statement to the press: Her horse Whisper suffered from shivers, a neuromuscular disorder. Veterinarian Hans Stihl had treated Whisper with the pharmaceutical Modecate, which contains fluphenazine. Stihl had assumed that the product's traces would have left the horse's body after six days, and Isabell had believed him. However, this did not seem to have been the case: The medication was administered on May 16; the doping sample was taken on May 30.

"I am aware," read her statement, "that I have given some reason to doubt my integrity and my ethics and that of our sport. I apologize to all those who are associated with me and equestrian sport."

This is how a new story started, one that brought Isabell to the verge of hopelessness and that still has an effect, even today. She has preserved her rage, which found root in her then, after the first phases of despair passed. A positive doping sample from one of her horses could not be argued away. She had to accept the allegation that she had broken the rules, simply because she had trusted her vet's recommendation, as she had always done, without questioning it, and she had believed his prognosis. However, it was not the first time Hans Stihl had been implicated in a doping case, and her explanation appeared, at the very least, imprudent to the equestrian world's inner circle. Nobody doubted that some kind of punishment was justified, not even herself. But the radical verdict that the public, and worse, the German Equestrian Federation passed on her, along with the general mistrust that followed the doping accusation (magnified due to the experiences with Ahlmann and Kutscher), exaggerated her misconduct, transforming it into a monster that threatened her very existence.

*I had the feeling that everything that had happened before the drug test no longer counted, and I was deemed the worst person in the world. I stood there in shock and didn't know what was happening to me. The last thing I had ever wanted was to ride a horse that had prohibited substances in his body. I now had this feeling that there was a person hiding behind every tree, waiting to come out toward me, pointing a finger, and* saying, "Look, everyone! This is one of those bad people who dope their horses."

I was so disheartened that I thought about ending my career. For the first time, I questioned the purpose of what I was doing. But, the same moment I thought: "No, you can't stop this way. Not as a result of 'name and shame.'" My family and Madeleine, who stood steadfastly by my side, gave me the support that I needed to fight. I had the will to prove to the world that I was good enough to come back.

The FN's conduct was a complete disappointment. The greatest irony is that I had access to documents showing that a number of high-ranking officials had used the substance I was accused of abusing during their competition years. People who, today, feigned complete innocence, as if you had to spell the name on the medication for them. The case has forever marred my relationship with these officials. Never again will my relationship with the Federation be one of mutual trust. At the same time, the whole story is more complicated than it looked to many on the surface.

The circumstances under which Whisper ended up in Isabell's barn are part of the explanation for the doping case. She came by Whisper the same way that she obtained Bella Rose, through her former employee Matthias Bouten.

Matthias showed Whisper to me on video and said that he was fascinated by the gelding. The horse's movements were extraordinary, but he was extremely difficult and quite dangerous at times. I tried him, and, indeed, I was also impressed by his potential. His challenging behavior didn't put me off. His owner, Hans Elmerhaus, warned me, though. He literally said, "Mrs. Werth, you know what you are doing. But, if you *ask me, the horse has a screw loose." I replied that I was aware the horse was difficult and that the task to turn him into a dressage horse would be a difficult test...and with Satchmo and Hannes, I had a strong, successful string of horses already at the time. "But," I said, "I enjoy a good challenge, and if we succeed, we will end up with an exceptional talent." For me, the challenge, combined with his remarkable potential, that was what was most fascinating about Whisper.*

*When he came to us as a six-year-old, everyone was stunned by his movement. We did know at the time that he showed symptoms of "shivers," a disorder that is hard to explain and has not been fully researched until today. It affects the horse's central nervous system. It is mandated, and rightly so, that a sick horse may not be used in competition; I fully support animal protection laws. But shivers is not an "illness" as such—symptoms only emerge, at least at first, in certain situations. For example, one common sign is when a horse lifts a hind leg for the farrier or to have his feet cleaned, he keeps his leg up a little longer before he puts it down. The limb trembles as it is held suspended.*

*In the beginning, the disorder seemed insignificant to us. It was eclipsed by his oversized movement and his feisty attitude. Over time, however, as shivers is progressive, an irregularity in the shape of a delay of the hind leg in trot extensions became visible. Signs of shivers can sometimes occur in one, sometimes in two, or even in all four legs. With more training, the delay became stronger, and it was prominent as soon as we moved toward more difficult exercises.*

*It was my dream to bring Whisper to the international dressage arena, and Dr. Stihl successfully treated the gelding's extended trot with the relevant drug, after other treatments had failed.*

*I tried everything in my power to optimally support and care for this horse. I considered my actions to be absolutely justified. At the same time, I was facing a public that believed me guilty. I was forced to confess over and over: "Mea culpa. Mea culpa." Inside, I actually felt completely differently about it. I didn't know what I had done wrong. I would do it again just the same to help Whisper, if the vet advised me to do so. But, because of the general mood back then, the public didn't believe that I had only wanted to help my horse.*

*Knowing what I know today, I would never again take on a horse with shivers, even though it runs counter to my belief that there is always a way forward with a talented horse. At the time, I thought I would manage.*

*It was basically a series of unfortunate circumstances. Whisper wasn't even supposed to compete at Wiesbaden. My goals for him were long-term, and a class like the one there was not really important with regard to his competition plan— quite the contrary. The horse I had originally planned to ride, Der Stern, had fractured his splint bone and was on stall rest, and when I called the show organizer to cancel my entry in the Prix St. Georges, she asked if I could ride another horse as they had only very few pairs entered for the class. And so I thought I could take Whisper to let him gain some experience.*

*Dr. Stihl also took a hit during this case, but he only acted according to the best of his ability. He accompanied me to the hearing in front of the FEI tribunal in Lausanne and made no secret of his error in judgment. He had trusted his long-term experience at the time. We have never denied that Whisper was treated with the medication, and we made the reason public. I was open about it—we never tried to cover anything up or whitewash anything. We didn't even request the analysis of the B Sample to prove the accuracy of the result.*

Support for Isabell finally came from the highest level, in the person of Haya bint al-Hussein, Princess of Jordan, the then-president of the FEI and a former competitive rider herself. She told journalists, "I don't believe for a second that Isabell would risk a great career for something like this. She is innocent and not a cheater; I believe this from the bottom of my heart. She was very ill-advised."

However, the royal vote did not prevent the FEI tribunal from suspending Isabell from competition for six months at the beginning of September 2009, and to further take her to task after their ruling. The tribunal, made up of three people and chaired by Norwegian FEI judge Erik Elstad, accused her of negligence in the maintenance of her horses. The tribunal chose not to accept Isabell's argument that she, an experienced professional rider, had trusted Stihl blindly, stating that the substance fluphenazine should have been widely known as problematic since the Cian O'Connor case.

> I was not aware of the link between the two. On the packaging, it didn't say fluphenazine, it said Modecate. I did not research the individual substances. This whole situation taught me to question treatments a lot more often and more thoroughly, although that still can't save me from making mistakes. I am not a pharmacologist. As a rider, I am generally responsible for what happens to and with the horse. Regulations call this the "Person Responsible." Yet, in fact, this responsibility can't be met, because I can't oversee and evaluate all processes.

The sentence was lenient, despite the tribunal's stern reprimand. The six-month ban from competition had already started with Isabell's suspension in June and ended on December 22. The European Championships in Windsor took place during this time, and the German team, without Isabell, came third after the Netherlands and Great Britain. Isabell's son Frederik was born in October, so she would not have been able to compete for several months anyhow. In addition, the tribunal evidently demonstrated foresight: Had the suspension run one day longer, Isabell would have not been allowed to qualify for the next Olympic Games, to be held three years later in London. National rules stated that a doping suspension of more than six months precluded a nomination for the next Games.

National coach Holger Schmezer heaved a sigh of relief at the thought of London. But the officials at the FN were not satisfied with the decision of the FEI tribunal. Admittedly, the Federation did not file an appeal as they did in Ahlmann's case, with the rationale that Isabell had not committed her misconduct at a championship, and thus, not while "riding for the team." But, on recommendation of the Steiner commission, they excluded Isabell from the national team until the following June—when qualifications for the World Equestrian Games in Kentucky the following year were on the horizon. At that time, it did not look good for the German team. She was needed again.

Whisper's competitive career in international dressage was over before it even really began. Matthias Bouten rode him in some lower-level competitions, and after that, the gelding became a schoolmaster for Isabell's apprentices. Then, he was retired. His twitching foot became worse with time, but he has not lost his home in Rheinberg and will stay here until the end.

*The only thing I can accuse myself of is that I took on the challenge. It appealed to me that this horse was so difficult. I am always intrigued by the possibility of overcoming problems that seem unmanageable for others. It matches my personality, and it is how I started my career with The Doctor, and it is how*

*I have often found success. I could have said to myself, "Why are you making your life difficult?" Then this horse would have never ended up with me. But with that attitude, I would not have had the chance to ride many other horses, horses with which I was and still am very successful. If I question my choice in taking on Whisper, I would be questioning my secret to success. And calling it a mistake that I am what I am.*

The World Equestrian Games in Kentucky in 2010 came around, with Isabell on Hannes, and the German team came third once more. It was followed by the European Championships in Rotterdam in 2011, where El Santo came into play: Those were the Championships where Ernie had basically ceased to perform his piaffe. Placed seventh, Isabell experienced a new low. The question arose, if, in the midst of all these crises, she should even be considered for the Olympic Games in London in 2012. Isabell fought, but Ernie's blatant weakness could not be fixed quickly. She decided to give up on London. Johnny was taken into consideration as a reserve mount, but he was rather inexperienced, and Isabell did not want to ask him to try and fill such a demanding role. Instead, she threw herself into solving Ernie's problems with all her might and impulsively decided to compete him in the championships in Langenfeld, Germany, as a schooling round for the insecure gelding.

*I said, "Come on! Let's use this to get some practice." And, at that show, out of all competitions, I end up chosen for a bizarre, in-competition, drug test that, very probably, could not be used before a court of law. I was informed before my start time that I would be checked, but nobody came. After my test, I dismounted and asked where I should go for my doping test. After tediously asking my way through a number of*

*people, a steward finally took me to the vet. I could have sim-*
*ply put my horse back on the trailer and gone home. But I had*
*no reason not to subject to the testing.*

And again, Isabell was confronted with a positive result. This time, it was not labeled "doping," but its softer relative, "prohibited medication." Traces of the substance cimetidin had been found in Ernie, a substance that is used to treat the overproduction of gastric acid. However, what was contradictory was that cimetidin is allowed at international competitions that are held under the regulations of the FEI, but is prohibited at national competitions under the control of the FN. But Isabell was not just irritated because of this jumble. To her knowledge, Ernie had never been treated with the medication. She had no clue how it had gotten into his system and how its byproducts had made it into his urine.

Now, not only was she facing another exhausting process under Federation rules, she also had to consider the possibility that a contamination, which she could not explain, had occurred in her barn. This occurrence had to be sorted out urgently if she did not want get into trouble with any of her other horses. The pressure was extreme.

*I told them the only thing I was asking for was time. I had*
*to find out why this horse had provided a positive sample.*
*We turned everything upside down, starting with the path*
*the test sample took, and working back toward the routines*
*at my barn. We didn't find anything for a long time, and we*
*considered all possibilities—from contamination to manipula-*
*tion. As a human, I can completely trace my food chain, but*
*it is almost impossible with an animal. There is a good reason*
*that top athletes only drink from unopened bottles and cover*

*up their glasses with coasters at the bar at night—they fear their drinks may be contaminated with a substance. It may sound a little paranoid, but, in truth, in a situation like this, you do consider that other people may want to do you harm. You think about who could potentially be an enemy and who could be capable of doing something so perfidious. After all, here it was, the second time that everything was on the line.*

*We discovered that the handling of the doping samples in Langenfeld had been full of mistakes. Allegedly, it had been stored anonymously in a computer room, but we found out that this could not be one hundred percent true. They had locked another doping sample in a different refrigerator, because one jumper rider had asked so conspicuously about the storage situation that the organizer worried he might steal it. I don't think this qualified as particularly anonymous. We discovered that the samples had then been taken, packed in a garbage bag, in a Porsche, to an anti-doping lab in Cologne. They had not been officially mailed, as they should have been. I found the carelessness in handling the drug samples frightening and outrageous, considering the very serious consequences that a positive test could have on a rider, but I discovered that nobody but me was interested in this topic. Normally, riders don't try to defend themselves in these situations. They accept a lenient punishment, maybe a few weeks' suspension in the winter, and they don't think about it anymore. But for me, it was about my career, my sport, and, above all, my reputation.*

*I found that the medical product cimetidin did indeed exist in my barn. Ernie's stall neighbor Warum Nicht (Hannes) was treated with it. He had fractured his hip and was given the pain-reliever and anti-inflammatory aid phenylbutazon daily over a long period of time. To protect him from suffering side effects, he was also on a stomachic. The vet could just as well have given him a substance that was permitted at the national level; GastroGard® is one alternative, but it is a lot more expensive, and with his serious injury, there was no risk that Hannes would compete in a show in the near future.*

*The question remained: How did the cimetidin make it from one stall over into Ernie's body? A mix-up in which horse was medicated was impossible, and besides, the lab had only found cimetidin and not phenylbutazon. We racked our brains. It was enough to drive you crazy.*

Different from other areas of the law, in sports, the principle applies that the court of a federation does not have to prove the culpable offense of an athlete or rider in the case of a positive doping sample to assess a penalty. The positive doping sample is sufficient. Those who claim not to know how the substance made its way into their own body or the body of their horse do not benefit from the principle of the presumption of innocence. This principle is overridden, as, otherwise, the opportunity to punish someone using illegal substances would only arise in very rare cases. If one had to prove that a person took medication deliberately and fraudulently or, in equestrian sports, administered it in the same manner, then the anti-doping fight in sports, already quite ineffective, would be fully brought to a halt.

To enforce this procedure, which largely denies athletes the right to call on an official court of law, German sport federations demand that the athlete sign a written agreement. Without a signature, the athlete cannot participate on a German national team. Some athletes regard this as extortion; they do not want to waive their rights. Behind this is the fear of doping tests that could be wrongly classified as positive and, thus, could destroy a career.

The athlete, or the rider as the Person Responsible in equestrian sports, would have to prove his or her innocence in a court of law ordered by the federation to be exonerated. Even if the positive drug test was potentially the result of a mistake, the accusation remains. In public law, the procedure resembles that of dealing with those said to have been driving under the influence. A positive test is enough to lead to a fine.

Isabell had to absolutely offer a logical explanation that would be accepted by the court. This explanation had to have a probability of at least 50 percent and she had to prove due diligence in the care of her horses—this is what is written in the rules and regulations of the German Equestrian Federation. She discovered that there had been a case of cimetidin medication in the German state of Hessia several weeks before, and the proceedings in that case had been immediately stopped after a veterinarian had admitted to the treatment. But Ernie had *not* been treated. There simply was no explanation.

*I even had water samples from our well tested to see whether they contained any substances. Coincidentally, we also had our water system checked during that time. We had problems with the power supply, and on occasion our circuit breakers tripped and the entire water system failed. This meant that, during that time, the automatic waterers in the horses' stalls no longer functioned. After we got them up and running again, of course, all the horses drank at the same time, and a vacuum formed through which some of the water could have flown back into the pipes. We asked ourselves if it was possible that water from Hannes' water bowl had ended up in Ernie's stall and that this water had contained remnants of Hannes' medication.*

*We suspected it was a possibility. Because Hannes did not like his cimetidin, his groom always put it in a big syringe and injected it into his mouth, but a lot stuck to the end of the syringe. So the groom cleaned the syringe in the automatic water bowl so that Hannes would get the rest with the water.*

*We tested the theory with colored water in the Viebrock Model-Home Park—the company that had built my barn—and it showed that the contamination could have happened this way. We sighed with relief. The medication could have indeed found its way into Ernie like this. After all, the tests had only found very minimal traces. Finally, we had an explanation.*

To see the explanation in action for themselves, the FN disciplinary committee came to Isabell's farm in late June 2013 and were given a demonstration of the water system. The gentlemen nodded and Isabell was hopeful.

Her father Heinrich accompanied her to the hearing in November of that year. The committee, chaired by Jörg Offeney, a lawyer from Hanover, suspended Isabell for six months. The committee described the explanation that the substance had entered Ernie's stall through the water system as "highly unlikely" and stated the probability of 50 percent was "far from being sufficiently met." Instead, the committee felt it likely that Hannes had licked the bars of his stall and that Ernie had adopted the substance into his system in this way. In this case, a violation of due diligence was present, and a suspension of six months, as well as a 2,000 Euro fine, was deemed appropriate. This was a drastic punishment for the inadvertent administration of a stomachic, which was not even prohibited at international level.

Isabell could have appealed the decision and was fiercely determined to do exactly that. Previously, her lawyers from the firm Kleefisch and Baumeister had tried in vain to have all three members of the disciplinary board removed on the grounds of partiality. Due to the press statement of the German Equestrian Federation on the decision of the disciplinary board, she even obtained an interim injunction against Soenke Lauterbach, since, in her opinion, he had not reported the significance of the water situation assessment accurately. But, the injunction was lifted shortly after. Isabell was ready to fight; this much was obvious.

*The entire disciplinary proceedings were completely unacceptable. It was claimed that the water theory had a probability of 49 percent at the most, and that, on the other hand, the theory that the horse had licked the substance off the metal bars had a likelihood of 51 percent, and so, I was suspended for six months. It was purely arbitrary. I knew that I would fight this case through, all the way to a regular court of law. In this case, I could not accept a conviction and, least of all, a suspension. It was contrary to my sense of justice. I didn't just need my lawyers to find out what happened. I also needed them to defend me when I went toe-to-toe with the Federation. I would resist by all means available.*

The FN's court of arbitration decided in March 2014 that Isabell had broken the rules in the case of the prohibited medication of her horse El Santo. However, it was considered a "minor violation." Professor Manfred Kietzmann, pharmacologist at the Veterinary School of Hanover, had drawn up a report stating that the traces of cimetidin in Ernie's body were so minimal that the substance had not developed any effect at the show where he was tested. It was additionally taken into account that the substance was only prohibited under national, but not under international regulations. Isabell was still to accept the fine and bear the considerable costs of the proceedings.

She still did not want to let the matter rest.

*I said I would fight to the last breath. Until the last authority. But then, when the news came that the legal action had been abated, Madeleine said, "Please, stop." After all, she was a member of the Board, and everyone was harassing her. And so, I accepted the abatement, even though I still felt I was innocent of any wrongdoing.*

*It was difficult for me, but it went without saying that I put Madeleine's feelings first. As she said, at least it would be over. When Madeleine was awarded the German Riders Cross in Gold with Rhinestones, the highest accolade awarded by the German Equestrian Federation to distinguished equestrian figures, I was certainly very happy for her. But I also reflected on the entire experience one more time. The Federation had invited me and Ludger as surprise guests to the ceremony in Stuttgart. Suddenly, we were the "golden riders" again.*

Isabell learned a lesson from Ernie's case and has taken appropriate steps to counter a repeat incident—which shows the degree of absurdity riders are forced to undergo due to the doping problem. Nowadays her barn is equipped with surveillance cameras to keep track of all that happens there. At least she can do that at home. She has to rely on the diligence of show organizers with regard to stabling at competitions, an area that is not always as well monitored as it is at the Olympic Games. And even there, an over-ambitious participant could want to somehow harm their fellow competitor. The fear of sabotage is great; the feeling of powerlessness, worrying.

*I used to laugh when it was said that runner Dieter Baumann tested positive for a drug because he had ingested a substance with his toothpaste. But now, I believe almost anything—that is how much I have researched the subject. I start to sweat when I imagine all that can happen, which I cannot then influence. I am at somebody's mercy at all times. Not long ago, Madeleine and I were driving home from a show in Isernhagen and spoke about it. Somebody had pried open our tack boxes one night, and some riders were without saddles and bridles the next morning. Obviously, it was a free-for-all and anyone could have done whatever he or she pleased...even given prohibited substances to a horse. Or hurt a horse. Or a self-appointed animal-rights activist could have shown up, one who disapproves of horses living in stalls, and could have opened their doors. All of this puts me in a state of helpless fear.*

*Or let's take capsaicin, traces of which were found in Christian's horse. It is, for example, frequently found in anti-chew products. Some people put anti-chew spray on the polo wraps used to protect the horse's legs so that the horse doesn't rip them off. Just imagine: the horse nevertheless pulls them off with his mouth, and two hours later, a vet comes by with the test kit. I would have a two-year suspension just like that, and I would be unable to defend myself. And this has about as much to do with doping as a cow has in common with Sundays.*

*You can never feel completely safe. This powerlessness is the only thing that could ever spoil my job for me.*

The fight against doping has been and still remains a contradictory topic—the measures are continuously tightened, since those resorting to doping become more and more devious. Simultaneously, those trying to control the problem repeatedly overstep the limit of what is acceptable. Riders are part of the testing pool for sport federations, just like sprinters and weightlifters. And many admit: If there was a pill, which, by taking it, would make them able to ride better, they would surely be tempted to take it. However, those substances that are commonly abused in sports—the muscle-booster steroids, for example, or the blood-thickener erythropoietin—would be of little use to a rider. Nonetheless, there was one positive test in 2016, involving jumper rider Thomas Frühmann, who came in second at the Olympic Games in Barcelona, fifty-five years old at the time, and not necessarily known for his austere lifestyle. The substance, which a cyclist might have tried to use and conceal, was an integral component of a high-blood-pressure medication that was essential for Frühmann. He had forgotten to apply for a special approval from the World Anti-Doping Agency. He received a reprimand.

This is not the only case of rider doping, but it is by far the most prominent case. It is, therefore, difficult for Isabell and her fellow riders to accept that they are monitored by the National Anti-Doping Agency with the same intensity as other "normal" athletes. A top athlete has to accept that somebody could ring his or her door at the crack of dawn and request a urine sample…even when the horse is the true athlete in one's discipline. If not prepared for this, riders jeopardize their reputation, and, potentially, their career.

*I have to indicate three months in advance where I will be, at what time. For every day, I have to indicate one hour when I am absolutely available for a drug test. Only once, during my career, they didn't find me at home because I had left early for a show in Mannheim. I wasn't on vacation somewhere. I hadn't "disappeared." I was at work. They accused me of a missed testing, which entails a reprimand at the first violation, but if you should receive a third violation within eighteen months, you would already have a three-month suspension.*

*The entire system contradicts my understanding of my basic rights, my rights of freedom, and my personal rights. We put up with these restrictions on behalf of the fight against doping, but I think the politics of sports are nowhere near justifing this.*

*I also find the testing derogatory. When, at a show, I am asked into a mini-restroom that is hardly big enough for two people, together with a female anti-doping agent, I am allowed to only wash my hands with water, because they are afraid I might have a doping substance under my fingernails, with which I will later contaminate the sample. We have to use the restroom in front of them and pull up all our clothing so that they can see that there is nothing underneath. In addition, the distance from the toilet to the door is less than two feet, and the proximity to a stranger during the process is hardly bearable. While you are taking a pee, she almost sits on your lap. It is humiliating.*

Those who want to have a relaxed conversation about doping should probably not choose to bring up the subject with Isabell! She flies into a rage when faced with the topic. She has gotten through her two cases and is at peace with herself and the public. However, her relationship with the German Equestrian Federation has been of a sober nature ever since.

*I no longer feel like I was ruined. Instead, I have the impression that most people understand that what happened to me was something like strokes of fate. I think the equestrian public knows I am not one of those who cheat or manipulate. I believe that I have convinced people that I am good at what I do and that my success doesn't come from a tube or a bottle.*

*You can't cheat your way through such a long career with so many horses.*

# 11  WEIHEGOLD

With Weihegold, everything was different. The beautiful black mare was not an enigmatic discovery as a young horse. She did not demand others adjust to her whims. She did not enact dramatic tantrums. From the beginning, she was gentle, quick to learn, and cooperative. But, despite her extreme potential for piaffe and passage, hardly anybody would have initially foreseen the kind of grand performances she would eventually be capable of.

Weihegold was not a pain in the neck, she did not look rebelliously for opportunities to spook, she did not put up any resistance—but she also did not test her limits. She was no volcano; she was still waters. Weihegold as a potential championship horse? At first, nobody really believed in her—nobody but Isabell. Though she was lacking certain airs and graces, Weihegold would become a star. Her talent, her beauty, and her absolute willingness to perform made up for any lack of genius.

Weihegold is not an Isabell-type horse. She is not a sparring partner on a playground of temperaments. And yet, it was Weihegold who carried her forty-seven-year-old rider into a new phase of athletic maturity in 2016. With the team gold medal at the 2016 Olympic Games in Rio de Janeiro, she crossed an impressive boundary: Isabell has been the most successful Olympic rider in history ever since. With her six gold medals, she surpassed the previous record-holder, the legendary German dressage rider Reiner Klimke. She also added a fourth silver medal in the individual competition—altogether her tenth Olympic medal. Mind you, this was accomplished with horse number three, after Gigolo and Satchmo.

And that was not all. The greatest compliment she received in Rio came from the individual Olympic Champion, whom she could not keep at bay for a second time during the final Freestyle, but on whom she put quite a bit of pressure in the end. British rider Charlotte Dujardin declared in front of the gathered press that it was Isabell who taught her to fight. "She is everyone's role model," she said. Isabell, who sat next to her, had a lump in her throat when she heard this. And she felt a sadness when her young rival from Great Britain stated that the career of her phenomenal gelding Valegro was over, despite the fact that he was only fourteen—quite early for a healthy horse. But Charlotte said her impressive dark bay had won enough...she had already become a double Olympic Champion with him at the Games on home soil in London four years previous, and then also World and European Champion.

"What a shame," Isabell said in Rio. "It's fun to compete against the best. He probably would have had a few more good years."

*Valegro has shaped an era. It goes without saying that he would have remained number one if he had not been retired from competition. But the day where he would have been beaten at a championship would have come for him, too. What I found most impressive about him was his presence. He came in and everyone was looking. He filled a room with this presence. He was so confident, did everything with great naturalness, paired with dynamics and power, and always with a good contact—you never saw a rein bounce. I will never forget one particular Grand Prix Special from Charlotte and Valegro. That was in Hagen, Germany. It was a world-record ride. It was electrifying. A wonderful performance: seamless, natural, pretty, effortless, but with lots of power. For me, the memory of this ride is one of a few very special highlights.*

Ever since those golden and silver days of Brazil, twenty years after her tearful double victory in Atlanta with Gigolo, the picture of Isabell Werth those in the dressage world had in their minds has changed quietly. In Rio, only a few tears were gleaming in her eyes when the national anthem was played for the German team. When the flags were raised, there was no nearly superhuman tension inside Isabell that had to be released. She had not fought tooth and nail like she usually did; all she did this time was let her ability and her horse's talent shine. Now she radiated the joy of a winner—one who was, in fact, ready for an encore. Her colleagues' envy and ill will, usually ubiquitous in her small, often hermetic world, seemed to finally be exhausted after all the years. The entire industry unanimously admired her accomplishment.

"It just was not meant to be." Isabell often had to console herself with this sentence, when, once again, luck seemed to turn against her—when she had missed the Olympic Games because of difficulties, when she lost a horse or simply had things go wrong. Now she stood there, gifted and honored, without the usual traces of a fight on her face, without the usual adrenaline rush in her veins, maybe even a little astonished that such gentle victories were possible. "Today," she happily stated, "it was meant to be."

With Weihegold, Isabell had achieved the best result in the Grand Prix Special, the test that decided the team competition in Rio. She had even beaten Charlotte and Valegro, the two stars everyone expected to appear at the top of the list. They had allowed themselves a few uncharacteristic slips. That is how it is in sports: It is not the form on paper that counts, but what happens in the here and now. And Weihegold had given everything she had on that day.

Isabell needed all her experience and ability to present the black mare in such top shape on the right day, at the right time. She and Weihegold had to get to know each other in a very short time, because originally Isabell had planned everything very differently. She had wanted to shine in Rio with Bella Rose—her classy, highly talented, but continuously injured Bella Rose. And when she realized that Bella would not be sound in time, Isabell still believed she could fall back on Don Johnson. But then Johnny also injured himself while playing in his stall and was out of commission for months. And so Isabell decided to dare to ride Weihegold.

She had not done something like this for decades: bring a horse to a championship competition that she had not trained herself from the beginning. But the feat was accomplished. In April, she had to give up hope of riding either Bella Rose or Don Johnson in Rio. In August, she stood at the top of the Olympic podium, together with Kristina Bröring-Sprehe, who had ridden the noble stallion Desperados, Dorothee Schneider, rider of the powerful Showtime, and Sönke Rothenberger, a young, promising parvenu, just like his gelding Cosmo.

*For me, Rio was a kind of resurrection. Four years before, I had not competed at the Olympic Games in London due to the difficulties I was having with Ernie and because Johnny was not yet mature enough. It was a very difficult time, in which I had to build things from the ground up. And then…I had to face the injuries of Bella Rose and Johnny. Despite my bad luck, I got to ride Weihegold in Rio de Janeiro, and there I felt others recognized that I had pulled myself "out of the hole" once again. This might have been the reason why, for many, I was more of a focus than was the performance of my horse. This was a new experience for me. I was surprised by the huge response that I received.*

*The Rio Games were completely different than Olympics I had experienced before. During my ride in the Grand Prix Special, where I got the best score of the entire class, I was far from being as agitated as I had been with some of my other crucial performances. I went in and pretty much just wanted to ride a good test. After all, I knew I couldn't expect an experience to rival those I had with Gigolo and Satchmo. And yet, I still worked myself into an emotional high. Weihegold was on the ball, and this time, I was not the one being chased. On the contrary: This time, I had nothing to lose. I was under no pressure from people's expectations. Privately, I knew that something great was possible, and of course that gave me a thrill. After all, my first class during the major test in Aachen, just before the Olympic Games, had gone well. I had that performance in the back of my mind.*

*The Grand Prix Special in Rio was close to the optimum of what was possible at that stage. Effortless, elegant, and still, not without taking risks.*

*The Freestyle also went well—there was one mistake in the rhythm that was not crucial. Valegro was out of reach with his more than 93 percent. But I had a blast and the silver medal was the cherry on top. I had told myself before the competition, "Don't get carried away—you can't hope that Valegro will again make the kind of mistakes he did in the Special." And he didn't make another mistake.*

No, he did not. The time for slip-ups was over. As soon as Charlotte entered the arena, the muscular neck of her powerful horse rounded before her, and the two of them casting an impressive shadow on the sand, everyone knew that they would not allow themselves a second day of weakness. Her Freestyle to Brazilian music was not only flawless, it was confident. In the piaffe, the bay horse moved his feet to the rhythm of samba music, and when the two of them halted in front of the judge at C for their final salute, it was certain: Nobody could contest the Olympic Champion of London 2012 for the gold medal, not even a reborn Isabell with her black mare. As always, Isabell remained realistic and did her job—and got to add another silver medal to her collection.

*I never really thought about the fact that it was possible that I could become the most successful Olympic rider ever during the Rio Olympics. I told myself that nothing is as old as the success of yesterday. But the realization of such an accomplishment is lovely. It gives me a nice, satisfied feeling. And it confirms my philosophy: that training young horses myself and bringing them up through the levels is the right way. It is also evidence that sometimes it is right to calmly say, "No, I don't always have to be a part of everything to be successful." I have already achieved a lot of things that many people just dream of, so it is a lot easier for me to say no to certain things. Totilas, for example. I had to work hard to have the composure in such a situation to make the right decision.*

This newfound composure gave Isabell a completely new aura. Still, preparing Weihegold for the Olympics had brought with it its own risks. A ride "on the edge" might not be what was ever expected of the mare, but a completely different balancing act had been necessary. Initially ridden by her employee Beatrice Buchwald, Isabell had, of course, helped shape Weihegold's development, but she had only taken on the ride at the beginning of the year. The question at that time was: How would Isabell manage to turn the talented young horse into an Olympic mount in such a short time, while keeping Weihegold motivated, and without asking too much and still demanding the mare's best performance at the right moment? Precise work in horse management was needed.

*The mare is an honest, uncomplicated horse and makes it easy for her rider. She is always willing to work, and she is focused on what is asked of her. She always makes a gigantic effort, and I have to take that into consideration. Because she is always ready to go to her limits, it risks her falling into a kind of "red zone," and I can't continuously challenge her to do that.*

*We have walked an exciting path together; I knew from the beginning that there was considerable potential. After all, I did not pull the ride out of a surprise bag… I had worked with the horse, together with Beatrice. I knew how the mare ticked and when to pay attention. She knew all the movements, but there were some things lacking when it came to fine-tuning and her physical presence. I had to learn, show by show, how to structure her preparation. Dressage horses make their final progress with regard to strength and stamina through competition experiences, because those are exactly the situations where you approach performance levels differently and exploit all possibilities in a way you wouldn't normally do when training at home.*

In July, at the CHIO in Aachen—which is very similar to a championship because it demands a high workload of the horses over three days—she had not optimally managed Weihegold's strength and stamina. It was no wonder, really, as it was the first time that the mare had to complete three competition days of this caliber. They completed the first class, the Grand Prix, in excellent form, but then Weihegold's performance level decreased. There was no comparison with Gigolo, the tough guy who always wanted to get going, who drew from a vast reservoir of energy, and who blossomed under pressure. Isabell was faced with a diametrically conflicting task, and the experience in Aachen was to prove to be decisive in Rio.

> *I had to learn the hard way in Aachen with regard to Weihegold's preparation leading up to competition. The process was very helpful. I found that I had to give her a day off very late in the training schedule and then build her up for four days. The fifth day in Rio was the first day of competition, then we had two days off, and I used those days to rest…we only did light gymnastic work. That's always the difficult question: How much do you work a horse to maintain form and strength, and yet how little do you work him so that you don't tire him out, sacrificing performance?*

Every horse is a new teacher: Weihegold became a part of Isabell's career as the last resort, sort of a "Plan C," even though Isabell's original plan had been very different. And she turned out to be a jackpot. The black mare was another kind of learning experience for Isabell: With her, Isabell was confronted with the forces of the "horse free market." To this day, she is grateful to owner couple Christine and Frank Arns-Krogmann for the fact that they see so much more in Weihegold than just an investment that has to bear fruit. If that had been the case, they would have long since had to pick up their horse, possibly even before the Olympic Games in Rio, and sell her to the highest bidder. Offers for a gifted horse like Weihegold, whose quality has already been proven in competitions, can take on astronomical dimensions. Seven-figure sales prices are hardly exceptional.

When you consider that while owning a competition horse may bring you pleasure, but that, first of all, he brings expenses—such as, for example, board, training, and veterinary fees—and that these costs can hardly be recovered through prize money or offspring, these offers become all the more tempting. Even more so as many different deals concerning potential revenue are proposed between riders and owners. Added to this is the daily risk that the horse may become sick or injured at any time and then the millions the horse was once worth dwindle down dramatically.

With all of this in mind, it is most ideal that Madeleine Winter-Schulze, without ever having to think about profit, can afford to equip top riders such as Isabell Werth or Ludger Beerbaum with horses simply because she enjoys those horses' quality.

*This situation results from the fact that training a dressage horse from the beginning is difficult and not many people are good at it. And so, some riders and their sponsors prefer to make a late purchase of a "made" horse. In these cases the important thing for the rider is to be able to request all the movements and have the horse know everything. The importance not lie*

*in the developing the proper foundation, which constitutes my*
*passion and my life's work: the journey of training a horse.*

This means that the value of a trainer, who, technically, teaches the basics and works toward competition success increases, but it also increases the probability that, at the same time, the rider loses the horse she is building up. Many horse-and-rider pairs have gone separate ways as a result—pairs that, in fact, helped make equestrian sport attractive to the public. Past "dream teams" in show jumping, such as Fritz Thiedemann and Meteor, Hans Günter Winkler and Halla, and later John Whitaker and Milton, still ring a bell with older generations. Today, many rider-horse combinations break apart before the public even takes notice of them.

Consider how American owners sold the mare Bella Donna, ending the high hopes of Meredith Michaels-Beerbaum and the German show jumping team prior to the World Equestrian Games in 2014 and the Olympic Games 2016. Bella Donna was sold to the army in Qatar for a lot of money and was never seen in jumping championships again. This was a painful moment in Meredith's career. The most prominent example in dressage is, once again, Edward Gal and Totilas, who were separated by an astronomical sum. The best friend and partner was turned into a commodity overnight. But the stallion's owners knew exactly what they were doing. They sold him before wear and tear would have decreased his million-dollar value.

Weihegold did not come to Rheinberg as a blank sheet of paper in 2012. She was already seven years old and had successfully completed the traditional "youngster tour" in Germany, beginning with the diamond ring for the winning mare of the Oldenburg stud book. She was the dream horse of passionate breeder Christine Arns-Krogmann from the Oldenburg

Münsterland region, who had bought her as a very young mare with money she had saved. She and her husband Frank were convinced that the horse had a very bright future ahead of her. The renowned trainer Jo Hinnemann recognized the quality of the then rather plain, black mare, cute at most, and took her on for further training. However, the day came when the owners wanted to change training barns. This was when Isabell came into play, as professional rider Beatrice Buchwald had moved from Hinnemann's barn to hers six months earlier. They agreed that Beatrice, who had ridden Weihegold for a few months before, was to continue the horse's training for the time being.

*The horse very much appealed to me, because she was so uncomplicated. She was not spectacular, she wasn't giving us a grand performance, but she accepted everything easily and was so eager to learn. Her hind leg, stepping energetically forward and under her body, raised high hopes for piaffe and passage, and when we started those exercises, she proved to be quite talented. I said early on that she was a super exciting horse, potentially a horse for the German team, and I started talking to the Arns-Krogmanns with the aim to secure Weihegold for our barn. Beatrice had just won the Nürnberger Burg-Pokal Finale with her, which was the most important competition series for young dressage horses, and Weihegold promised to turn into an interesting Grand Prix horse. Together with Madeleine, we arrived at an agreement to lease Weihegold so that Beatrice and I could continue riding her. But then, a new problem emerged.*

Initially, Isabell had a plan in her mind that later turned out to be all too bold and unrealistic. She hoped to ride on the team in Rio, side by side with her rising star and employee Beatrice Buchwald. Beatrice would ride the uncomplicated Weihegold for a solid team result, and Isabell with the brilliant Bella Rose would ride for top scores in the team and individual ranking. This was one of the reasons why Isabell continued to actively help with Weihegold's training and saw to it that she was presented well at shows.

At the show in Oldenburg in 2014, she rode the mare herself, both to let the horse gain experience and to affirm to the officials that Weihegold indeed had the potential to become a horse for the team. It was a big surprise: Right off the bat, and among a top field of competitors, Isabell and Weihegold came second in the Grand Prix as well as the Special with 73 and 77 percent respectively. Shortly after, Beatrice and Weihegold won the Louisdor Prize, an important young horse tour series.

Her success and top scores resulted in two consequences for the now nine-year-old horse. Weihegold was awarded the Otto Lörke Prize, a highly prestigious award for young promising horses at Grand Prix level. And her owners, the Arns-Krogmanns, received an offer of purchase from Austria. It was a respectable offer in the seven digits. Suddenly, all prior agreements became obsolete.

*As difficult as it was for me, I understood that you have to consider a sale when such a high offer is involved.*

Isabell nevertheless continued to try to secure Weihegold for the Olympics and, eventually, found a new solution in the shape of an investor who agreed to raise a sum in the millions to buy the horse for his wife. The deal would have made the horse available to the Werth barn until Rio; after the Olympics, the horse would have left. Isabell continued to strategize with the "Rheinberg Team" scenario on her mind. At the time, she still assumed that Bella Rose would be sound in time for the Olympic Games. A contract was written up—but before it was signed, the phone rang in Rheinberg: The bond the current owner had with the black mare could not be undone, even with compensation in the millions.

*Christine had just had her third child. Her husband called and said: "I have good news. We won't sell."*

And they came to a new agreement. Madeleine continued to lease Weihegold, together with the German Olympic Committee for Equestrian Sports. This was done with great foresight, as it became slowly clear that Isabell might potentially need the mare as backup for her own Olympic game plan. The idea began to feel more and more consistent to Isabell, since Weihegold herself moved to the forefront in more ways than one.

The Olympic year of 2016 started off with another premiere: In January, Weihegold, with Isabell in the saddle, performed her first Freestyle at the World Cup competition in Amsterdam. By now, Isabell was working with Weihegold more frequently at home. Her concern was that with Beatrice, who was still just learning her way with the most difficult movements, the pair would overwhelm themselves. It is true what they say: Horses ridden by those who have to practice harder will also have to work harder. By now, Weihegold had developed insecurities in the piaffe and needed to regain confidence with Isabell in the saddle. But Amsterdam became a lot more than just that.

*It was a huge surprise. She came sixth in the Grand Prix. But she was spectacular in the Freestyle a day later. It was a breakthrough. It was like she had raised her hand to get our*

261

*attention. We won with 83 percent. Several times the judges awarded 9 out of 10 points for certain movements. And that is how things took their course. I rode her again at the World Cup competition in Neumünster, Germany, in February. At that point, I qualified for the Games with her, and when we knew it was all over for Bella and Don Johnson, Beatrice acknowledged, "Well, that's that now."*

Beatrice took the rider change hard. After all, she had originally hoped for her own spot on the German Olympic team with Weihegold, and now her boss had taken over the ride on the horse. However, there are probably very few people in the world who would have had what was needed to get Weihegold into the shape needed to win Olympic gold in such a short time, and to do so without overwhelming her. Still, the disappointment weighed heavily, and the two women parted ways at the end of the year.

*I enjoy supporting my staff in their training and also making suitable horses available to them during their different phases of learning—in consultation with the horses' owners, of course. It is part of their job as well as a great opportunity for them to ride the horses that I have in training. They will benefit their entire professional career from the many things they learn from this.*

The experience could not ruin the period of feeling on top of the world that began for Isabell the day the Olympics in Rio started: The energy and effortlessness of those days, where everything had been proven and nothing had to be won anymore, lasted a long time, even months, and could still be clearly felt at the World Cup final in Omaha, Nebraska, the following March. Here, in the most important indoor competition of the year, Isabell came to the stage as someone who could, once again, afford to let herself and her horse shine. She and Weihegold, with whom she had grown even closer, were enthusiastically celebrated in the Freestyle. The horse had continued to develop physically, and at the show in Amsterdam in January 2017, the two had received a dream score for their Freestyle: 90.720 percent—Isabell had never scored that high in all her long career. Finally, she could max out Weihegold's abilities, as the mare had the necessary strength to fully display her talent. A 90.704 percent in the Freestyle in Omaha was the second-best score of her life, but the audience was hardly interested in the numbers anymore, since they had already guessed that they were witnesses to an exceptionally outstanding performance. The après show party started before the test was even over. Isabell rode toward the corner of the ring in extended trot, a sudden smile beaming from her face. What was on her mind?

She was excited for the final line...the turn right when she would let her horse carry her to the test's finish and let her elation show in the passage and piaffe. Isabell and Weihegold basked in the admiration. "Weihegold should be celebrated," Isabell said about the mare a little later.

She won the dressage World Cup for the third time in her career. She had first done so twenty-five years before with the mare Fabienne. But this time, it was not competition that brought her the title, but one big celebration. Isabell was so unused to the positive energy during the prize-giving ceremony that she kept sitting on her horse long after she should have dismounted. Then, she jumped up on the podium way too early, where she sprayed champagne like a Formula One champion, then brought the bottle to her lips and took a big swig. After, she let runner-up American Laura Graves and the third-placed Britain Carl Hester drink before giving the bottle to all three grooms. Isabell's groom, Steffi Wiegard, cried bashfully into Weihegold's coat while the German National anthem played.

Then came the victory gallop. And then another one. It seemed as if none of the eight-thousand American Isabell Werth fans in the arena wanted to go home just yet. But Isabell kept true to herself: In her moment of greatest effortlessness, when no pressure constricted her anymore and no special willpower was necessary to master the challenges of the day, she thought about all the difficulties she had faced over the years. "I know what it feels like to be at the bottom," she said shortly after the gallop, still out of breath. "And I am glad that I am at the top."

Of course, life went on after this overwhelming highlight, and as Isabell already knew: Your competitors never rest. In Omaha, Laura Graves clenched her delicate fists. The champagne that Isabell poured into her in a state of exuberance may have had a bitter taste. Laura honestly admitted that she did not have a chance to touch Isabell and Weihegold that day, but she also left little doubt that this was not to be her last word. The young woman explained, with a threatening vibrato in her voice, that she studied her rivals down to every detail. And that she particularly studied Isabell. She said she learned from all of them, and she knew what she had to work on at home in Florida. Her gelding Verdades is a rather big-boned, old-fashioned driving horse type: He has the stately appearance and the fantastic mobility of the coach horses that noblemen once used to harness to their carriages.

Laura first beat Isabell and Weihegold a few months later in the Grand Prix Special at the CHIO in Aachen in the summer of 2017. Isabell and her black mare made a few unusually careless mistakes—and as quickly as that, Laura had passed them. The day after, however, Isabell rode her American rival into the ground in the Freestyle. They didn't have a chance... even more so, since Isabell was enthusiastically celebrated in the arena for her performance while Laura was still waiting outside, ready to enter, and Verdades became more and more excited due to the noise.

A few months later, at the World Cup Final in Paris in 2018, Laura surprised Isabell, who was favored by everyone, with a win in the Friday Grand Prix. Weihegold had felt confined in the overly small ring and, subsequently, gave herself room to breathe in the canter tour, which cost valuable points. After this success, however, Laura may have spooked, asking herself what Isabell would do this time during the Freestyle.

Indeed, the effect of Laura's win on Friday was blatant. Isabell's face became very serious. She frowned. She took a deep breath. And it was almost visible how, deep down, her sources of adrenaline, which might have become a little dry over the years, began to open up and, finally, to sputter to life. She was then in full competition mode as Weihegold celebrated her strengths in piaffe and passage in full glory, every hair lying in the right direction, and the two of them performed the perfect Freestyle.

Again, it seemed Laura and Verdades did not stand a chance against the champion on her elegant mare. Isabell won her fourth World Cup title; Laura had to accept another defeat. She obviously found it difficult to mentally digest the experience, but when she had recovered, she explained determinedly: "I will be back, even stronger."

On her own team in Germany, resistance also surged up against Isabell's dominance. Eighty miles south of Rheinberg, in Bad Homburg, near Frankfurt, a young rival prepared to launch an attack on the great champion: The economics student Sönke Rothenberger, with his Dutch gelding Cosmo, is the son of former Dutch Olympic riders Sven and Gonnelien Rothenberger. Not even half Isabell's age, Sönke had already been her teammate once, in Rio de Janeiro. His gelding had been extremely naughty in Rio, but this did not change the fact that they were rising stars. With his hoof, Cosmo had inflicted an ugly cut on his groom during the prize-giving ceremony. It had to be sewn together with several stitches. But the groom was already back from the hospital, happily attending the victory party, while Cosmo ate his feed in the barn as if nothing had happened.

Rothenberger and Cosmo delivered the scratch result for the team score, but that their effort was not needed for the Olympic victory was mainly due to the strong rides of his fellow riders. He ranked in the top ten with his only nine-year-old horse. It was obvious: This horse, with his great fundamental quality, had not yet shown everything he was capable of.

And Sönke was not just hungry for success. He also had the necessary willpower and toughness to put pressure on Isabell and her mare Weihegold in the long run. He felt riding was like juggling, he once said, a job of keeping ten plates up in the air at the same time. In other words: to ideally present every detail of every movement of a test. He added that, in his opinion, the art of doing this was Isabell's particular strong suit, and on the day where he would succeed in juggling, he would beat her.

But, at the German Championships in 2017, one year after the Olympic Games, his plan did not work out. Isabell was in the lead in all three classes—the Grand Prix, the Grand Prix Special, and the Freestyle. Sönke and Cosmo came second three times. Once again, "The Boss" of dressage did not let anyone get the better of her. And maybe this would not have been a surprise if she had ridden for the title with Weihegold. But no, the true shock lay in her mount: From the second string of horses at the Werth facility, which continued to be depleted due to Bella Rose's absence, another superstar suddenly stepped into the spotlight: Emilio, who was once considered a "problem horse," now suddenly showed his best game as if there was no tomorrow. Another top-class product had emerged from the master school in Rheinberg. Everyone was astonished: It was as if Isabell rode on a wave of luck that was not going to run out any time soon.

The bay gelding moved so energetically to the sounds of Beethoven's Ninth Symphony that those who knew him thought they were seeing an all new Emilio before their eyes. The originally slightly plump bay of former days had transformed into an elegant, beautiful ballet dancer. Isabell had taken "Ode to Joy" from Bella Rose's Freestyle in homage to the entire equine family, because Emilio had the same grandfather as her dream mare, the Anglo-Arab Cacir. And he came from the same experienced family of breeders.

It was as if Emilio felt that his career window had opened on this June weekend in 2017, since Weihegold was suffering from a harmless leg inflammation that had to be treated with medication. Qualification for the European Championships in Gothenburg that summer was open to Isabell and Weihegold, and now, to Emilio, too. Suddenly, Weihegold was Isabell's Number 1 horse...and Emilio was Number 1A.

*Emilio is an extremely dynamic horse with lots of impulsion that now knows how to use his physical abilities positively. When Emilio moves, every fiber of his body does, too. It has taken time to get Emilio's body and mind to merge into one, as calm is not his thing. He is always alert, always holding his breath. As soon as he starts moving, everything is okay, but in general he is skeptical of most things and highly sensitive.*

The young Emilio was so suspicious and sensitive that his breeders, Heinrich and Wilhelm Strunk, had great difficulty starting him. There was nobody in their professional barn who could manage to get on five-year-old Emilio, and it became clear that if nobody succeeded in doing so, no one would want to buy the horse. No one would want such difficulties in their barn, and no one would want to risk an accident—unless it was a distinctively confident rider, who had dedicated herself to solving horse problems. Unless it was Isabell, and her employee at the time, Matthias Bouten.

*What to do with Emilio became a valid question. If he was a danger, they would consider destroying him, unless they could find someone to take care of him. I said, "Okay, Matthias, we'll take him. But you have to take care of him, and you have to do so in a way that enables us to eventually work with him." In fact, Emilio had already put several riders in extremely dangerous situations, and nobody knew what to do about it. In the beginning, he had still let a rider get on. But as soon as he was in the indoor, he started running and could not be stopped, going round and round, faster and faster. Eventually, he just didn't let anyone get on anymore.*

*Matthias managed with lots of patience. But it took six months. He noticed that the horse always got scared when something moved upward behind him. That was the moment when the horse started to panic and run away. Nobody knows why. Matthias longed him with a puppet tied to his saddle to get him used to the rider, but that was not successful. Only when he gave him an eye patch did they make some slow progress. Then, he tried blinders, like on a carriage horse. Mattias and Emilio carefully built trust, and eventually, it became possible to get into the horse's saddle without him losing it. Today, everything is just fine. Matthias really did a fantastic job. I took over the ride on Emilio when Matthias left my barn.*

*The horse has remained extremely sensitive. He is still terrified when the farrier comes. He has never had a negative experience with the farrier that I know of, but he is still scared.*

*I continue to try to avoid everything that could scare him. He has gained a lot of trust and can make it through prize-giving ceremonies, but I do try stay away from situations where he would want to get away, so that he doesn't remember any old experiences that might cause the problem to repeat itself. So far, this has been successful. All I can say is, I've had some good luck.*

The luck did not end with the German Championship title. At the close of 2017, Emilio had won two World Cup qualifiers and was the world's number three horse in dressage. And he continued to improve the following year.

But Weihegold was long since sound again for the European Championships in Gothenburg in August 2017. Another summer season together saw the relationship between rider and horse become even closer than before; Weihegold was now at the peak of her abilities. And this was indeed necessary to parry the attack coming from within Isabell's own team. In Rio, one year before, the mare had been the newcomer and nobody had really focused on them. But those times were over. Isabell had gone back to her old role: She was once again the rider to beat.

Sönke Rothenberger pretended to be calm, but the knife had been sharpened. His Cosmo—now ten and considerably more mature since Rio—had improved in the movement where he had trouble, the piaffe, and had reined in his forwardness. When the horse started his extended trot, pushing energetically from behind, the audience became wide-eyed with admiration. The extended trot, of all things—the not-so-perfect movement for Weihegold, whose specialities were piaffe and passage—was the ace card that Sönke intended to play against Isabell. She knew that. The quiet of the intermezzo was over and the European Championships injected her with a full dose of the combat agent that she thrived on: adrenaline.

The dramatic build-up was almost Hollywood-like: On Wednesday in the Grand Prix it was still a walk in the park for Isabell; on Friday in the Special it was a stimulating kick; in the Freestyle on Sunday it was a fight to the finish. Isabell entered the ring in Gothenburg three times with Weihegold, and she won the title three times—first with the team and then in the individual competition, twice. The young university student and his gelding Cosmo succeeded in hassling her more fiercely every time. On the last day, he turned up the barbecue on which the student wanted to grill the maestro with an almost perfect Freestyle. Isabell could prevent a defeat only with the utmost effort. She could not afford to make a mistake, not even the smallest one. And if that was not enough: She also had to increase the risk and ride the well-behaved mare on the razor-sharp line between goose bumps and failure. She risked everything, and Weihegold gave it her all.

After their Freestyle, possibly the best one she had ever performed with Weihegold, Isabell sat on her horse with a serious expression, awaiting the scores. The question was: Would their best be enough to keep her competitor, who had ridden a dream-like performance, at arm's length? It was enough...but barely. The difference was still 5.4 percent in the Grand Prix; it shrank dramatically in the Special to 1.235; and in the Freestyle she had a very thin lead of 0.368. Isabell's face relaxed when her victory was definite. The day with another big failure, which she anticipated out of habit, receded into the distance.

After a short moment of reflection, Isabell quickly expressed gratitude for the seventeenth European Championship title of her long career, which Weihegold helped her win. Once again, the mare had been ready to go through fire and water for her rider. Isabell was also grateful to Sönke for inspiring her to take it to the next level. He did think, for a short moment, that he had topped her. The judges saw him past the 90 percent mark, and a fight for the championship with two 90-percent rides had never been heard of before. Monica Theodorescu, the German dressage team coach, sent a prayer of thanks to her deceased father George, her great teacher. It was an outstanding triumph for her as a trainer to have such strong riders competing. As a former championship rider herself, it might have been difficult for her at times to be content with the role of advisor and manager, but on that August day in 2017, she had arrived at the top of the world as a trainer.

*Gothenburg was just awesome. Before, in Aachen, I had been thinking to myself that it would be difficult to do it again. That Weihegold kept it up for three days, and that she pulled off three tests at such a high level, was her absolute highlight so far. Monica says that there is currently no other horse that fulfills the requirements of a Grand Prix as well as Weihegold does—the movements that an advanced test is made of: piaffe, passage, pirouettes—and with such ease. This is what we mean by "Losgelassenheit."*

The suspense in Gothenburg served the sport of dressage well, but it is likely that Isabell's victory would have been far more pronounced with a more modern scoring system. For the European Championships, the FEI had not implemented an already existing reform for the Freestyle competition. Namely, that, similar to gymnastics or figure skating, a technical basic score is given, reflecting the level of difficulty. This is supposed to help make the scoring system more objective. If the degree of difficulty had been scored in this way, Isabell's lead over Sönke would have been much bigger, considering the fireworks of highly difficult movements in her Freestyle. But this scoring system was only mandatory in the World Cup.

*Of course I knew that I was the one being chased, and the judges saw it, too. Cosmo, with the advantage of his trot— under those circumstances, it was quite the declaration of war.*

Weihegold's strengths in her par excellence movements, the piaffe and passage, were obvious. But, of course, judges also tend to look to create some diversity in the results. They have the tendency to emphasize a favorite's weaknesses and to look at a competitor's strengths. But what did that mean for the future? When faced with the same scenario, would Isabell succeed again in fending off the attack at the next showdown?

*I was just happy how Weihegold had developed—that she was so focused in the ring, that she gave it everything she had and did not make a single mistake. And for the future, the saying, "New game, new chance," holds true. As we say, first of all, everyone has to ride.*

The dressage world bowed, once more full of respect. Everyone had been able to see that twelve-year-old Weihegold had given her best in Gothenburg. It was, again, a very special moment to witness a horse that was so willing to bend over backward for her rider at the zenith of her athletic career. The question of how long they would be able to keep their form defined Isabell's further plans with Weihegold. She did not want to overwork the horse as she wanted to preserve her strengths for as long as possible. The walk on the tightrope continued.

*Weihegold is not a soft horse, but I have learned over the years that I can't continuously max out a horse's potential. That was something that, for example, Satchmo taught me: I have to accept a horse's limits. Eventually, excessive ambition is only counterproductive. Sometimes, more is less.*

This also made sense to Weihegold's owners, who decided after Gothenburg to extend the lease for another four years, until after the Olympic Games in Tokyo in 2020. Again, the decision was one made for the pleasure of owning an extraordinary horse rather than making a lucrative sale. The mare did not have to walk the path of many top horses that change hands for a lot of money. The dream team was not torn apart.

*I don't want to sound arrogant but if Weihegold had ended up with someone else, I would have been very skeptical about such a project. It would most likely be difficult for another to do better than what we had accomplished. If an unexperienced rider had gotten her, the "Totilas effect" may have occurred. A rider has to learn together with the horse how to access superior performances. And when the two have finally found each other, it may be too late, and the horse's health has gone. Fortunately, Totilas' example now keeps some riders from buying themselves expensive, successful, "made" horses. After all, you don't want to make a fool of yourself. But the risk might be worth it to a Japanese rider who wants to make a good impression at the next Olympic Games in Tokyo. Thankfully, for me, this question no longer needs to be answered. We have found an agreement that works well for everyone.*

So...Tokyo 2020. They would be Isabell's sixth Olympic Games. She will be fifty-one, and, at the end of Weihegold's lease, fifty-two. But this does not mean that her career in the saddle will end. Her greatest future hope, Belantis, will only turn eleven in the next Olympic year. And in equestrianism, whose base is experience after all, the following is true: As long as the horse is young, the rider should be just fine. But Isabell would love to find a professional rider to one day become her successor at the Werth facility.

*I would like to build someone up over maybe the next five years with whom I agree when it comes to horses and training and someone with whom I get along well. Someone I am confident about that this person can continue running my facility. It has to be someone who will fit the role with regard to talent, character, and people skills. And someone who has a feeling for certain situations. I don't want to carry the responsibility alone, and I don't want success to be solely dependent on my person.*

This is a thought that should also suggest itself to Weihegold, as well—if she is at all capable of looking toward the future! Because there is one thing that she likes even more than giving her rider her all at shows: that is eating, eating, eating.

Technically, she is on an athlete's diet during show season. But, at some point, she will want to call it quits and enjoy life. Put the piaffe and passage aside; oats are better! The sport of dressage may be nice for a few years, but the day will come where she will also work toward building a round little belly, like her happy barnmate, good old Satchmo.

# 12 ALLOW YOURSELF TO BE CARRIED

One rainy afternoon in December, Isabell and I sit together inside Operncafé, where, traditionally, Frankfurt's upper crust meet to drink champagne. Of course, we talk about horses. A few hours before Isabell won a class at the Frankfurt Festhalle show. She has only brought one horse to the show and her family has stayed home...for once, she has a few hours to herself. We have ordered wine and toast to the pleasure that our book project has thus far brought us.

Cheers! Soon it will be Christmas.

Again we talk about what it is that has brought us together, and what the fundamental theme of our book should be. It is about the love of horses, which we know we share with many people—probably even a silent majority. Those people who smile dreamily and nod when they read or hear the common rider meme: "Two legs move my body, four legs move my soul."

As if any more proof is needed, an elegant woman walks up to our table, already in her coat, and says she didn't want to leave the restaurant without wishing Isabell Merry Christmas. She is a horse lover herself, she tells us, and Isabell is her idol. It is a little bit awkward on both sides—after all, the lady does not wish to be intrusive, and Isabell is not a professional soccer player for whom such approaches from fans would be completely the norm. I can sense, though, that even today, an encounter like this still touches the heart of the experienced Isabell.

*There is a large number of people who, somehow, somewhere, sometime had something to do with horses. It really is remarkable. And when you hear these people talk about it, you realize how much the encounter enchanted them. They carry a large affection in their hearts, which, at times, may be buried, and then when they come across horses again, it is like a particularly beautiful memory coming back to life. It is this enthusiasm and fascination that drives us forward without exception—me just the same as a passionate pleasure rider or a breeder who can't and doesn't want to stop thinking about horses. The fact that I ride at the top level of the sport and so demand athletic efforts from my horses is without a doubt. But what brings us as riders to the barn every day is something else. And it is the source of it all.*

*It is the unconditional desire to devote yourself to horses every day anew. It is a never-dwindling interest in their personalities, their quirks, and talents. It is to lose yourself in observing a horse and to develop a vision of his potential possibilities. I can't take in enough "horse." I would love nothing more than to sit on my orange crate for days and look at nothing but horses. It has always been like this and this is what it will always be, even in twenty years when I have long since stopped being out and about at shows.*

*The pleasure of being with horses is what is most important. Success is simply the icing on the cake. The love for and fascination with discovering a horse, and thus his talent, is the foundation of my bond with these animals. This is what drove me to my pony as a child. And it is why I have been able to bring thirty horses to the top of international dressage—not just two or three, or some "made" horses that were bought for me.*

Isabell is focused at shows. Her face is serious. She wears correct attire and her horse is always impeccably turned out, not a hair facing the wrong direction. Competition requires a basic level of tension from horse and rider, and the outside onlooker might not always notice that horse and rider are competing for the fun of it. But sometimes, and even if it happens right in the middle of a big fight to win, you can very clearly feel it: the tight bond that connects the rider with her horse. The blind rapport. The keen compliance of the horse. A moment of harmony. And the flash of a smile here and there.

Sometimes Isabell allows the public extra insight into the personal moments of her work. A few years ago, for example, she shared a video online of her riding the then nineteen-year-old retired Satchmo in her indoor in Rheinberg. No saddle—she rides him bareback. He also does not wear a bridle...and certainly not a double bridle. Only a halter with a lead rope attached to it. Riding this way, she demonstrates movements of the highest level with her old friend, without any kind of equipment, simply with her seat and her body language. Satchmo seems frisky and cheerful, like a youngster, and she visibly enjoys "becoming one" with her long-time partner. You can see, they are both having fun. The times of their old quarrels are forgiven and forgotten. When you see this, every amateur rider can only marvel...and wish. The feeling of relaxed harmony paired with such virtuosity has to be wonderful. Probably really a few moments of utter happiness.

Not everyone who has seen the video feels this, however. It is distressing that a critical tone appears in some of the comments posted in relation to the video, despite numerous favorable posts. One of the commentators, for example, does not like Isabell's seat. Someone else assumes that Isabell's horse is an enslaved creature that suffers, although Satchmo had every opportunity in the situation—bareback and bridleless—to explicitly express his discontent. Instead the horse seemed to enjoy the rounds of the indoor as much as Isabell. Equestrian sports certainly deserve criticism every now and then, but you have to wonder what such hostility feeds on.

Isabell does not want to justify herself for her sport. She knows what she is doing, and she can accept responsibility for her choices. But sometimes, something like the pressure to have to justify herself echoes in the answers she gives in reply to the frequently launched attacks from outside.

*Of course I also make mistakes in my horses' training. It is the same as raising children. Nobody can claim that they have never been in a bad mood, that they have never treated their children unfairly or punished them wrongfully. It is the same with horses. You have to react immediately and spontaneously due to your close physical cooperation with a horse. You react intuitively with your body, and usually, you can't assess the situation from a distance first. Reflexes may be used that you can't immediately control if you have a bad day. I feel that I only demand as much of my horses as they are capable of giving and that the mistakes that I make over time only account for a fraction of my actions. If I have the feeling that I treated my horse unfairly, or if something isn't going smoothly, then I can't sleep the following night. I can't let it go, and I try to find a better way. I continuously question myself. At the same time, I also have to consider every horse's quirks. The perception of the rider's aids varies greatly from horse to horse. There are horses that react very sensitively even to the smallest of aids. And there are horses that are a lot less sensitive, and the aids that have to be given are considerably stronger.*

*But, no matter how similar or not similar the feelings of humans and horses may be, I can sense that my horses are happy when they have done something right. Sometimes they even seem to burst with pride, and it pleases me when they let it out. They grow with the challenges and build up confidence. I wish everyone could feel something like it at least once.*

*Of course, there are horses that show great composure, and others that will only work if you make them. And there are horses that love what they do. They want to take part so badly and are excited and highly motivated. As a professional rider, a healthy and sound horse is my greatest asset and capital, and I will do anything for the horse's well-being. This should be obvious to everyone.*

Again and again, Isabell is confronted with the serious claim that horses should have a right to self-determination, like humans. This is linked to the postulation that, since horses have not taken an active part in the decision to be ridden, riding is not legitimate. Since the horse's natural state was not pulling a carriage, this should also be forbidden. And, in general, horses belong in the wild and not in a barn. But, the core question in all of this is: Do humans have a right to ask an animal to carry them?

In any case, humans have assumed this right for thousands of years. Where would humanity be without the horse and the horse without humanity? Their symbiosis has a very long history. But now, in the era where humans no longer need the horse to survive and to manage their day to day existence, where horses have become superfluous in the industrial sector, the agrarian sector, and the military, the connection between man and animal should be entirely severed due to the protection of the horse's right to self-determination?

*I won't be able to win these arguments. You can always contend that we have never asked horses whether we are allowed to sit on their backs. Yes, of course: I decide that I ride. And I decide when I want the horse to do a flying change. And, of course, the horse won't spontaneously perform a Grand Prix test when turned out in the field. Opinions will always differ on this key issue. I say that I may choose an animal for a partner, and whether it is a horse, a dog, or a cat, I should do it with the necessary respect for the creature—this takes priority before anything else. I also don't force the horse to behave unnaturally when I ride him. I school his basic talents and improve upon them. And I can't appreciate enough what horses not only do for me as an athlete but also for me as a person.*

Those who criticize the principle of equestrianism form a minority, but a vehement one, which is the current way of the world. The knowledge and competence of experts like Isabell, with regard to working with horses, is not generally respected. It is similar to other popular fields: Only very few people really are in the know, but everyone knows better.

It looked a lot more favorable for equestrianism a hundred years ago. Back then, nobody in our society could have imagined a life without horses; they were an essential part of a person's daily routine. Horses were ridden to get from Point A to Point B. They pulled mail coaches and trams, beer carts and covered wagons, lent their strength to farming equipment and brought the harvest home. And they went to war with mankind.

Today, most adults no longer know how to ride; they drive a car instead. They no longer dream about a pretty team of horses, but about a SUV. Certainly, if there were no more horses in today's life, many people would miss them. And the horse should not be underestimated as an economic factor. But it would no longer hit society as hard on an existential level as it would have in previous times. Pleasure riders would have to change hobbies; the racetracks, which are in the midst of a crisis anyhow, would have to close; and there would be no more shows. The industrial sector built around equestrian activities would have to find new areas of specialty. But many people would be poorer without horses, and an entire chapter of the collective knowledge of humanity, developed by many generations with meticulousness and dedication, would be lost.

*The horse used to be our mode of transportation. Riding, being around horses is, in my opinion, a cultural heritage that has to be preserved. Those people who think that it all has to end obviously don't have any connection to animals, and they don't know how much man and beast can grow together. It can be an exhilarating relationship for both parties. These people come from an artificial world where many words may be said, but the practical relevance is completely missing. Of course, we could say, "Let's open the barn doors!" Perhaps the horses would run outside and survive somehow. But this life would not correspond to the socialized and civilized standards of our horses. They are products of developments in breeding over a long time, and they are completely drawn to people. We no longer live in the time of wild horses and wide-open prairies.*

One of the major misunderstandings out there is that the horse does not need people, that he even rejects people, and prefers a life in freedom. Reality is quite the opposite: The horse needs man more than ever, someone who secures his place in the world, who protects his habitat and his health in our overdeveloped urban landscape. To rather be dead than be "dominated" by humans? This may be true for animals that are snatched from the wild, and which genetically do not have the need or the ability to integrate into our social structures. But domestic horses have adapted to life with mankind for thousands of years and they benefit from it.

*There is only a small percentage of horses that don't get involved with people because they have had a bad experience, or because they have a "genetic temper deficit," as we like to say. These horses are really extremely rare because such character traits have been selectively bred out. Today, in the era of pleasure and sport horses, we almost only have the light body type—really heavy types, suitable for carriage pulling and farm work, have become less common. But apart from the horse's outward appearance, breeding has also changed his disposition. He is now used to being domesticated and led by humans. I will even go so far as to say horses are dependent on us. Our horses completely trust us and have fully integrated into our social world. They are absolutely content to engage with humans. They are often rather grateful to be guided by someone. If this weren't so, they would use their strength against us, and we would have no chance.*

*Horses always want to do right by us. They gratefully accept our offers to take them with us and guide them. The horse has adapted to an evolving civilization, and this is the role he plays in it today. If we weren't allowed to ride horses, soon there would hardly be any left. There would only be a few in zoos and perhaps some costly protected wild horses in the Western United States, in Dülmen, Germany, or in the Camargue in France.*

It is a fact that horses never had it as good during the history of their domestication as they do today. The eyes of the public are on them, and many a suffering horse receives more attention than a suffering person. Horses are no longer a commodity.

And it is not false sentimentality to point out that everywhere horses do and did their duty, they fulfill another job: as a source of warmth and comfort, as "someone" who, for a moment, can make a troubled human feel the "tender indifference of the world." How many tears we've cried into the sweet-smelling manes of horses over time is not known, but it amounts, without doubt, to endless streams.

Where to begin when you look at the fate of horses back in the days when industry, agriculture, and the military were not as mechanized as they are today? Wherever heavy pulling, carrying, or lifting was needed, horses worked alongside humans and shared their living conditions. With only a few examples we can outline the tough life of horses in earlier time periods.

They led miserable existences in the mining industry until almost the seventies. Horses were lowered down into the pit in a harness and maybe only saw daylight again many years later, when their eyes could barely handle it. In the mines, they pulled heavy trolleys to collection points, day in, day out. Their underground stables were cramped, badly ventilated, and dark, and there was not a single fresh blade of grass in their feed. The miners took care of them and lamented the unjust world where a well-behaved animal, willing to work, had to work so much harder than a lazy one, which nobody wanted to deal with.

The history of horses in war is another gruesome tragedy. Once, the number of deployed horses could decide battles, and the equestrian skill of the cavalry was essential for survival. The number of total horses that died as victims of human acts of violence, whether harnessed to Roman war chariots, as living weapons on battlegrounds, or as silent and fast means of transportation during the American Indian wars, has not been calculated, but billions of horses were sacrificed on the shambles of political failure.

It is estimated that between fourteen and sixteen million horses were used in the First World War alone. Only very few excelled as riding horses for officers. They were literally harnessed in the armies' service. And even though the mechanization of war had already begun, heavy weapons, such as large field guns, had to be pulled by six to twelve horses. Approximately eight million horses died. They died as miserably as the soldiers: shot by the enemy, ripped apart by grenades, injured and sickened in the unhygienic conditions, starved and exhausted, or even served as an emaciated soldier's last meal. It is reported that the life expectancy of a horse on the Western Front was all of ten days at the end of the First World War. And, horses still played a significant role in the Second World War despite technical progress.

Several years before his death, former cavalry officer Philipp von Boeselager, one of the conspirators of the 20 July Plot to assassinate Adolf Hitler, described the close relationship of a soldier to his horse in war. His Czech gelding Moritz, a black horse with a noble head, accompanied him through the war and also returned home with him. It seemed as if Moritz took particular care of his rider during long rides by moving so nimbly that von Boeselager never came close to brushing his knee along a tree.

"We rode as close to the enemy as possible, then dismounted. Then the sarge took the horses to take cover. After, we fought like infantrymen. When the encounter was over, it was radioed in to bring the lead horses to the front. They came back and we mounted again. When the horses came back, it felt like home. It was a very special moment; it is hard to imagine. Every soldier fished for a sugar lump in his pocket or a piece of bread, because he was so happy to be with his horse again. You could see how the soldiers cuddled close to their horses. There was peace in this moment."

At the end of the Second World War, the existence of horses was severely threatened, more than it ever had been before. And also that of those who bred horses. Tractors replaced the horse in agriculture, and heavy machinery took over in the industrial sector—horses became unemployed. Only the democratization of the idea that a person could ride and own horses just for pleasure brought a new boost to breeders. The horse was transformed from a work animal to a friend for pleasure and sport. He lost his place in the male domain to motorcycles and cars, and found himself more and more in the hands of teenage girls who, very often, are happy to spend hours cuddling and grooming him, while saving their pocket money for riding lessons.

At the top level of the sport, equestrianism developed into an astonishingly well-functioning money machine. Prize money rose to enormous amounts, at least in show jumping, as did the prices for highly talented sport horses—more so as the super-rich (and especially their daughters) started to enjoy themselves at exclusive show venues surrounded by like-minded people. Horse breeding experienced another boom.

Even so, nobody would have guessed that a price in the millions could ever be realized for a top sport horse when the paradigm shift began in post-war times. Today, high-priced horses are sometimes almost excessively protected and "wrapped in bubble-wrap." And everything is done to maintain their value. Of course, equestrian sports struggle with similar issues as any kind of athletic pursuit, with performance manipulation and excessive demands. But, essentially, horses have become more independent of physical work than humans themselves. It still depends on the character of the person into whose hands horses fall, but many live an almost "royal" existence today.

If someone could have told a mountain farmer of the past, a miner, or a soldier in a war, what would happen on a far away day in April 2013 in Kronberg, Germany, he would have probably laughed. The Frankfurt prosecutor's office and a team of independent experts showed up at The Schafhof Stud, the spacious luxury property where multimillionaire Ann Kathrin Linsenhoff resides with her family and horses. The purpose was to determine whether the famous dressage stallion Totilas was kept in a way that was cruel to animals, despite his noble living conditions. The animal rights' organization PETA (People for the Ethical Treatment of Animals) had reported Totilas' owners and his rider the previous October. PETA operates highly publicly and effectively—one of its more recent famous cases before an American court was that of the "monkey selfie," where they sued for the photo rights of a macaque who had taken a selfie with a professional photographer's camera, claiming the animal owned the copyright and revenue related to the image.

The Linsenhoff family, who makes sure nothing is lacking in their stable, was irritated by the accusation but had to open their barn door to the public officials. The result was the proceedings were closed—evidently, the maintenance of Totilas did not conflict with any law, but only with the sentiments of a certain group of people, who perhaps in other cases rely on expertise and valid reasons for lodging a complaint, but in this one simply vehemently made their voices heard.

There is still the real world between the extremes. The people who live with horses, have maybe grown up with them, and who are the base that allows equestrian sports to thrive. People who were raised in equestrian traditions or maybe have developed a brand-new fascination for horses. Horse people from all backgrounds can, for example, be found in Aachen, Germany, every summer. The annual CHIO in Aachen is the highlight in the social calendar for many. It is the most glamorous equestrian show that the industry has to offer in the world. There, the bleachers are full, the concentration of hats is as high as that of hoodies, and the seats are so in demand that they are passed down from generation to generation. Those who love and appreciate the equestrian tradition have fiercely celebrated themselves at this indestructible festival for more than one hundred years and everyone uses it to reenergize. Here, everyone knows who he or she is: the breeders, owners, pleasure riders, competitive riders, sponsors, trainers, coaches, equestrian officials, and pony kids.

*Aachen feels a little like my living room. My home. I went to Aachen the first time in 1989. With Weingart, I rode in the old dressage arena with the wooden bleachers. I had only seen the show on television before then, and it was the ultimate experience for me to be able to ride there...and it still feels special today. My awe and fascination for the event are just as great now as they were then. I always want to give my best possible performance in Aachen, because of the atmosphere and the audience, which is so knowledgeable and enthusiastic—like nowhere else. That is why you "owe" a top performance in Aachen. Fostering tradition is taken as seriously as commercial development of the sport. This is why you find everything there: You can eat curried sausage and drink wheat beer, you can go to the sushi bar or to the gourmet caterer. It is all there. It is a mix of sport, social gathering, VIP-event, and folk fest. It has always kept its down-to-earth attitude and its roots in tradition.*

It is not only the ladies and gentlemen with the buttons on their traditional jackets, the conservative, often Anglophile families with their solid, rural roots, that dominate the landscape at the Aachen CHIO. Another species of horse crazy meets here on a massive scale...people who have dedicated their lives to horses: the mostly invisible yet omnipresent grooms. They are probably the ones closest to the horses, and they do the work without publicity or glory. They bring their charges water and let them drink; they groom them and hand-walk them; rub them with ointment and brush them; they tack them up, and then later take the saddles off their steaming backs. The relationship between horse and groom is often a relationship of trust, characterized by a deep affection.

Wonderful grooms, who identify eminently with their job, have worked for Isabell. Hacki, for example, accompanied her to shows for years. He was well known on the circuit and did not have to be introduced to anyone. Hacki was originally employed by The Doctor. He began as a driver with the company who shipped Isabell's horses to shows, and when the company quit the horse transportation business, Hacki was taken on by Dr. Schulten-Baumer, and The Doctor bought his own horse trailer for Hacki to drive. When Isabell left The Doctor's barn and moved to Mellendorf, Germany, Hacki went with her. For years he was, quite naturally, part of Isabell Werth's entourage, and it was a hard blow for him, when, one day, he could no longer manage the physical work. His knees no longer put up with it. He was heartbroken when he had to give up his life in the barn and at shows.

Then Isabell's head groom was Anna, who worked for Isabell for ten years before she met a high school teacher, married, and had two children. As soon as the first child was in kindergarten, she came back and took on a part-time position at Isabell's.

Anna's successor Steffi was, originally, an administrative assistant in a hardware store. She reduced her job to minimum work hours so she could spend more time with Isabell's horses. She works at the hardware store from Monday to Wednesday and in Rheinberg from Thursday to Sunday. In addition, she also got her commercial driver's license. Steffi is a workaholic for the sake of the horses. She is so meticulous that the rest of her team always starts to clean everything in the barn on Wednesday night, before she arrives on Thursday. Sometimes, you can see Steffi in the background on the television screen, during the prize-giving ceremony. She cries easily, just like her boss.

The love for horses is the common thread that connects all these people into a network, although they come from very different worlds. Anyone who has ever heard the sound with which a mare welcomes her newly born foal into the world—a friendly, low nicker—knows that modern horses have preserved their independent existence, despite their closeness to humans. And those people become curious. You can't help but start thinking more about horses and their nature. Maybe the opportunity even presents itself to observe with how much confidence and inner independence this mare will raise her baby to become a social being.

In earlier times, when horses were still part of every human's day-to-day life, stories of gentle animals that had contributed to people's lives with their instinct and power were probably told in every family. Maybe there was a story about the mare who was teamed up with her own daughter in harness and taught her the art of pulling a carriage. Or about the workhorse that refused to cross a bridge with a heavy harvest load, even though the farmer who was driving eventually became angry and rough. And later, it was discovered that the bridge was damaged and would have collapsed under the load.

In Germany, great admiration was shown for the mare Halla for decades—the horse who, in Stockholm in 1956, carried jumper rider Hans Günter Winkler to an Olympic victory almost on her own. Winkler got in the saddle, screaming in agony, as he had torn a muscle in his groin that morning. With the help of a painkiller, and a lot of coffee after, to clear his senses, he went on to compete in the second Olympic round. He could barely point his horse in the right direction, but Halla still jumped the entire course without any rails down, and thus became a symbol to all for loyalty and intelligence.

*Again and again I notice that, in certain moments, horses react fractions of a second faster than I do. That they know something that I don't and that they instinctively react to it; they are simply more clever. These are the moments when they teach me humility.*

Isabell's life as a rider is almost always about control. About education. About guidance. In principle, the hierarchy is clear. And yet, there are moments of vulnerability in her life, when with her horses, she does not act the part of "boss" or "protector." When instead she puts herself under the protection of a horse.

*Satchmo is the horse that I rode right up until just before my son Frederik was born in October 2009. I trusted him with me. I knew Satchmo would take care of me...that nothing would happen on his back...that he knew he had to look after me now.*

Satchmo, who could be very hot on other occasions, who had repeatedly thrown Isabell into the dirt in his youth, pricked his ears, and very carefully walked through the arena as if he absolutely knew that, in that moment, his four legs carried two souls.

# Isabell Werth's Most Important Horses

**Fabienne**—Westphalian, chestnut mare
Sire: Feuerschein | Dam's sire: Dilettant
Born 1980, died 2010

**Gigolo FRH**—Hanoverian, liver chestnut gelding
Sire: Graditz | Dam's sire: Busoni
Born 1983, died September 29, 2009

**Antony FRH**—Hanoverian, dark bay gelding
Sire: Argument | Dam's sire: Wenzel I
Born January 1, 1986, died December 9, 2013

**Amaretto**—Westphalian, bay gelding
Sire: Angentinus | Dam's sire: Ehrenfried
Born 1986, died 1999

**Satchmo**—Hanoverian, bay gelding
Sire: Sao Paulo | Dam's sire: Legat
Born 1994

**Warum Nicht FRH** (Barn Name: Hannes)—
Hanoverian, chestnut gelding
Sire: Weltmeyer | Dam's sire: Wenzel
Born January 1, 1996, died July 30, 2015

**El Santo** (Barn Name: Ernie)—Rhinelander, bay gelding
Sire: Ehrentusch | Dam's sire: Rhythmus
Born February 5, 2001

**Don Johnson** (Barn Name: Johnny)—Hanoverian, bay gelding
Sire: Don Frederico | Dam's sire: Warkant
Born December 14, 2001

**Bella Rose**—Westphalian, chestnut mare
Sire: Belissimo | Dam's sire: Cacir
Born 2004

**Weihegold**—Oldenburger, black mare
Sire: Don Schufro | Dam's sire: Sandro Hit
Born 2005

**Emilio**—Westphalian, bay gelding
Sire: Ehrenpreis | Dam's sire: Cacir
Born 2006

**Belantis**—Gray stallion from the State Stud Brandenburg
Sire: Benetton Dream FRH | Dam's sire: Exposé
Born April 3, 2009

# Isabell Werth's Greatest Successes

## Olympic Games

### 1992 in Barcelona
Team gold
Individual silver
with GIGOLO

### 1996 in Atlanta
Team gold
Individual gold
with GIGOLO

### 2000 in Sydney
Team gold
Individual silver
with GIGOLO

### 2008 in Hong Kong
Team gold
Individual silver
with SATCHMO

### 2016 in Rio de Janeiro
Team gold
Individual silver
with WEIHEGOLD

## WORLD EQUESTRIAN GAMES

**1994 in The Hague**
Team gold
Individual gold in the Grand Prix Special
with GIGOLO

**1998 in Rom**
Team gold
Individual gold
with GIGOLO

**2006 in Aachen**
Team gold
Individual gold in the Grand Prix Special
Individual bronze in the Freestyle
with SATCHMO

**2010 in Kentucky**
Team bronze
with WARUM NICHT

**2014 in Caen**
Team gold
with BELLA ROSE

**2018 in Tryon**
Team gold
Individual gold in the Grand Prix Special
with BELLA ROSE

## European Championships

### 1989 in Mondorf
Team gold
with WEINGART

### 1991 in Donaueschingen
Team gold
Individual gold in the Grand Prix Special
with GIGOLO

### 1993 in Lipica
Team gold
Individual gold in the Grand Prix Special
with GIGOLO

### 1995 in Mondorf
Team gold
Individual gold
with GIGOLO

### 1997 in Verden
Team gold
Individual gold
with GIGOLO

### 1999 in Arnheim
Team gold
with ANTONY

### 2001 in Verden
Team gold
with ANTONY

### 2003 in Hickstead
Team gold
with SATCHMO

## 2007 in La Mandria
Team silver
Individual gold in the Grand Prix Special
Individual silver in the Freestyle
with SATCHMO

## 2011 in Rotterdam
Team silver
with EL SANTO

## 2013 in Herning
Team gold
with DON JOHNSON

## 2015 in Aachen
Team bronze
with DON JOHNSON

## 2017 in Göteborg
Team gold
Individual gold in the Grand Prix Special
Individual gold in the Freestyle
with WEIHEGOLD

## 2019 in Rotterdam
Team gold
Individual gold in the Grand Prix Special
Individual gold in the Freestyle
with BELLA ROSE

# Acknowledgments

Above all, we would like to thank each other—for the intensity of our meetings and the inspiration that came from working together. Only through our work on this book have we become aware that we have known each other for more than twenty-five years and that this longstanding relationship is a special gift. Sincere thanks are due to our partners Wolfgang Urban (Isabell) and Manfred Wagner (Evi). Without our partners' love, loyalty, and patience we would not be what we are now.

———

Many thanks to Isabell's parents, Brigitte and Heinrich Werth, for they have always been there along the way and have contributed to this book with their grounded perspective. And, of course, thank you to Madeleine Winter-Schulze, who remains steadfastly at Isabell's side and opened her door in Mellendorf for Evi's research. Evi thanks the newspaper *Frankfurter Allgemeine Zeitung* for giving her decades of experience, which have found their way into this book. And special thanks goes to co-editor Holger Steltzner, who gave her the necessary freedom to realize a complex project like this one. Evi would also like to thank Seravina, Hankey, and Goody, who, during the book's writing, did not tire of explaining the nature of horses all over again.

Isabell's thanks to the horses is given in the shape of this book.

# Index

Plate numbers, noted in *italics*, correspond to image numbers in the photo insert.